Fasting and Feasting in Morocco

Mediterranea Series

General Editor: Jackie Waldren, *Centre for Cross-Cultural Research on Women, University of Oxford, and Administrator, Deya Archaeological Museum and Research Centre, Spain*

This is a new series which will feature ethnographic monographs and collected works on theoretical approaches to aspects of life and culture in the areas bordering the Mediterranean. Rather than presenting a unified concept of 'the Mediterranean', the aim of the series is to reveal the background and differences in the cultural constructions of social space and its part in patterning social relations among the peoples of this fascinating geographical area.

Other titles in the series:

William Kavanagh
Villagers of the Sierra de Gredos: Transhumant Cattle-raisers in Central Spain

Aref Abu-Rabia
The Negev Bedouin and Livestock Rearing: Social, Economic and Political Aspects

Fasting and Feasting in Morocco

Women's Participation in Ramadan

Marjo Buitelaar

BERG
Oxford/Providence

First published in 1993 by

Berg Publishers

Editorial offices:
221 Waterman Street, Providence, RI 02906, USA
150 Cowley Road, Oxford OX4 1JJ, UK

Library of Congress Cataloging-in-Publication Data
Buitelaar, Marjo.
Fasting and feasting in Morocco: women's participation in Ramadan
/ by Marjo Buitelaar.
p. cm. -- (Mediterranea)
Includes bibliographical references and index.
ISBN 0-85496-321-9
1. Ramadan--Morocco. 2. Morocco--Religious life and customs.
I. Title. II. Series: Mediterranea (Oxford, England)
BP186. 4.B85 1994 92-39822
297'. 36--dc20 CIP

British Library Cataloguing in Publication Data
Buitelaar, Marjo
Fasting and Feasting in Morocco:
Women's Participation in Ramadan
(Mediterranea Series)
I. Title II. Series
ISBN: 0-85496-321-9

ISBN: 0-85496-321-9

Printed in Great Britain by SRP Ltd., Exeter

Contents

Foreword

It is a very pleasant task to welcome this study, which originated as a dissertation, and see it being made available to a wider readership. Here we have, as far as I know, the first comprehensive ethnography of fasting in an Islamic society. Many Moroccans, like the majority of Muslims elsewhere, think of Ramadan as the most important religious celebration in the annual ceremonial round. Anthropologists who have conducted research in Muslim societies must have noted that in no other month does Islam penetrate daily life so pervasively as during Ramadan. Yet, oddly enough, the scant attention paid by anthropologists to the fasting month contrasts sharply with the importance Muslims attach to it. A focus on the details of fasting is not only of interest in and for itself. As this book shows, it also elucidates wider issues of Islamic society and culture and addresses several theoretical questions in anthropology as well.

This lively, detailed and readable ethnography draws on intensive fieldwork carried out in three different Moroccan places and on the author's mastery of the local dialect. Marjo Buitelaar became an adopted member of three households, immersed herself (as Malinowski would have urged her to do) in daily life, in particular in the world of women, and lived through three Ramadans as well as the months preceding and following the fasting month. Part of the ethnographic knowledge presented in this book is thus based on subjective empathy with the women whose daily life she shared.

This study echoes Clifford Geertz's emphasis on 'thick description' as the core of ethnography, an attractive mixture of description, argument and analysis. The author adds to this small portraits of the women, who are not only the subjects of this ethnography, but who also shaped it. Moreover, the author is candid about her own experience, not in the sense of fieldworker's exhibitionism, but in order to reveal some of the circumstances under which ethnographic knowledge is produced.

Fasting and Feasting in Morocco is both a case study in the anthropology of religion and a study of gender. Basic themes addressed in this book are ritual, gender, power and identity as well as the links between religious prescriptions and behaviour. Contributing to one of the major issues in the study of religions, Marjo Buitelaar shows that there is no clear distinction between what has been called 'official' or 'orthodox' ('male') Islam and 'popular' ('female') Islam. Many women have internalised the dominant (male) view that they are more impure/sinful than men and as a consequence have to 'work' harder to come closer to God. Since menstruation and childbirth profanise and break the fast, women are more preoccupied than men with earning spiritual rewards, and with collecting religious merit (also on behalf of the male members of their household). They employ their own strategies to counteract their structurally weaker position in the dominant gender configuration and ideology. Marjo Buitelaar shows that female ritual performances are no less important than the more visible male performances in the mosques.

A closely related theme is the link between 'universal' Islam to which fasting during Ramadan belongs and 'local' (Moroccan) Islam. Although Moroccans refer to the universal community of believers, fasting also takes on local meanings. There are local nuances in the cultural notions of purity, Islamic community and religious merit. Ramadan is also set in the overall cycle of celebrations and analysed as a special month. Here we also see some specifically Moroccan features.

This book is a valuable contribution to Islamic and Mediterranean studies in yet another sense. Mediterranean culture is increasingly becoming part of public life in Western Europe. There are now approximately one-and-a-half million people of Moroccan origin living in the European Community. This study of a central feature of their religious life enhances our understanding of 'others' who have now become our neighbours. *Fasting and Feasting in Morocco* will be of interest not only to anthropologists, but also to Arabists, theologians, feminists and people outside academia who work with Muslims.

Henk Driessen, Institute of Cultural and Social Anthropology, University of Nijmegen, The Netherlands

Acknowledgements

I would like to express my gratitude to the Nijmeegs Instituut voor Comparatieve Cultuur en Ontwikkelings Studies (NICCOS) in whose research programme this project was embedded, and the Catholic University of Nijmegen and the Stichting Antropologie, who provided research facilities and financial support. I am indebted to Karin Fierke, who faced the unrewarding task of trying to make my English sound less Dutch, and Geert Jan van Gelder and Jan Hoogland, who corrected my transcription of Arabic words. Nothing seemed to escape their attention, and the errors that remain are to be blamed on unjust stubbornness from my side.

Each in his or her own way, my supervisors Henk Driessen, Willy Jansen, Jan Peters and Albert Trouwborst have guided me through the various stages of writing a doctoral dissertation. At difficult times, it was their faith in me that kept me going. I wish to thank them for their repeated readings, comments and encouragements to keep struggling to find my way through my material. I am also grateful to the members of Albert Trouwborst's 'promovendi-overleg' for their critical comments.

I would like to thank numerous friends, colleagues and relatives for the support, suggestions and distractions they offered. Some of them I wish to mention in particular. The interest and original comments of Annemoon van de Broek, Cora van de Veere and my mother Aad Buitelaar-van de Berg have made me realise the importance of the contribution and involvement of friends from other professional fields. In the same respect, the advice and friendship of Wilma Roos, Maria Smetsers and the other members of our 'women's study club' have been invaluable. Our discussions have helped me clarify my arguments.

Without the help, hospitality and sympathy of various people in the field, this book could not have been written. First I wish to thank Moustapha Lemaamer for accommodating me during the first few weeks of my stay in Morocco. I owe a lot to Abdelmajid and Loretta al-Ghazouani for introducing me into some Marrakchi families and taking me in when I was ill. They provided a haven to which I could turn for distraction, encouragement, or simply a hot shower. I thoroughly enjoyed my visits to Jolijn Eikeboom and Rob Rutten in Rabat and Salé and I thank them for their hospitality and friendship. It is hard to imagine how this book could have come into being without the continuous advice, support and friendship, both in the field and at home, of my dear friend Léon Buskens. His confidence and unfailing sense of humour and talent of being there when needed made this Moroccan adventure all the more rewarding. I owe him much more than the *jubanîya* that he was prepared to put at stake and it is to him that I dedicate this book. My most profound debt is of course to the people in Berkane and Marrakech with whom I lived and worked. I thank them for accepting me into their lives on a temporary basis and teaching me the things I tried to convey in this book. In particular, I wish to thank the women sharing the courtyard of the house where I lived in Sidi Sousan. For reasons of privacy in this account their names have been altered. Their willingness to allow me a prolonged look into their everyday world is the basis of this study and I am most grateful for their help.

Note on the Transcription

Although the Moroccan Arabic dialect deviates from Modern Standard Arabic (M.S.A.) in several ways, I have chosen to transliterate Arabic words primarily according to the system in H. Wehr's (1976) *A Dictionary of Modern Written Arabic*, for two reasons. Having initially been educated in M.S.A., this system is most familiar to me and I have used it in the field to write down Moroccan Arabic words. Also, adopting Wehr's system will make the Arabic phrases more accessible to a wider group of Arabists than only those who are familiar with the Moroccan dialect.

In order to do justice to the authenticity of Moroccan Arabic, in all chapters except the first, which does not contain Moroccan terms, some adjustments will be made. These generally do not concern religious terms, which tend to be closer to M.S.A. than other words. Most adjustments concern vowels, that sometimes disappear in Moroccan words or are reduced to an /e/ as in the English word 'men'.

Two consonants have been added which do not exist in M.S.A.:

The /g/ is pronounced like the /g/ in the English word 'goodbye'.
The /ṛ/ is added to the emphatic consonants marked with a subscript dot under the symbol. The sounds of such emphatic consonants are lower in pitch than their non-emphatic counterparts.

Other consonants are transliterated as in Wehr's system. It must be noted that the Moroccan pronunciation of the /j/ differs from M.S.A. It should be pronounced like the /s/ in the English word 'pleasure'.

For those not familiar with Arabic:

The /q/ is similar to the /k/ but pronounced further back in the mouth.
The /ġ/ is pronounced like the /r/ in the French name 'Paris'.
The /ḵ/ is pronounced like the /ch/ in the German name 'Bach'.
The /ṯ/ is pronounced like the /th/ in the English word 'thumb'.
The /ḍ/ is pronounced like the /th/ in the English word 'this', but lower in pitch.

The /š/ is pronounced like the /sh/ in the English word 'shame'.
The /'/ is the glottal stop. It is the break between vowels as heard in the exclamation 'uh oh'.
The /ᶜ/ is similar to the glottal stop but pronounced further back in the mouth.

Except for words which appear more often in plural form than in singular form, such as *ᶜulamâ'* and *jnûn*, plurals are formed by the addition of /s/. Names of persons, groups, places and months will be written as they are translated into English in Wehr (1976). Those which Wehr does not include will be simplified in the same way. In quotations from other books, the author's transliteration will be respected.

Woman cleaning her cooking utensils as a preparation to Ramadan

Baker selling Ramadan pastries

Streetscene during Ramadan: a man in traditional Moroccan attire, a banner with a religious text and mendicants at the entrance of the mosque

Woman preparing hrîra, the Ramadan soup

Introduction

The Argument

Fasting during Ramadan is one of the 'five pillars' or religious duties which Muslims must perform. For an entire month, fasting people abstain from food, drink and sexual relations between dawn and dusk. Towards the evening, the call for the sunset prayer from the muezzin, the crier in the minaret who calls people to prayer, is anxiously awaited, since it announces the moment to break the fast. The self-control exerted during the daytime then makes way for self-indulgence. People gather around the table and eat lavish meals. Afterwards, some townspeople stay at home to watch television, while others go out to attend the special Ramadan prayers in the mosque or to stroll along illuminated shopping avenues, buying sweets from one of the many street vendors. Unlike the other months of the year, during Ramadan towns are bustling with activities until late in the evening, and most people do not go to bed until after midnight.

For Moroccans, and probably for many Muslims elsewhere as well, Ramadan is the most important religious ritual of the year. Although most people agree that, especially in summer, fasting may be an ordeal, the fasting month is much looked forward to. One question about Ramadan from the side of an interested foreigner suffices to trigger off elaborate and vivid accounts of life during this sacred month.

Despite its special significance to Muslims, Ramadan has been largely neglected as a topic in the ethnography of Islam.[1] I could only find a study by Hofmann (1978) in which several chapters are devoted to Ramadan in Indonesia and one by Buskens (1987), who did preliminary research on Ramadan in Morocco. It was the study of the latter which gave the initial impetus to my own research. Apart from these relatively extensive accounts of Ramadan, most publica-

1. Cf. Buskens (1986) for a partially annotated bibliography of Ramadan.

tions are short articles (Antoun 1968; Benkheira 1986; Fallers 1974; Jomier and Corbon 1956; and Zaki Yamani 1987). The majority of these articles are of a descriptive nature and do not search for meanings of the fast as I do in this study. This is also true for some monographs which include small sections on Ramadan (Ben Talha 1965; Davis and Davis 1989; and Fernea 1969). An exception must be made for Eickelman (1976: 137), according to whom fasting distinguishes 'men of reason'. This analytical approach is lacking in the books of folklorists and travellers who occasionally mention Ramadan (Burton 1964; Lane 1842; and Westermarck 1926). With the exception of Snouck Hurgronje (1888–9), who devotes a chapter to the practice of fasting during Ramadan in his book on Mecca, and Nabhan (1991), who focuses on the concluding feast of Ramadan in Egypt, Islamicists and Arabists have studied Ramadan mainly on the basis of texts. Unlike this study, they do not concern themselves with the relationship between fasting prescriptions and practice (cf. Goitein 1966; von Grunebaum 1958; Lech 1979; Wagtendonk 1968).

One of the reasons why the practice of fasting has been neglected as a topic for extensive analysis may be that, as such a fundamental part of religious duties, it is presumed to be carried out along similar lines everywhere, strictly following the doctrinal rules. As a consequence, ethnographers, who generally show preference for the unique and the exotic in Islamic cultures in the Middle East, pay more attention to religious practices and views which deviate from doctrinal prescriptions (cf. Antoun 1976; Denny 1985).

The primary goal of this study is to contribute to our understanding of the way this Islamic duty is carried out in practice. My aim is to convey the ideas and feelings expressed by people performing the fast. By describing how they integrate fasting into their daily routines of going to work or school, managing the household, going shopping, socialising with friends and neighbours and other activities that make up the day-to-day living of most urban Moroccans, I address the question of the meanings these people attach to the fast and in what ways their fasting practices are embedded in a local world-view.

To a large extent, this study is an attempt at what Geertz calls a 'thick description' of the fast. In this sense, it is related to the ethnographic accounts of Morocco written from the perspective of Geertz's school of interpretative anthropology, such as Eickelman (1976), Geertz (1968), Geertz, Geertz and Rosen (1979), Rabinow (1975) and Rosen (1984). Three notions will be presented which make 'abstaining from food, drink, and sexual contacts' meaningful acts from a Moroccan point of view. I will also indicate what these meanings of the fast tell us about Moroccan society at large (cf. Geertz 1973; 1983).

The first time I conducted fieldwork on the practice of Ramadan, I was rather disappointed by the answers I received upon asking people why they fast: 'In order to be Muslims', 'Ramadan makes one healthy, strong', 'To learn to be patient', and 'In order for rich and poor people to be equal'. Variations in these more or less standard responses were put forward almost unthinkingly by virtually anyone to whom the question was posed. Such statements are part of scriptural Islam, and do not deviate much from what I had taken down in notes on the goals of fasting during the first university course I took on Islam.[2]

During the three successive years that I participated in the fast, I gradually came to realise that these formal Islamic statements are elaborations of some of the basic assumptions shared by Moroccans about how the world 'really' is (cf. Eickelman 1976: 123). These basic attitudes are taken for granted to the extent that they are seldom articulated. They are composed of several closely related key concepts around which patterns of meaning are constructed.

By a constant search for what my informants emphasised in their action and topics of conversation during Ramadan, and by studying how such articulations 'fit' together, I have deduced three notions around which to centre my argument: *umma,* Islamic community; *ṭahâra,* purity; and *ajr*, religious merit. In several ways, each of these key notions shapes the practice of fasting and, in turn, is shaped through this practice. As Eickelman (1981: 175) puts it: 'Patterns of meaning are generated in the everyday world of social experience, shape that experience, and in turn are modified by them.' The selected notions contain both a cognitive and an emotional, evaluative component. They integrate aspects of Moroccan world-view or the assumed structure of reality, and aspects of Moroccan ethos, that is, the approved life-style (Geertz 1973: 126–7). *Umma* indicates the capacity of the fast to unite all Muslims. *Ṭahâra* refers to the importance of purity in the Moroccan ethos. Fasting is conceived of as a purification process, which renders both the body and the mind healthy, as well as having beneficial effects on society at large. Gaining *ajr* is inherent to fasting, and, in addition, many fasting people perform good deeds that render *ajr*.

2. The series of lectures entitled 'An Introduction to Islam'was given by Professor Dr J. R. T. M. Peters of the Katholieke Universiteit Nijmegen. Four goals of fasting were mentioned:
1. rendering the body healthy
2. teaching compassion for the poor
3. teaching self-discipline
4. demonstrating obedience to God.

The lecture notes (dd. 26.10.81) further read that in pursuing these goals, both the mind and the body are restored to good health, which is the key to happiness.

Presentation of the material under the headings of *umma*, *ṭahâra* and *ajr* inevitably implies an exclusion of other notions. However, in the course of the argument, several related local notions will be mentioned, while I will also describe how these three key notions are interrelated.

Eickelman (1976: 125) points out that the notions which make up any world-view 'are not in a rigid, fixed relation with one another'. As they are used by individuals, shifts in emphasis on one or several of the key notions occur. For example, one elderly informant was much more preoccupied with performing deeds for *ajr* than were the younger members of her family. Women tend to put more emphasis on *ajr*, while men are identified more with *ṭahâra*. Also, while I contend that people in both towns where I conducted fieldwork 'tune' to and interpret their performance of the fast in regard to these notions, my informants in Berkane were more explicit about them than informants in Marrakech.

Shifts in emphasis occur not only in different settings but also through time. Information on the emotions, ideals, opinions and behaviour of individuals as presented in this study hardly ever finds its way into historical records, thus hampering comparison. Tracing the historical development of the meaning of the fast is, therefore, beyond the scope of this study. Focusing on local level interpretations of key concepts presents an indigenous view of experience rather than that espoused by Moroccan religious scholars. Formal opinions (*fatwâs*) and contemporary Islamic literature on fasting will therefore only be touched upon in so far as they affect the behaviour and views of my informants. In the same respect, attention to the economics of fasting will concentrate on the budgets and choices of individuals rather than the economic effects of fasting on a national scale.

The focus on how the key notions of *umma*, *ṭahâra* and *ajr* shape and are shaped by the ways Moroccans think and feel about the world will, in the last chapter, be complemented by addressing the problem of their practical social effects. To this end, I will adopt Turner's analytical approach to ritual. In contrast to Geertz, whose primary concern is, as Ortner puts it, with 'Meaning, with a capital M', that is, 'the larger significance of things' (Ortner 1984: 131), Turner is primarily interested in the instrumental aspects of symbols:

> Ritual activities, too, appear to be purposive; even if they do not seem to be directed to the achievement of any practical results, they nevertheless have effects upon the participants which influence their subsequent behaviour . . . Ritual is a periodic restatement of the terms in which men of a particular culture must interact if there is to be any kind of a coherent social life . . . it actually creates, or re-creates, the categories through which men perceive reality. (Turner 1968: 6–7)

Turner argues that it is the strength of religious symbols to integrate and establish unification. In his analysis of symbols, he concentrates on what symbols refer to and how they facilitate social change such as in rites of life crisis (cf. Ortner 1984: 128–31).

An important concept developed by Turner is liminality. Liminality is derived from the Latin word *limen*, which means threshold. It refers to the ritual state or condition which 'represents the midpoint of transition in a status-sequence between two positions' (Turner 1974: 237). When analysed as specific articulations of liminality, the notions of community feelings, purity and religious merit draw attention to the boundaries that are expressed and established through fasting. It will be argued that fasting can be viewed as a rite of initiation and serves as a point of temporal orientation.

Douglas's (1966) theory on body symbolism is also clarifying in studying the boundaries that are the focus of people's attention during Ramadan. It points to the fact that the preoccupation of Moroccans with the boundaries of the human body during the fast represents a concern with boundaries between more complex social structures. As Douglas puts it: 'Rituals work upon the body politic through the symbolic medium of the physical body' (Douglas 1966: 128).

Most scholars distinguish between two levels of Islam: 'formal Islam' on the one hand, and 'informal Islam' on the other (cf. Eickelman 1981; Gellner 1969; Waardenburg 1979). In general, 'formal Islam' is understood to include beliefs and practices which are validated in Islamic law, and refers to the 'reflective' or 'explicit' ideology of the elite, which is articulated by religious scholars. Beliefs and practices which deviate from Islamic law are labelled 'informal Islam', which refers to 'unreflective' or 'implicit' ideologies of the mostly uneducated masses (cf. al-Zein 1977).[3] The relation between these two levels of Islam has been conceived of as dichotomous, complementary, or dialectical (ibid.).

Recently, there has been a growing awareness that the execution of even the most universal and detailed prescribed Islamic duties contains local practices and meanings, the articulations of which exceed or deviate from the formal opinions expounded by religious scholars. Bowen (1990), for instance, argues that, in Indonesia, performance of the *ṣalât*, the five daily prayers required of Muslims, can take on local socio-political meanings. Combs-Schilling (1989) analyses how, in the Moroccan celebration of the Feast of Immola-

3. Many different terms are used to indicate this basic distinction. Formal Islam may also be called 'normative', 'universal', 'official' or 'orthodox' Islam, while 'popular', 'local', 'heterodox' Islam are terms which refer to informal Islam.

tion, metaphorical equivalence is established between Ibrahim, the Prophet Muhammed, the monarch, and all male heads of households, thus creating bonds of closeness which underscore the legitimacy of the king. Tapper and Tapper (1987) demonstrate that, during the celebration of the birth of the Prophet in a Turkish town, gender-specific versions of *mevlud* (panegyrical poems about the Prophet) recitals express and legitimate both men's and women's beliefs in key religious mysteries.

In this study, I join this line of research. I will give several examples of Moroccan practice and views which diverge from, but do not necessarily contradict, prescriptions of the fast. More importantly, I will demonstrate that even where Moroccans formulate the significance of fasting in terms of universal Islamic values, in everyday speech and action these statements take on local meanings.

Edwin and Shirley Ardener (1972; 1975) distinguish between dominant models of the world, which are promulgated by dominant groups in society, and counter or muted models, held by subordinate groups in society. Following up on these ideas, I distinguish between dominant Islam, which is propagated by the local religious establishment and largely accepted by most Moroccans, and alternative models of Islam which represent the aforementioned 'shifts of emphases' in meaning. In what follows, these alternative models do not necessarily contradict the dominant model but may exist within it.

The false assumption that a clear distinction can be made between 'orthodox Islam' and 'popular Islam' often goes hand in hand with the association of women with 'popular Islam' and men with 'orthodox Islam' (cf. Davis 1983: 107; Tapper and Tapper 1987: 72). This corresponds with the relative 'invisibility' of women in Islamic institutions and the depreciation of their religious practices within dominant Islam. An additional aim of this book is to make women's participation in the fast more visible. I will demonstrate that although their practices may differ at some points from those of men, this does not entail that women operate outside dominant Islam. Also, while the ideas held by women may be at variance with the opinions expressed by men, they do not necessarily conflict with doctrinal prescriptions of the fast. Inspired by Dwyer's study on the images and self-images that men and women have about the nature of males and females in the Moroccan town of Taroudant (1978a) I will argue that subtle distinctions between what men and women emphasise during the fast may refer to male-female differentiation in perceptions of what it means to be a man or a woman.

Berkane and Marrakech

This study is based on three months of fieldwork in Berkane and nine months in Marrakech. Berkane is an agro-town located in the foothills of the eastern Rif in northern Morocco. Only a small hamlet until the turn of the twentieth century, Berkane owes its growth to the French who, in 1911, set up a military camp in Berkane and established a centre of European settlers in the town. Until 1942, the population of the town remained below 3,500, but by 1950, Berkane had grown to 8,000 inhabitants. The departure of the French brought about a great influx of Moroccans, so that in 1960 the town counted 20,000 inhabitants. This number grew to 30,000 in 1970 (Noin 1970; Seddon 1981: 239). At the time of my fieldwork in 1987 Berkane had 70,000 inhabitants.[4]

The market of Berkane is of regional importance as a distribution centre for fruits, vegetables and cereals. The town has a factory where oranges are packed for export (Troin 1975). The distance between Berkane and the provincial capitals of Oujda and Nador is about 60 and 100 kilometres respectively. Both towns can be reached by bus or by 'big taxi'.

Marrakech is one of Morocco's oldest and largest cities, with an estimated population of 610,000 inhabitants.[5] It is the capital of southern Morocco and a centre of administration, small-scale, mostly agricultural processing industry (olives, apricots), crafts and tourism. The tourist industry, encompassing both crafts (souvenirs) and services, is the most important economic activity of the town. Fifty per cent of the tourists who visit Morocco, that is 800,000 people, come to Marrakech every year (Daoud 1988: 42). In all the families I visited, at least one family member was, in one way or another, involved in the tourist industry.

Marrakech is situated in the Haouz plain, bordering the western foothills of the High Atlas Mountains. The distance from Marrakech to other main cities covers 155 km to Safi, the closest port on the Atlantic coast, 242 km to the economic metropolis Casablanca, and 530 km to Fes, which was the capital until the French Protectorate.

Like many cities in the Maghreb, Marrakech is basically divided into two parts. When the French settled in the town in 1912, they left the old town or medina with its labyrinth of alleys intact and

4. Taking a growth rate of 3%, this figure is based on the figure of the census in 1982 (Annuaire Statistique 1989: 16).

5. This estimation is based on the figure in 1982 (Annuaire Statistique 1989: 16) adjusted with an annual growth of 3%. Other information in this section is largely based on Deverdun (1959), Mandleur (1972) and Schwerdtfeger (1982).

built a modern European township outside the city walls. When the French left in 1956, the houses in Gueliz, as the *ville nouvelle* was called, were occupied by rich Moroccan families, who fled the overpopulated medina. Due to this overpopulation, several spontaneous quarters have developed outside the city walls. In 1979, these peri-urban settlements concentrated 115,000 inhabitants, a fourth of the total population of Marrakech (Sebti 1985: 64). One of the most recent spontaneous quarters is Hay Fakhara, which is located on the cemetery opposite the gate to the tanners' quarter. The houses of Hay Fakhara are constructed of mud, and lack electricity, water and sewage facilities.

This study concentrates on people who live in the medina of Marrakech, but I also paid regular visits to informants in Hay Fakhara and Gueliz.

Fieldwork

I visited Morocco for the first time in 1983–4, when I spent six months in the town of Sidi Slimane to do research on the significance of the public bath (*ḥammâm*) for women (cf. Buitelaar 1985a; 1985b; 1986). I greatly benefited from that experience when I embarked on the Ramadan project. For example, it supplied me with foreknowledge about the importance of purity for Moroccans. The fieldwork for the present study was done between 1987 and 1990. The first period, from April to June 1987 in Berkane, involved preliminary research and covered the Islamic months Shaban, Ramadan and Rajab. I returned to Morocco in March 1988, and lived in Marrakech from April to November of that year. In 1989 I visited my host family in Marrakech for a period of six weeks to witness Shaban and part of Ramadan. I returned to Morocco for another six weeks in April and May of 1990, but only stayed in Marrakech for a few days. I then travelled through Morocco to get a more general impression of the fast in Morocco.

When I began my research, I preferred to do fieldwork in an Arabic-speaking town in one of the regions from which the majority of Moroccan migrants in the Netherlands originate (the Rif mountains and Sous valley). Berkane was chosen because relatives of an acquaintance in Nijmegen were willing to accommodate me. The family consisted of a woman in her sixties whose husband had been working in France for over twenty years, one married son with his wife and son, two unmarried sons in their twenties and an unmarried daughter of 18 years old. The women in this family spent so much time with the married daughter of my hostess, who had three children and lived with her husband and his three unmarried sisters, that the two families almost constituted a single household.

Despite the generous hospitality of this family, I chose not to return to Berkane for the second and major part of my fieldwork for two reasons. Firstly, many people, especially the elderly, often switched between Moroccan Arabic and a dialect of Riffian, while the Arabic dialect they spoke differed much from the dialect I had learned in Sidi Slimane. More important, however, was the fact that my freedom of movement was greatly restricted. After I had been with the family for three weeks, I decided that I had met enough friends and relatives by accompanying my hostess on her visits to begin seeing these women alone. One day, when I was about to leave the house, I was stopped by my hostess. Some long, difficult discussions ensued. The chances of finding a new family before Ramadan was to begin, a week later, were small. I had no choice, therefore, but to agree to her conditions that in exchange for the hospitality and protection of my host family, I was not to leave the house unless accompanied by either my hostess or one of her sons. This, of course, hampered the fieldwork considerably. Despite these hindrances, it will become clear in subsequent chapters that my stay in Berkane was a useful experience which allowed comparison with later experiences.

Hoping to find a new host family through friends in Rabat, I returned to Morocco the next year, six weeks before the advent of Ramadan. Having been told in Berkane that inhabitants of large cities tend to be lax about fasting, I decided to try to make contacts in the medinas or old quarters in one of the royal cities, preferably in Fes, the centre of ancient civilisation and hometown of Morocco's old elite.

As it turned out, one week before Ramadan was to begin, I moved in with a family who lived in a house, inherited by them from their father, in Sidi Sousan, a division of the tanners' quarter in the medina of Marrakech. Four of the five rooms situated around the spacious courtyard were occupied by family members without husbands or wives. The woman who let me share her room was in her mid-twenties. She had not yet been married, which in Moroccan conception meant that she was still a *bint,* a girl. She shared her meals and evenings with her older sister who occupied another room of the house. This sister was widowed and had a son who was eight years old. As it was this woman whom I paid for my meals and lodgings, I will refer to her as 'my hostess' throughout the book. She also prepared meals for her mentally retarded brother, who occupied the room next to hers. Like his adult nephew, who occupied yet another room of the house, this man kept to himself. He never entered the rooms of his sisters, who, in turn, never entered their brother's and nephew's rooms. The courtyard was also shared by a paternal aunt, who occupied a room with her husband and two grown-up children, a daughter and a son. Since all the women had to go out to earn money from time to time, we were all on equal footing in this respect and everyone accepted my leaving the house every day, as long as I told my hostess where I was going. Spending much time with these women, discussing with them every night what I had learned during visits that afternoon, while they told me about their whereabouts that day, we became closely involved in each other's lives. I came to regard them as my key informants.

It is through the women with whom I lived that I met most of my other informants. Having learned from my previous research experience in Sidi Slimane, I chose not to reach too far beyond their networks. To establish good rapport with Moroccan women means maintaining intensive contact, that is, visiting them at least once a week. I nearly always found my informants in the company of 'close' relatives, friends or neighbours, who insisted upon my visiting their houses as well. Being accepted in a wider circle of friends in turn reinforced the relationship with the initial informant. Choosing informants was rather a matter of limiting the number of contacts than finding means to extend them, the more so since I came to Sidi Sousan one week before the beginning of Ramadan, which is the pre-eminent month to invite guests. Despite the fact that I had only just arrived, I was invited to break the fast with a different family almost every evening during Ramadan. From these initial contacts, I developed more intensive visiting patterns with women from three families in the medina, which were supplemented by casual conversations with their neighbours, friends and relatives.

For contacts with families outside the medina I could not work through the networks of the women with whom I lived. I was introduced to a family in Gueliz, the former French quarter of Marrakech, by a friend of a colleague in Rabat. This contact did not trigger off other contacts. As I have described elsewhere in regard to the former French quarter in Sidi Slimane (Buitelaar 1986), families in the *ville nouvelle* keep to themselves and women tend to lead secluded lives in comparison to women from other quarters. A chance encounter in the public bath with a woman from Hay Fakhara, a recent squatter area just outside the city wall on the other side of the river Issil, provided a valuable entrance to a network of women in this bidonville of mostly poor newcomers to Marrakech from the surrounding countryside.

Besides the women with whom I lived, there were seven women from the aforementioned families whom I visited at least once a week and whom I consider important informants. Through them, I had less regular contacts with about fifty to sixty women, most of whom, except for the comparatively rich family in Gueliz, were from middle or lower social strata, (having been) married to small traders or craftsmen such as tanners, carpenters and tailors. Nearly all women were exclusively Arabic-speaking and illiterate, with a few exceptions such as my hostess, her sister with whom I shared the room and an older nurse and her grown-up daughters.

Most of the information which I present in this study is the result of informal conversations with women. This informal method could be followed because I had chosen to study in depth the lives of a small group of women whom I had the opportunity to visit frequently over an extended period. One advantage of this method was that it was more natural for my informants, who when I attempted to interview them, were soon distracted by visiting friends or children demanding attention or else became bored talking for more than fifteen minutes about the same subject. I never tape-recorded conversations, and only jotted down short notes in the presence of informants. These helped me to write down the conversations upon coming home. The quotations in the text are therefore not always *ad verbum*, but should be read as very close approximations.

The Moroccan ethos of hospitality greatly facilitated my access to women. However, it must also be said that, as a rule, just as I sought contact for my own academic purposes, the women with whom closer relationships developed all had their own objectives for seeking my company, although most of them could not state their intentions as clearly as I did. My expectations that women would be glad to share most of their experiences with me in return for small presents and being distracted with stories about my own experiences obviously did not match the expectations of some women who saw in me a future Muslim, a passport to Europe, or an extra source of income. For example, after some time I learned that, despite the occasional visits by a close friend from Rabat, whom I had introduced as my 'fiancé', one woman hoped I would raise interest in her son. Another woman had ambitions to convert me to Islam, while a key informant from the squatter area hoped to gain access to networks of 'established' Marrakchi women through me. I did my best for this latter lady, but had to disappoint others.

In several instances, when after a few months it became clear that I could not meet certain expectations, tensions arose. In most cases, despite disappointments, relationships were saved by the ongoing process of negotiation of reality between informants and myself. Tacitly bargaining over terms of reciprocity, we learned to adjust our expectations. I continued to visit the lady who hoped for my conversion, for example, but she would no longer invite me to join her on her visits to the shrines of saints and was less eager to 'teach' me about Islam.

Ethnographers elsewhere may have similar experiences, but I think the inevitability of it in nearly all my contacts is illustrative for the way Moroccans organise their relations with others. In chapter 7 I will describe in more detail how, in my view, Moroccans tend to interpret communication in terms of favours paid and favours received.

In sex-segregated societies such as Morocco, female researchers tend to have better access to male domains than male researchers have to the domains of women. Despite gender differences, which cannot be overcome readily, female researchers may profit from being an outsider in making contacts with men, since men are expected to deal with the 'outside'. Male researchers who seek contacts with women have the double handicap of having to overcome gender differences and of having to penetrate the barrier with which women protect themselves and are protected from contacts with the 'outside'.

If, however, a female researcher wishes to establish intimate relationships with women, I would argue that she has to become an 'insider', meaning that she chooses to move within the world of women and keep her contacts with men, who are relative outsiders to this world, limited. In my contacts with Marrakchi men, I therefore restricted myself to casual conversations with the husbands, brothers and sons of my female informants. I generally spoke with them in the presence of their female family members only, although I profited sometimes from the opportunity to have a more private conversation while being escorted home by a man.

Apart from my own observations, which in themselves are already influenced by participating predominantly in women's domains, most of the information presented here was supplied by women. Inevitably, therefore, the study is characterised by the gender biases of both the researcher and her mostly female informants. Indeed, as Bynum (1986: 13) contends, religious experience is always 'gendered'.

Notwithstanding my focus on the activities of women during Ramadan, the amount of information I have collected about men's activities justifies presentation. In my view, the religious practices of women and men cannot be separated. The extent to which the meanings analysed here are specific to women cannot be ascertained until they have been compared with more detailed material on fasting by men. It would be interesting to complement this study with similar research conducted by a male researcher. Comparison with the study of Buskens (1987) and the remarks made by Eickelman (1976) about Ramadan suggest that, indeed, minor or even some major 'shifts of emphasis' would occur.

Outline

The first chapter deals with the prescriptions on fasting in the Koran and the Traditions, followed by a summary of Malikite interpretations of these prescriptions. Because the scholar al-Ghazali is often quoted in Moroccan newspapers, a section concerning his treatise on fasting concludes the first chapter.

The second and third chapters describe the activities that take place before, during, and following Ramadan. I will first describe how people take leave of 'ordinary' life and prepare themselves for the fast by purging their homes, bodies and in some cases even their minds. This will be followed by an account of the course everyday life takes during Ramadan, which serves as the basis for the conceptual analyses of the meanings of the fast in terms of the key notions of the Islamic community, purity and religious merit. These notions will be studied in the three succeeding chapters.

First, it will be argued that fasting emphasises the boundaries of the Islamic community, the significance of which can be identified at different levels of Moroccan society. Second, the idea of fasting as a purification process with beneficial effects on both physical and mental health but with slightly different outcomes for men and women will be elaborated upon. Third, the importance of collecting religious merit during Ramadan will be focused upon.

In order to answer the question of how specific the significance of these notions is for the fast, chapter 7 indicates the extent to which these themes recur during the other religious feasts of importance to Moroccans: the Feast of Immolation, the celebration of the Islamic New Year and the celebration of the birth of the Prophet. In the final chapter the key notions are analysed as attributes of liminality. It will be argued that in the lives of individual Moroccans, the first time that they participate fully in the fast can be interpreted as a rite of passage which initiates them into Muslim adulthood, while, more importantly, local categorisation of Ramadan as the beginning of the cycle of religious celebrations marks it as a collective calendrical rite.

one

Prescriptions on Fasting in Islamic Law

Ramadan, as it is practised today in Morocco, is based on fasting precepts derived from two sources. The most important source is the Koran, which Muslims believe to be the literal word of God, revealed to the Prophet Muhammed. The prescriptions from the Koran are supplemented and specified by the Sunna, the customs or traditions of the Prophet. These traditions are expressed in Hadiths, narratives relating the deeds and utterances of Muhammed and his companions. Together the Koran and the Sunna constitute the Sharia, the Islamic Law.

Although the Koran and the Sunna together form the basis for Islamic law, these texts as such do not yield an elaborate set of rules that constitute a legal system. In order to generate such a system, the texts had to be interpreted. Accordingly, the science of *fiqh*, jurisprudence, was developed. By the end of the third century after the Hegira, Muhammed's emigration from Mecca to Medina, several schools of law had been founded.[1] Moroccan jurisprudence belongs to the Malikite school.[2]

The first section of this chapter examines the texts in the Koran on fasting. In the second section, the Hadith will be looked at more closely. Initially, narratives were passed on orally. Only later did men of learning begin to collect and even record them. Each narrative was preceded by naming the *isnâd*, the chain of authority upon which the tradition is based. Mainly by investigating these chains, sound traditions were distinguished from dubious ones and the latter were discarded. Different versions of traditions which

1. The year of the Hegira, 622 AD, is the starting point for the Muslim Era.
2. This school of law was named after Malik Ibn Anas (d. 796). It prevails in Muslim Africa, except for the east coast and Lower Egypt. The Hanafite school, named after Abu Hanifa (d. 767), is mainly to be found in the former Ottoman Empire (Turkey, Muslim parts of the Balkans and the Arabic Middle East), Central Asia, India and Pakistan. Another school was founded by Ibn Idriss al-Shafi (767–820). Its adherents are to be found in Lower Egypt, Eastern Turkey and the Muslim countries around the Indian Ocean especially in East Africa, the south-east coast of the Arabian Peninsula and in Indonesia. The most recent and smallest school was founded by Ahmad Ibn Hanbal (d. 855),the Hanbalite school. It is the official school of law in Saudi Arabia (R. Peters 1984: 171).

had equally reliable chains of authority were all written down. There exist many such compilations of traditions. Here, I have restricted myself to the work of Bukari (1862), which is considered to be one of the six most reliable compilations, and, together with that of Muslim (1955–6) the most widely consulted ones. In the third section, I will take a closer look at the rules on fasting which have been elaborated by the Malikite school of law.

It would be interesting to study the development of Moroccan jurisprudence from these early texts to the present day. This, however, falls beyond the scope of this study. When Moroccans talk about prescriptions regarding fasting, they do not refer to Malikite texts and, as a rule, do not concern themselves with what the *ᶜulamâ'*, the men of learning, have written about the subject, but rather simply state: 'this is written in the Koran'.

The chapter concludes with a section on the writings of the scholar al-Ghazali (1058–1111) about fasting. Not only are his writings still cited in Moroccan newspapers every year during Ramadan, but al-Ghazali has been very important in the development of Islamic orthodoxy. His views distinguish varying degrees of intensity which are discernible in the practice of fasting by different people.

The Koran on Fasting

The *ṣawm*, fasting during the month Ramadan, is one of the five pillars of Islam, i.e. the religious duties Muslims should fulfil. The others are the *šahâda*, the Muslim Creed, the *ṣalât*, the five daily prayers, the *zakât*, alms-giving, and the *ḥajj*, the pilgrimage to Mecca. Fasting during Ramadan is mentioned in Sura 2: 183–187:[3]

> 183. O believers, prescribed for you is the Fast, even as it was prescribed for those that were before you – haply you will be godfearing –
>
> 184. for days numbered; and if any of you be sick, or if he be on a journey, then a number of other days; and for those who are able to fast, a redemption by feeding a poor man. Yet better it is for him who volunteers good, and that you should fast is better for you, if you but know;
>
> 185. the month of Ramadan, wherein the Koran was sent down to be a guidance to the people, and as clear signs of the Guidance and the Salvation. So let those of you, who are present at the month, fast it; and if any of you be sick, or if he be on a journey, then a number of other days; God desires ease for you, and desires not hardship for you; and that you fulfil

3. All quotations from the Koran are from Arberry's translation, *The Koran Interpreted* (1955).

> the number, and magnify God that He guided you, and haply you will be thankful.
>
> 186. And when My servants question thee concerning Me – I am near to answer the call of the caller, when he calls to Me; so let them respond to Me, and let them believe in Me; haply so they will go aright.
>
> 187. Permitted to you, upon the night of the Fast, is to go in to your wives; they are a vestment for you, and you are a vestment for them. God knows that you have been betraying yourselves, and had turned to you and pardoned you. So now lie with them and seek what God has prescribed for you. And eat and drink, until the white thread shows clearly to you from the black thread at the dawn; then complete the Fast unto the night, and do not lie with them while you cleave the mosques. Those are God's bounds; keep well within them. So God makes clear His signs to men; haply they will be godfearing.

These verses date from the time Muhammed had already settled in Medina, where he came into contact with Jews. The Jews fasted on the Day of Atonement to commemorate Moses' descent after his second sojourn on Mount Sinai (Goitein 1966: 95). According to one tradition, when Muhammed was confronted with fasting Jews, he inquired about the meaning of their fast. They replied that the Day of Atonement was the sacred day upon which God had liberated Israel from its enemy. As a token of gratitude, Moses had introduced a fasting day. To this Muhammed responded by specifying the *ᶜâšûrâ'*, the tenth day of the Islamic New Year, corresponding to the Jewish Day of Atonement, as a compulsory fasting day for Muslims (ibid.).

After having broken off his relations with the Jews about a year later, Muhammed abolished obligatory fasting on the *ᶜâšûrâ'* and replaced it by a fasting period of several days. This is what the words 'for days numbered' (S2: 184) refer to. It is likely that by prescribing the fast of days numbered, Muhammed revived an old voluntary practice existing among Arabs of fasting a sacred period of time during the month of Rajab. This fasting consisted of complete abstention from food, drink and sexual relations until sunset, after which only one meal was allowed before fasting was resumed again until the next sunset (Wagtendonk 1968: 80). The severe character of this form of fasting is probably the reason why the Koran initially permitted breaking the fast in any situation and compensating for it by feeding a person in need, as can be read in S2: 184: 'and for those who are able to fast, a redemption by feeding a poor man'.

Yet, even in these early days fasting was preferred over feeding the poor, as can be deduced from the following lines in S2: 184, in which it is stated that it is better to perform acts of charity voluntarily, that is, besides fasting: 'Yet better it is for him, who volunteers good, and that you should fast is better for you, if you but know.'

Later, the fasting of 'days numbered' in its turn was replaced by fasting during the whole month of Ramadan. According to Lech (1979: 224), for some time the two forms of fasting co-existed. The reason for this was that the Prophet had to reconcile the demands of the ascetic few who preferred severe fasting, and the wishes of the more moderate many, who asked for a milder form of fasting that could be attained by all people.

Gradually, however, fasting during Ramadan gained ground over fasting 'days numbered', and Ramadan became a sacred month. The special character of Ramadan may account for the fact that it is the only month mentioned explicitly in the Koran. It was during Ramadan that Muhammed received his first revelation from God. This is what the words 'wherein the Koran was sent down to be a Guidance to the people' in S2: 185 refer to.[4] This first revelation occurred during a special night, the *laylat al-qadr*. The importance of this night is more specifically described in S97: 1–5:

> Behold, We sent it down on the Night of Power; And what shall teach thee what is the Night of Power? The Night of Power is better than a thousand months; in it angels and the Spirit descended, by the leave of their Lord, upon every command. Peace it is, till the rising of dawn.

Nowadays, the *laylat al-qadr* is celebrated in the night between the 26th and 27th of Ramadan, although the exact date is not known (Wagtendonk 1968: 83). According to a statement of the Prophet, as recorded in Bukari's compilation of traditions, it should be searched for among the odd days of the ten last days of the month:

> I had come to teach you about the Night of Power, but since a such and a someone were quarrelling, the knowledge about that night has escaped me. Maybe it is better for you. Seek it among the ninth, seventh and fifth last nights of the month. (Bukari 1862: 642–3, my translation)

According to the tradition as compiled by Bukari, the sins of those who spend the *laylat al-qadr* in vigil and prayer will be forgiven (ibid.: 609). The compilation by al-Tabari (1898–1901) states that during this night, God makes a decision and writes down who shall participate in the coming pilgrimage to Mecca (Wagtendonk 1968: 100).

4. It remains uncertain whether Muhammed had only his first revelation or whether the Koran was sent down in its totality. Speculation over this question has kept Islamic scholars debating for centuries. The matter is usually solved by stating that the Koran was sent down to the first of seven Heavens, from which Muhammed then received his first revelation (Wagtendonk 1968).

The revelation of the Koran is not the only reason why Ramadan became such an important month for Muslims. It is also the month during which Muslims in the year 624, under the guidance of the Prophet, triumphed over the unbelieving Meccans in the battle of Badr (ibid.: 88–95). This was interpreted as a sign of God's guidance and a reconfirmation of the legitimacy of the Koran. According to Wagtendonk (ibid.: 80), the words in S2: 185 'and as clear signs of the Guidance and the Salvation' imply both events: the revelation of the Koran and the victory in the battle of Badr.

Once fasting during Ramadan had replaced the fasting of 'days numbered', the prescriptions on how to fast had to be adjusted. This is reflected in the second part of S2: 185 and onwards. First of all, the possibility of replacing fasting, at all times, with feeding a person in need was qualified by the words: 'So let those of you, who are present at the month, fast it.'

What is translated here as 'who are present at the month' reads in Arabic *man šahida*, which can be interpreted in different ways. It can mean 'whoever is present', as Arberry, the author of the translation cited here, has chosen to translate the phrase. The same words, however, could also be interpreted to mean 'whoever witnesses', in the sense of seeing with one's own eyes or in the jurisprudential sense of 'bearing witness' (Lech 1979: 76). The consequences of this ambiguity will be touched upon in the next section.

After fasting during Ramadan had become an established practice, breaking the fast was only allowed to those who were ill or travelling. The fasting days thus missed had to be made up later in the year: 'and if any of you be sick, or if he be on a journey, then a number of other days' (S2: 185). According to a tradition mentioned in Bukari, one is allowed, but not obliged, to break the fast whilst on journey. The Prophet, however, did warn against extreme practices: 'It is not an act of piety to fast whilst on journey' (Bukari 1862: 623, my translation). In Bukari's compilation, it is also said that women do not fast during their menses. As in the case of ill people, the lost fasting days are to be made up later in the year. The elderly and people who perform hard work are also released from fasting, if they wish. They can compensate by feeding the needy (Wagtendonk 1984: 185). The words: 'God desires ease for you, and desires not hardship for you' (S2: 185) may be interpreted as a justification of this compensation, as is the aforementioned S2: 184. In S2: 185, the believers are provided with a reason to fast: to glorify God: 'and that you fulfil the number, and magnify God that He guided you, and haply you will be thankful'.

According to Wagtendonk (1968: 70,74), S2: 186 may be connected with the so-called *i^{c}tikâf*, the sojourn in a mosque for several days to worship God. This is a voluntary practice which is combined with fasting. The *i^{c}tikâf* may be observed at any time during the year, although it is most commonly practised during the last ten days of Ramadan. The word *i^{c}tikâf* is derived from *^{c}ukûf,* a pre-Islamic custom of dwelling in the vicinity of idols, in the hope of receiving a meaningful dream. Several verses in the Koran mention that idols do not answer. The words in S2: 186 'I am near to answer the call of the caller, when he calls to Me' may well refer to the reliability of God in contrast to the idols.

The transition from fasting 'days numbered' to fasting during Ramadan was marked by an expansion of the number of fasting days to a full month, and a restriction on the alternative of feeding the poor instead of fasting. These alterations were possible because the fasting rules had become less severe. From that time on, eating, drinking and having sexual relations were allowed between sunset and sunrise. This is the intent of the words:

> Permitted to you, upon the night of the Fast, is to go in to your wives; they are a vestment for you, and you are a vestment for them. (S2: 187)

> And eat and drink, until the white thread shows clearly to you from the black thread at the dawn; then complete the Fast unto the night. (S2: 187)

According to Bukari's compilation of traditions, S2: 187 was revealed to Muhammed when he received word of a man who had accidentally slept after sunset during the time when one was supposed to break the fast with one meal. Consequently, he had to wait another 24 hours before being allowed to eat again. As a consequence, he fainted. Although the Prophet himself was well able to observe the severe form of fasting, he forbade others to do so, saying: 'Eat the last meal of the night. Blessing is attached to this last meal' (Bukari 1862: 614, my translation).

As mentioned above, S2: 183–187 is the only pericope in the Koran which explicitly mentions fasting during Ramadan. Fasting is, however, mentioned in several other places in which the virtues of faithful believers are enumerated:

> It is possible that, if he divorces you, his Lord will give him in exchange wives better than you, women who have surrendered, believing, obedient, penitent, devout, given to fasting, who have been married and virgins too. (S66: 5)

> Men and women who have surrendered, believing men and believing women, obedient men and obedient women, truthful men and truthful

> women, enduring men and enduring women, humble men and humble women, men and women who give in charity, men who fast and women who fast, men and women who guard their private parts, men and women who remember God oft – for them God has prepared forgiveness and a mighty wage. (S33: 35)

In various other verses regarding more specific situations, fasting is presented as an act of penance. Two of these verses concern the pilgrimage to Mecca. In S2: 196 fasting is mentioned as a means of redemption for shaving one's head prematurely during the pilgrimage (Lech 1979: 10):

> Fulfil the Pilgrimage and the Visitation unto God; but if you are prevented, then such offering as may be feasible. And shave not your heads, till the offering reaches its place of sacrifice. If any of you is sick, or injured in his head, then redemption by fast, or freewill offering, or ritual sacrifice.

The verse in S5: 95 concerns compensation for having killed game while on pilgrimage (ibid.):

> O believers, slay not the game while you are in pilgrim sanctity; whosoever of you slays it wilfully, there shall be recompense – the like of what he has slain, in flocks as shall be judged by two men of equity among you, an offering to reach the Kaaba; or expiation – food for poor persons or the equivalent of that in fasting, so that he may taste the mischief of his action.

In verse S4: 92 it is suggested to fast as a form of penance for having accidentally killed a Muslim (ibid.: 9):

> It belongs not to a believer to slay a believer, except it be by error. If any slays a believer by error, then let him set free a believing slave, and bloodwit is to be paid to his family unless they forgo it as a freewill offering. If he belong to a people at enmity with you and is a believer, let the slayer set free a believing slave. If he belongs to a people joined with you by a compact, then bloodwit is to be paid to his family and the slayer shall set free a believing slave. But if he finds not the means, let him fast two successive months – God's turning; God is All-knowing, All-wise.

To conclude this list of verses in which voluntary fasting is mentioned in the Koran, there are two verses in which fasting is presented as a recompense for having breached a vow (Lech 1979: 9):

> God will not take you to task for a slip in your oaths; but He will take you to task for such bonds as you have made by oaths, whereof the expiation is to feed ten poor persons with the average of the food you serve to your families, or to clothe them, or to set free a slave; or if any finds not the means, let him fast for three days ...(S5: 89)

To a man who repudiates his wife by pronouncing the forbidden formula 'Be as my mother's back', fasting is one of the options to compensate for doing so (ibid.):

> And those who say, regarding their wives, 'Be as my mother's back' and then retract what they have said, they shall set free a slave, before the two of them touch one another. By that you are admonished; and God is aware of the things you do. But whosoever finds not the means, then let him fast two successive months, before the two of them touch one another. By that you are admonished; and God is aware of the things you do. (S58: 3–4)

Fasting in the Hadith

The fasting prescriptions in the Koran are few and vague. This must be understood against the background within which these texts were generated. When the Prophet Muhammed still lived in Medina, the community of believers was so small that the meaning of fasting from sunrise to sunset was clear to everyone. The example of the Prophet was close at hand. According to Lech (1979: 223), even when the Muslims conquered Mecca, Muhammed deliberately saw to it that the prescriptions were kept rather general, so as not to confuse new believers or run the risk of having them reject rules which they had not yet grown accustomed to. Many tribes had converted to Islam for purely political reasons. Since they were not interested in precise rules, they did not ask for them either. It is therefore unlikely that a very detailed set of rules had already been developed during Muhammed's life (Lech 1979: 223).

Due to the rapid expansion of Islam, the generations following Muhammed saw themselves confronted with many questions. Distances were becoming too large to turn to the centre of the caliphate to have these questions answered. Deriving rules from the categories of *ijmâ*^{c}, consensus, and *qiyâs*, analogy, as secondary sources to Islamic law, had not yet been introduced. Furthermore, regions on the outskirts of the caliphate were probably influenced by non-Muslim customs, so that an unequivocal understanding of the prescriptions for fasting during Ramadan, if they existed at all, was more and more threatened (ibid.: 225).

One of the major problems was who should determine when to begin fasting the month of Ramadan. The words *man šahida* in S2: 185 can be interpreted in various ways. One opinion favoured the *ru'ya* principle, which entails that the beginning of Ramadan is only to be determined by seeing the *hilâl*, the first crescent of the new moon. But this could lead to problems if the moon was hidden behind clouds. The question of whether every individual Muslim had to witness the new moon or whether it would be sufficient for the religious leaders to do so, and then declare that Ramadan had begun, was also left unanswered. Therefore, others were in favour of the *ḥisâb* principle, which implies calculating the exact duration of Ramadan, which, as a lunar month, variably consists of twenty-nine or thirty days. This, however, would mean that the prescription of watching the new moon would be ignored. Neither principle was without drawbacks, so over the years a combination of the two was formulated. A calendar was drawn up based on calculations, but was corrected in practice by the *ru'ya* principle.

To avoid accidentally missing the first fasting day of Ramadan, in case the exact beginning of the month was unclear, fasting on *yawm aš-šakk*, the day of doubt, was introduced, the practice of fasting the last day of the preceding month, Shaban. This tendency to extend Ramadan also occurred at the end of the month. In cases where it was not clear whether Ramadan had been completed or not, people began to continue fasting on the first day of the following month, Shawwal, and eventually even on the first six days of that month.

Given this ambivalence, the importance of the traditions of Muhammed increased. Soon the sunna was not just a collection of sayings and doings of the Prophet, but was interpreted as the guideline for religious conduct, consisting of prescriptions which complemented and specified those of the Koran (Leemhuis 1984: 92).[5]

It must be noted that the compilations of traditions are not consistent works, but contain divergent and even contradictory statements. In the chapter on fasting in Bukari's compilation of traditions, we find not only complementary and specific prescriptions, but also motives for fasting, descriptions of occasions when fasting is recommended or disapproved of, as well as examples of fasting habits of the Prophet and the people nearest to him.

Given the *ru'ya–ḥisâb* controversy, it does not come as a surprise that some prescriptions provide guidelines for determining the exact moment to begin and conclude the fast. The Sunna rejects the *ḥisâb* principle and, consequently, fasting on the day of doubt. The problem of determining the exact length of a single fasting day is also touched upon. When asked about this problem, the Prophet is said to have replied that there should be enough time between

5. Lech (1979: 226) argues that tracing the chain of authority (*isnâd*) all the way back to Muhammed is, historically speaking, unsound in cases where Hadith offers specifications regarding issues that did not yet need any specification at the time of the Prophet. He even discards the traditions when analysing the meaning of pericope S2: 183–187. In his view, the verses have to speak for themselves (ibid.: 26). Because I am not here concerned with a complete analysis of the text but seek a better understanding of the way this pericope has been interpreted by Muslims, I do not follow his rigorous rejection.

the new fasting day and the last meal late at night for the recitation of 50 Koran verses.

Other prescriptions specify the conditions under which fasting is invalid. According to some, during the fast it is permitted to bath, gargle, brush the teeth, rub the hair with oil – if this is part of one's daily routine – apply *kuḥl*, antimonium, on the eye-lids, and to vomit, as is bloodletting and tasting food so long as it is spat out again. Fasting will also remain valid if water is inhaled accidentally during ritual purification, and if one accidentally swallows a fly. Even when one breaks the fast from absent-mindedness, by eating or having sexual contact, the fasting day remains valid, because: 'If anyone forgets and eats or drinks, let him complete his fast, for it was Allah who caused him thus to eat or drink' (Jeffery 1962: 100). Furthermore, when one wakes up in the morning in an impure state as a result of having enjoyed sexual relations during the night, the fasting day will remain valid if one purifies oneself immediately. This was in fact the way Muhammed himself acted. On the other hand, the fasting becomes invalid when one does not behave properly: 'If one does not give up saying false words and doing false deeds in Ramadan, giving up eating and drinking means nothing to Allah' (Jeffery 1962: 92). When someone is insulted or assaulted by another person, he or she is supposed to reply by stating twice: 'I am fasting'.

If someone dies while still owing fasting days, due to a break in previous fasting or illness, a close inheritor fasting in his or her place can make up the lack.

These prescriptions clearly show the importance of the concept of *nîya*, intention, in determining the validity of fasting. In other narratives collected by Bukari, motives for fasting are presented. Fasting people are precious to God: the scent coming from the mouth of a fasting person pleases him more than the fragrance of musk. The sins of those who fast shall be forgiven and their good deeds will be multiplied by ten. Fasting protects one from the fires of hell and provides happiness twice; firstly, in the legitimate breaking of the fast, and secondly, when standing in front of God on Judgement Day. There is a gate to heaven, al-Rayyan, through which only those who have fasted may enter. In some special cases, fasting, together with praying and alms-giving, can be a way to solve financial problems or mend neighbourly quarrels. Fasting can even be employed as a means to resist temptation: 'Let him who is able to marry take a wife, for it is the best way of averting lascivious glances and of providing chaste enjoyment, but let him who is not able (to marry) fast, for it will be a remover (of unseemly passion) for him' (Jeffery 1962:93).

Some narratives do not contain prescriptions or arguments in favour of fasting, but simply provide information on utterances and customs of the Prophet in regard to fasting. In a statement which, as will be demonstrated in subsequent chapters, is of great importance to Moroccans, Muhammed proclaims that during Ramadan, the gates of heaven open and the gates of hell close, so that the *jinn,* the demons, are temporarily locked up. Other narratives relate the generosity of the Prophet, which reached its apex during Ramadan: 'The Prophet – upon whom be Allah's blessing and peace – was the most generous of men with his goods, but he was never more generous than during Ramadan ... So at these times, when Gabriel met with him he would be more generous than the rain-bringing wind' (Jeffery 1962: 92).

Since the life of Muhammed constitutes the best model for the faithful, pious Muslims strive to adopt his habits. Unless, of course, the Prophet himself advised against it, as he is reported to have done in regard to the practice of a form of fast during which only one meal may be consumed every twenty-four hours, and sexual relations are to be abstained from completely. In yet another narrative, Aisha, one of the wives of Muhammed, relates that the Prophet did in fact touch his wives while fasting. But she immediately adds that her husband possessed more self-control than other men. About Aisha herself, it is stated that in the month of Shaban she made up for the days she had missed during the previous Ramadan due to menstruation. During the month preceding Ramadan, Muhammed used to practise voluntary fasting more often than he did during the rest of the year. Several other favourite dates are mentioned upon which he fasted voluntarily and recommended others to do likewise. A case in point is the *ᶜâšûrâ',* the tenth day of the Islamic New Year, which, as we have seen, was initially observed as an obligatory fasting day, but later was only recommended as a fasting day.[6] The Prophet did not fast while standing on Mount Arafat on the ninth day of the pilgrimage to Mecca, as had been the custom during the pre-Islamic era. However, he did not forbid others to do so. He recommended fasting on the 'bright days', the 13th, 14th and 15th days of the month.[7] Voluntary fasting, however, must be kept within limits: 'Fast, but then break the fast. Get up for prayers, but then sleep. You have a duty towards your eyes, towards yourself, and towards your family' (Jeffery 1962: 116). Even for the most devout it is sufficient to fast only

6. In Islamic law, all human action is classified into five categories:
i. *mafrûḍ* = obligatory
ii. *mandûb* = recommended
iii. *mubâḥ* = indifferent (said of actions which are neither rewarded nor punished but which are permissible)
iv. *makrûh* = reprehensible
v. *ḥarâm* = forbidden

7. These days are called bright days because they surround the full moon.

three days monthly, because such pious acts are multiplied by ten, thus amounting to thirty days. Should somebody, none the less, wish to fast more often, he or she can then take David, who ate one day and fasted the next, as an example. In any case, it is forbidden to fast more than three days in a row, as well as on Friday, unless this is part of a fixed period of fasting. Likewise, it is forbidden to fast on *ᶜîd al-fiṭr*, the feast that concludes Ramadan, as it is on *al-ᶜîd al-kabîr*, the sacrificial feast during the pilgrimage to Mecca.

In Bukari's collection of traditions, the chapter on fasting is followed by a brief chapter on collective prayers in the mosques during Ramadan at night. These gatherings were instituted after the death of the Prophet by Caliph ᶜUmar, who believed it beneficial to perform the voluntary Ramadan prayers collectively instead of individually or in small groups. Participation in these so-called *ṣalât at-tarâwîḥ* is recommended.

Interpretations by the Malikite School

Before turning to the texts of two Malikite scholars, some preliminary remarks should be made. Firstly, it should be noted that the official doctrine of any school of law is not to be found in the works of the old masters, as in this case Malik's *al-Muwatta'*[8] is, but in subsequent works, recognised as the authoritative exponents of current teaching by common opinion of the school. These works are now generally handbooks from the late medieval period. Subsequent works derive their authority from these handbooks (Schacht 1964: 71). Secondly, these handbooks contained no clear codes: Islamic law is not a corpus of legislation but the living result of legal science (ibid.).

Two Malikite works that have retained their importance in contemporary North Africa are the *risâla* by Ibn Abi Zayd al-Qayrawani (d. 996), and the *mukṭaṣar* by Kalil Bin Ishaq (d. 1315 or 1374; Bousquet 1960: 74–5). Moroccan *ᶜulamâ'*, men of learning, still base their *fatwâs*, religious decrees, on these books. The purpose for which the two works were written differs: the *risâla* was intended to be a sort of catechism for teaching both adult and young believers about their religion, so that they will be able to conduct a religious life. The *mukṭaṣar*, on the other hand, served from the very beginning as a kind of lawmanual to be memorised by professional lawyers.

The contents of the chapters regarding fasting in these two works do not vary greatly from the information supplied by Bukari's compilation of traditions. The main difference is that the

8. Which in fact was not written by himself but consists of a record of his teachings written down by his followers in several closely related versions (Schacht 1964: 44).

narratives about the deeds and utterances of the Prophet have either been transformed into prescriptions on relevant issues or have simply been omitted. Some prescriptions mentioned in the collection of traditions are merely repeated, while others are further specified. In treating the *muḵtaṣar* and the *risâla,* I will not provide a complete inventory of all these prescriptions, but will restrict myself to those bearing upon the themes of the chapters to follow.

Both texts state that the beginning of Ramadan should be determined by the appearance of the first crescent of the new moon. In the *muḵtaṣar*, it is further specified that the witnesses should be two *ᶜudûl*, professional witnesses. They should inform the *qâdî*, the religious judge, who then proclaims the fasting month to have begun. Fasting the day of doubt as a sort of precaution is rejected, but people who choose that day for voluntary fasting, to compensate for previously missed fasting days, are free to do so.

In both the *muḵtaṣar* and the *risâla* attention is paid to the issue of who should actually fast. Children should begin fasting when they reach puberty; in the case of girls when they have their first menses, for boys from the time they begin to have 'nocturnal pollutions' or wet dreams (al-Qayrawani 1975: 119). From that age everyone is obliged to fast, except for menstruating women, whose fasting is invalid. In cases, however, where people fear fasting to have negative consequences for their health, they are excused or even compelled to break the fast or abstain from fasting altogether. Pregnant women, for instance, should break the fast if they fear fasting will be harmful to the foetus. Breastfeeding women are also obliged to refrain from fasting if they fear fasting will affect the well-being of the baby. The fasting days thus missed have to be compensated for later in the year. If travellers and people who are temporarily ill break the fast, they should compensate the lost fasting days later during the year, whereas the elderly and chronically ill can make amends by feeding one poor person for every fasting day. Al-Qayrawani (1975: 119) remarks that according to some, this form of recompense is also necessary for pregnant and breastfeeding women who do not fast.

The fact that prescriptions about who is and is not to fast ultimately leave it to the individual to decide whether or not they are excused from fasting, once more shows the importance of *nîya*, one's intention to fast. This is further illustrated by the statement in the *muḵtaṣar* (1975: 130) that no fasting day will be valid unless one formulates the intention to fast the entire month on the very first night of Ramadan. Stating the intention, either to oneself or out loud, is in turn closely related to another condition that should be met for the fast to be valid: one is to possess reason. The fasting of mentally retarded people is invalid, as is the fasting of people who have fainted at some time between the formulation of the intention and the completion of the fast. Yet another condition is that one should be pure before the fast.

'Holding one's tongue' and watching one's actions while fasting, that is, not arguing or fighting with other people, are recommended. Making haste to break the fast after sunset and delaying the latest meal at night are further recommendations. Deliberate vomiting falls under the category of objectionable acts, as does the tasting of food and the chewing of foodstuffs before feeding them to infants. It is also reprehensible to engage in acts which usually precede coitus, such as sensual thoughts and glances, or kissing (Ishaq 1956: 13).

Other references deal with recommendable or objectionable acts during voluntary fasting. Fasting while travelling, even when covering a distance for which fasting is no longer obliged, is recommended. Voluntary fasting is also recommended while standing on Mount Arafat during the pilgrimage to Mecca, as is the fasting during the first ten days of the month of the pilgrimage by those who do not perform the *ḥajj*. Fasting on the *ᶜâšûrâ'*, the tenth day of the first month of the Islamic New Year, and preferably also on the nine days preceding it, is also recommended. In fact, Muharram in general is a good month to practise voluntary fasting, as are the months of Rajab and Shaban. On the other hand, fasting the 'bright days', the 13th, 14th and 15th day of every month, and during the first six days of Shawwal, the month succeeding Ramadan, is objectionable. Practising voluntary fasting when in fact one still owes days of compensatory fasting is also disapproved of. Furthermore, women may not practise either compensatory or voluntary fasting without the permission of their husbands.[9]

Different rules of validity and compensation apply to obligatory fasting on the one hand and voluntary or compensatory fasting on the other hand. Detailed information is provided on this issue, in the *muḵtaṣar* in particular, which can be summarised as follows: accidentally breaking the obligatory fast during Ramadan always renders the fast invalid and necessitates compensatory fasting. Deliberately breaking an obligatory fast requires not only compensation but also expiation, varying from feeding poor people to freeing a slave and/or fasting two months. Accidentally breaking a voluntary fast does not affect the validity of the fast, whereas deliberately breaking this form of fast necessitates compensatory fasting only.

'The Secrets of Fasting' by al-Ghazali

After having been a teacher for some time, the scholar al-Ghazali (1058–1111) resigned from his job in order to devote himself to

9. The husband's right of sexual access to his wife overrules the woman's will to fast.

mysticism. Strengthened by this experience, he strongly criticised the traditional science of law and philosophy for pretending to offer certainties which they could not substantiate. In his most important book *iḥyâ' ᶜulûm ad-dîn*, 'The Revitalisation of the Sciences of Religion', he argues that more scope for religious experiences and intuition, which would supply these sciences with new vitality, should be allowed. His line of thought proved to be very successful and has been important in the further development of Islamic orthodoxy (J. Peters 1984: 190).

In *The Revitalisation of the Sciences of Religion*, al-Ghazali devotes one chapter to 'the secrets of fasting'. From this chapter, his statement based on a tradition which states that 'fasting is a quarter of the religion' (al-Ghazali 1955: 80) is particularly well known and is cited in Moroccan newspapers every year during Ramadan. According to al-Ghazali, fasting has a special virtue in comparison to other religious duties, because it puts the endurance of believers to the test and involves a continuous battle against Satan.

Al-Ghazali distinguishes three degrees of fasting: first of all, the fasting of ordinary people, which consists of abstaining from food, drink and sexual relations; second, the fasting of the religious elite, which involves keeping all sensory organs free from sins; and third, the fasting of 'the elite of the elite', during which not only sin has to be avoided, but also sinful thoughts, in order to concentrate exclusively on God. This third degree of fasting can only be achieved by the prophets and saints. Men of learning should strive to attain at least the second degree of fasting.

This second degree includes the following requirements:

1. keeping the eyes downcast and turning them away from any scene or object that might engage the attention of the fasting person so strongly that he or she would forget God;
2. refraining from lies and slander as well as from opening the mouth to pronounce words that are harsh or *risqué*. Instead, one's tongue should only be used to recite the Koran;
3. preventing the hands and feet from engaging in reprehensible behaviour;
4. eating moderately after breaking the fast, since there is no point in denying oneself a lavish meal only to make up for it again later, and sleeping as little as possible whilst fasting;
5. fearing that God might not accept one's fast.

The intention of this last condition is to continue doing one's very best to attain the second degree of fasting. Fasting will only be accepted when it has met its purpose, namely if the believer is able to bear hunger and thirst. This is considered a characteristic of divinity the faithful should strive for: 'Man has an intermediary position between angels and animals; when he plunges into his passions, he debases himself to the rank of animals, and, when he fights them, he elevates himself to the rank of angels' (al-Ghazali 1955: 81, my translation). The distinguishing features of different modes of fasting, as emphasised in this citation from al-Ghazali, will be worked out in the chapters to follow, in which we will turn to questions relating to the degree and manner in which the prescriptions and directions described in this chapter are known and observed by Moroccans, as well as the meanings they attach to them.

Summary

Concluding this presentation of prescriptions and specifications regarding fasting, as described in the Koran and further elaborated in the Hadith and the works of Malikite scholars, let me briefly repeat the major points:

1. All adult Muslims who are in a good physical and mental condition should fast the month of Ramadan.
2. The first and last day of Ramadan should not be determined by calculation, but by witnessing the new moon.
3. From sunrise to sunset, those who fast should abstain from eating, drinking and sexual contacts.
4. Conditions that render the fast valid are that one should pronounce the intention to fast and be in a pure state.
5. The fasting of menstruating women and those who deliberately break the fast is invalid.
6. Those who fear that fasting will have negative consequences for their health (the ill, the elderly, pregnant and lactating women, people who perform hard labour) are released from fasting.
7. Missed fasting days must be compensated.
8. Voluntary fasting is recommended on the condition that lost fasting days have been compensated.

two

Shaban: Preparing for Ramadan

A few days before Ramadan was to begin, the aunt of my hostess emptied the cupboard and the shelves in her kitchen, gathered the cooking utensils around her in the courtyard, and spent an entire day scrubbing pots and pans with steel wool. In the evening, she called me into her kitchen and proudly showed me the new plastic decoration hanging from the shelves and the neatly arranged pots and pans on top of them, which shone like new. As far as she was concerned, Ramadan could begin: she was ready for it.

Cleaning the house is one of the ways people, and women in particular, prepare themselves for the coming fasting month. In fact, the whole month preceding Ramadan, named Shaban, is dedicated to these preparations. About a week before the advent of Ramadan, the changing streets in the medina of Marrakech make one realise that the fasting month is approaching. Many of the vendors, who sit along the side of the road behind a piece of cloth with a few displayed articles, have replaced their usual merchandise, such as washcloths and scrubstones for the public bath, with the bowls and wooden spoons that are used to eat *ḥrîra*, the special Ramadan soup. Other peddlers have substituted copies of the Koran for second-hand books and magazines. Small restaurants are decorated with glittering festoons and paper stars, like those used in Europe as Christmas decorations, and switch from serving quick lunches to selling *šebbakîya*s, the special Ramadan cookies. On Jemaa al-Fna, the central square in the medina of Marrakech, rows of stalls selling the same kind of cookies, which can also be found in all confectionery shops this time of the year, are set up. One confectionery, which is famous for the excellent quality of its *šebbakîya*s and other pastries that are eaten almost exclusively during Ramadan, rents a second shop for the months of Shaban and Ramadan in the middle of Semmarine, the *sûq* or bazaar of Marrakech and traditional shopping centre of the town. The smell of the *šebbakîya*s penetrates the whole medina.

Olives and dates are also much desired delicacies during Ramadan. Some days before the fasting month begins, small shopkeepers who usually sell anything from kitchenware to tools, suddenly have devoted plenty of room in their shops to crates of dates and jars or even washtubs full of olives and other preserves.[1]

Another sign that Ramadan is close at hand is the banners with texts from the Koran and Hadith about fasting. These banners are hung over the doors of most of the mosques of Marrakech, and notices appear on the doors of public buildings to announce the change in working hours during Ramadan (10.00–15.00 hrs).[2]

Most preparations for Ramadan, however, take place within the homes of people and are carried out by women. The various preparations are marked by an increasing degree of ritualised behaviour. Together they can be viewed as the preliminary phase of the fast. In this chapter I will describe this preliminary phase by first focusing on activities concerned with settling pending matters and bidding farewell to 'ordinary' life, such as organising parties, as is described in the first section, and fasting to make up for missed fasting days during the month of Ramadan of the previous year, as is described in the second section. The remainder of the chapter deals with purifying activities which enable people to begin Ramadan with a clean slate. In three successive sections I will describe how people prepare and purge their homes, bodies and, in some cases, their minds.

Celebrating Shaban

During Shaban, there is an atmosphere of enjoying the merriment and joys of life before committing oneself to the serious and reflective mood that Ramadan demands. It is a good time for organising parties. These may either be wedding parties, or *šeᶜbâna*s, specific Shaban parties.

Wedding Parties

Shaban marks the opening of the wedding season.[3] Many wedding ceremonies take place immediately preceding and following Ramadan. Many couples who have agreed to get married that year prefer to do so before Ramadan begins. When asked why people prefer to get married in Shaban, my informants provided several reasons. One, only jokingly, replied that the grooms want somebody to prepare the *ḥrîra* for them. Another reason which was mentioned to me was that next to Ramadan, Shaban is the most blessed

1. It would be interesting to find out how lucrative business is to these merchants during Ramadan. In this study however, I have restricted myself to the amount of money women say they spend on the extra foodstuffs wanted during that month.
2. Normal working hours are from 9.00 to 16.00 or 17.00 hrs.
3. It would be more accurate to say that Shaban marks the opening of one of two wedding seasons that sometimes overlap. A distinction should be made between the wedding season following the religious cycle, which we are concerned with here, and summer as the general wedding season.

month, so that it is a very good time to get married. The last reason which was given related primarily to the special character of Shaban as the preparatory month to Ramadan; once you have decided to get married, and you want a big wedding, you had better do it before Ramadan, 'to get it off your mind and settle in with your husband'. This shows that Shaban not only offers the last opportunity before Ramadan to have a big party, but it is also the month during which, I often noticed, informants make sure that all pending activities occupying their minds are completed, before the fast begins. It could also be argued that sitting together to wait for the signal of sunset, and then sharing the soup each night during Ramadan, creates a bond between the new husband and wife that forms a solid basis for their marriage. However, none of my informants actually explained the large number of weddings that take place during Shaban in this light.

During Shaban, betrothed young men who are not yet ready to marry confirm their promise to do so in the future by sending their fiancée presents. They are supposed to do this on the occasion of each religious feast, but only during Shaban, when according to informants the amount of presents exceeds those of other occasions, are processions organised to bring a cartful of presents to the house of the bride-to-be, where a party is held in honour of the engaged couple.

Shaban Parties

In addition to wedding ceremonies and the smaller gatherings organised by families of engaged couples, there are other parties which are held exclusively to celebrate that Ramadan is close at hand. These are called *še^{c}bâna*s. It was explained to me that such parties were organised *bâš nferḥu duḵûl ṛemḍân*, 'to rejoice and celebrate the coming of Ramadan'.

The women from one family or alley collect money to buy the ingredients to prepare cookies and food and to hire a band, preferably one with *šîḵa*s or female singers. Tasks are divided and the party is held in the courtyard of one of the homes during the afternoon or, as is becoming the fashion, at night. I have also heard of male adolescents organising such parties, but did not come across any reference to parties organised by married men.

Zahra, my hostess, was asked to participate on two such occasions. She did not go, however, since she would have to pay 20 dirhams for each party. This was too expensive for her taste. Moreover, *še^{c}bâna*s are no longer what they used to be, she complained: 'These days, it consists only of ordinary parties with a band, there is no special characteristic which make them good Shaban parties. These young people do not even seem to realise what a Shaban party is all about.' She then explained that in former days, no bands were hired for *šeᶜbânas*. Women would bring their *teᶜrîjas*, drums in vase-like shape, and make music themselves. Also, they would not just eat any *tajîn* or stew, but a special dish was prepared, called *gassa ṣ-ṣâbirîn*, the dish of the enduring people. It consisted of a couscous prepared with all the vegetables that were available in the market at the time, even vegetables that normally never go into a couscous, such as potatoes. This meal was considered to be very nutritious and to leave one saturated for a long time, thus helping one to endure the long fasting days in Ramadan.[4] Although *šeᶜbânas* in the old sense of the word are no longer celebrated, Zahra herself still prepares the *gassa ṣ-ṣâbirîn* every year and invites the families of her sister and aunt to share the meal with her.

Preliminary Fasting

During Shaban, many people begin fasting for a few days. It will be shown in this section that they may do so for several reasons.

Making Amends for Missed Fasting Days

For people who were not able to fast the whole of Ramadan the previous year, Shaban offers the last chance to make up for those missed days. In Marrakech making up for lost fasting days is called *tᶜerreḍ d-dîn*, to take care of one's religion. Someone who still has to make up some fasting days expresses this by saying *bqâ lîya dînî*, or, my religion is still left to me. This kind of fasting also concerns people who were ill last Ramadan, but the vast majority of people who still owe fasting days are women who interrupted the fast during their menstruation.

As was stated in chapter 1, according to the Hadith compilation of Bukari, the Prophet's favourite wife, Aisha, made up for her missed fasting days during Shaban. Women in Morocco, however, believe it is better to do so as soon as possible after Ramadan. It is said that women who make up the lost days before the Feast of Immolation gain a lot of *ajr*, religious merit, by eating the liver of the sacrificial ram. On the other hand, to women who have not yet made up the missed days, the liver tastes rotten and properly speaking, they should not eat it. Also, it is said that girls who marry before having made up for lost days will never have enough money to get by, nor will they be able to pay back any sum of money lent to them.

4. Legey (1926: 218), who describes similar parties in Marrakech, informs us that at the *šeᶜabâna*, a woman who had made painting henna her profession would sometimes be invited to paint the hands and feet of the participants. As the use of henna is considered *ḥarâm*, forbidden, or at least *makrûh*, objectionable, during Ramadan, the party was the last occasion to apply it before the fasting month started. It was therefore preferably applied in several layers, so that it would last a long time.

Implicitly, this belief makes reference to a comparison between having to make up for lost fasting days and owing money. This comparison is even more strongly suggested in the words that women in the town of Berkane in north-east Morocco use for making up for such days: *k̲allaṣa*. In Modern Standard Arabic this verb means to purify, to clarify, to pay duty, or to restore one's right. In Moroccan Arabic, however, it means simply to pay. In this sense, missed fasting days should be paid back. When explaining to me the meaning of fasting for previously lost days, some women made the comparison between this activity and paying back money that one owes. One girl used this comparison to explain why, if one has not made up for the lost days before the next Ramadan, one should not only do so after Ramadan, but in addition feed one poor person for each lost day: 'Borrowed money must be paid back. When you pay back too late, you have to pay interest. Well, with fasting it is the same thing; when you wait too long to pay back omitted days, you must pay a meal for a poor person on top of it.' Even though offering a meal to a poor person for each missed fasting day, not yet made up for before the next Ramadan, is an officially recognised regulation, in Marrakech it is said that if a woman does not make up for lost fasting days before the next Ramadan, after her death she will be suspended by the eyelids until Judgement Day. It is obvious, however, that belief in this threat is waning, or at least doubted; the person who told me about it assured me that in reality this is not true. Other people, to whom I posed the question, did not offer a straight reply, but just smiled and commented 'People say so'.

In any case, the number of days still to be fasted before Ramadan and plans when to do so are much discussed topics among women during Shaban. The ones who still owe fasting days look for partners to fast with because it is harder to fast when everybody else is eating than it is to fast during Ramadan, when the whole community is sharing the changed rhythm of alternately eating and not eating.

Voluntary Fasting

Finding someone to fast with is not hard during Shaban. Not only are there many women who still owe fasting days, but there are also quite a number of people who engage in voluntary fasting during this month. As was mentioned in chapter 1, during Shaban, the Prophet himself practised voluntary fasting more often than during any other month of the year, and Moroccans like to follow his example. They distinguish between *ṣawm al-farḍ*, fasting by religious duty, and *ṣawm al-ajr*, fasting for religious merit. In Marrakech, it is mostly older people who practise fasting for religious merit.

Some people who engage in this kind of voluntary fasting in fact already begin on the twenty-seventh day of the month preceding Shaban, named Rajab. This is the day following the *laylat al-mi*^c^*râj*, the night of the ascension made by the Prophet Muhammed from Jerusalem to the seven heavens.[5]

In Shaban, the day that is supposed to reap the most religious merit for those who fast it is the *nuṣṣ*, the 'half', the fifteenth day of that month. Women explained that this day is important because it is the day on which God decides who will live and who will die in the year to come.[6]

Some people who fast on the 15th of Shaban also do so on the two days preceding it. There are people who, both to 'warm up' for fasting during Ramadan and to obtain the great amount of *ajr* that voluntary fasting brings, fast every Monday and Thursday in Shaban. When asked why exactly these days, people said that the Prophet was born on a Monday. Nobody, however, could explain why Thursday is a good day to fast. In Berkane, a woman who was eager to please the ever-questioning anthropologist suggested, somewhat hesitantly, that maybe this was because Thursday precedes Friday, the blessed day, on which it is not good to fast. Generally, however, people do not stop to wonder why exactly these days are good for fasting. 'Because it is said so' is a good enough reason for them.[7]

Regarding voluntary fasting, married women are at a disadvantage in comparison to men. Men can decide independently whether they will fast or not, but married women need the permission of their husbands to do so (cf. chapter1). When I interviewed my hostess about this matter, she told me that the issue had been discussed in the television programme *rukn al-muftî*, 'the column of the Mufti'. A Mufti is an official expounder of Islamic law. This programme is broadcast every Friday night. Through letters, the audience can consult the programme on religious matters. The issues raised are then treated by one of the ^c^*ulamâ'* or religious scholars.

5. According to Westermarck (1926, II: 89), in former days people who could afford it celebrated this midnight journey by eating a good meal. Furthermore, schools were closed on the twenty-sixth and twenty-seventh days of that month, and in Tanger, women would go to the country before sunset to gather a certain grass, so that during the year to come, there would be an abundance of good things such as animals, food and clothes. In present-day Morocco, the *laylat al-mi*^c^*râj* is no longer celebrated actively. It was never mentioned to me when I asked about the important religious dates on the Islamic calendar.

6. Westermarck (1926, II: 89) mentions that this day is called *nhâr an-nusḵa*, the day of the copy. On the preceding night God is said to give a book to the angel of death containing a record of all living beings destined to die during the next year.

7. Roog (1988: 37) mentions that the Prophet was conceived on Thursday night during the first week of the month of Rajab. In Turkey this night is considered a holy night. This may explain why Thursday is a good day to fast.

My hostess recalled that it had been said in the programme that the voluntary fasting of women against the will of their husbands is not valid. A woman's first duty is to satisfy her husband. He must be able to sleep with her whenever he pleases, which would create a problem if she were fasting. A woman should, therefore, always consult her husband about her plans to fast any day other than those in Ramadan. In this respect, her husband has more control over her performance of religious activities, such as collecting *ajr*, than she does herself. When I mentioned this to women, most of them just smiled and commented 'That's the way the world is' or 'God is merciful, He will not hold it against us'. Two women stated that God would blame husbands who keep their wives from fasting.

It is difficult to estimate how many people actually practise voluntary fasting during Shaban. Who is fasting for religious merit is a topic of discussion among women. They all seem to know two or three people who always fast in Shaban, and they are invariably women. One wonders whether women engage in voluntary fasting more often than men, but it does not help much to ask people this question. Every time I directly asked about differences in observance of religious activities by the sexes, this was vehemently denied. I, none the less, have the impression that women fast more often than men.[8]

Latifa, the aunt of my hostess, also fasted the 15th of Shaban. She had announced it long before and had also fasted the 27th of Rajab. Her daughter Rahma promised to join her on one of the last three days that she still owed because she had eaten when she menstruated during Ramadan the year before. But when the 15th came, Rahma had too much work to do it on an empty stomach, and left her mother to fast alone. Zahra, who had said that she might fast with her aunt and neighbour, also let her down, because she did not have the strength. These examples illustrate that although not many people actually practise voluntary fasting, many more do have good intentions to do so.

Latifa did not mind having to fast all by herself. Since she is beyond the age of menstruation, when she fasts it is clear to everybody that she does so for religious merit, which is prestigious. More than once, she called attention to her fasting, by joining Zahra in her room when she received a guest, for example, where with a determined gesture, she declined the glass of tea offered to her. In the evening, she proudly presented us with a big bowl of *ḥrîra*, the soup eaten to break the fast, and assured us that the day had passed very quickly and that no doubt Ramadan would be beautiful this year.

8. This also seems to be the case in Jordan (cf. Antoun 1968: 100).

Preparing and Purifying the House

From early Shaban on, people begin thinking about what cooking utensils and foodstuffs they must buy in order to have everything on hand once Ramadan begins. In poorer families, the housewives may have saved money or now worry about how they are going to get some extra to buy everything they need. Latifa, for example, complained to me about her daughter having bought herself a new golden necklace and a pair of earrings in Shaban. Why in Shaban, of all times, when her mother was expecting to receive some extra money for her Ramadan purchases! She then listed all the items she needed to buy:

lentils, for 90 riyal per kg
chickpeas, for 90 riyal per kg
rice, for 140 riyal per kg
semolina, for 60 riyal per kg
wheat flour, for 3,000 riyal per sack
olive oil, for 320 riyal per litre
sunflower oil, for 140 riyal per litre
3 kg of charcoal, for 44 riyal per kg
fresh coriander to preserve, for 12 riyal
spices such as safran, pepper, ginger, garlic, cumin,
all 40 riyal per 100 gram.

Altogether this amounts to 4,096 riyal, which is 203 dirhams (approximately 24 US dollars). Normally Latifa spends about 15 to 20 dirhams per day on food. 'And that is only what I want to have for the *ḥrîra* beforehand, I don't even count the tomatoes and onions I have to buy fresh every day. Also, I am lucky this year that I don't have to buy any new soupbowls or spoons.' To this, her neighbour Zahra commented that one should buy some bowls or spoons every year, because there is *baraka*, blessing, in buying new items for each Ramadan. Latifa thought about this information, but then smiled and replied smartly that she had bought two jars to make lemon preserve, which was '*baraka* for her', using the same word *baraka* but in this case meaning enough, sufficient. Zahra herself planned to go to the Wednesday market the week preceding Ramadan to buy bowls and spoons. That day the market was overcrowded with people who had the same idea and had come to have a look at the extra stalls set up to sell items people want for Ramadan, such as the bowls and spoons already mentioned, shredders to make carrot-orange juice, plastic tablecloths, jars and steel wool.

The steel wool is needed because women thoroughly wash and polish all pots and pans a few days before Ramadan. This is part of a general cleaning-up of the house almost invariably undertaken by all housewives or maids before the fasting month begins. The furniture is removed from the rooms, the walls and ceilings are brushed, the floors mopped, and the covers of the couches and cushions are washed. The kitchen cupboard is emptied and all crockery and cooking utensils are rinsed. Also, many clothes are washed so that one does not have to wash much during Ramadan, when, on an empty stomach, it is an even heavier task to perform. More importantly, this washing, as with all the other cleaning activities, serves to begin Ramadan in an atmosphere of absolute cleanliness.

Purifying the Body

As was already stated in chapter 1, fasting is only valid when one is in a ritually pure state. In the view of Moroccans, several activities may have to be undertaken to attain this state of purity.

Visiting the Public Bath

After the house has been turned inside out, people go to the *ḥammâm*, the public bath. There, they may spend from one to three hours scrubbing themselves, washing their hair and, lastly, performing the *ġusl*, the major ritual ablution.

In general, Moroccans do not make a distinction between *ṭahâra*, the ritually pure state, and being *nqî*, clean in the profane sense of the word. Even though the *ġusl* may be performed anywhere, in their view it cannot be detached from all other activities that one undertakes in the public bath. One is not considered clean enough to perform the prayers after having had sexual relations, for example, unless one has also sweated a lot in the *ḥammâm*. In the same line of thinking, one is not in a clean enough condition to begin fasting if the house has not also been properly cleaned.

In this manner, religious connotations have been attached to activities, such as going to the public bath, scrubbing the floors and the toilet etc. before Ramadan, that do not strictly belong to the orthodox prescriptions concerning fasting.[9]

Suspending the Consumption of Alcohol

Another preparation for cleaning the body before the fasting month begins concerns only those people – mostly men and prostitutes – who drink alcohol. They should begin to abstain forty days in advance, since alcohol is supposed to remain in the blood for a period of forty days. Women stated this 'prescription' to me as if it were part of the official regulations relating to fasting. This, howev-

9. I have described the religious connotations surrounding the *ḥammâm* in greater depth in Buitelaar (1985a).

er, cannot possibly be the case, as drinking alcohol is forbidden by Islamic law altogether.

In addition, the selling and consumption of alcoholic beverages are officially forbidden for Muslims by Moroccan law. During most of the year, however, allowances are made for those who do not engage in such activities too openly. Shops that sell liquor wrap the bottles in paper bags and sell them under the counter. Cafés that serve alcohol do so behind non-transparent windows. It is only one week before Ramadan that the police begin to see to it that alcohol is no longer sold to Muslims.

Yet, none of the alcohol-consuming men whom I know stopped drinking forty days before Ramadan. In fact, our neighbour came home drunk as late as the 28th of Shaban, and only refrained from drinking during Ramadan itself.

Bloodletting

Some people, especially those who have a bad constitution or who have been recently ill, do not consider the cleansing activities mentioned above to be sufficient. In their eyes, the purging of the body is not complete without removing the bad blood. Some women still have their ankles and wrists scarified by a *šerrâta*, a woman specialising in scarifying. Lalla Fatiha, for example, was a bit embarrassed when I noticed the delicate pattern of fresh scars on her wrists and ankles a few days before Ramadan. When I had reassured her that I had heard about the *šerrât*, the scarification treatment, and found it interesting, she was surprised. She thought that Europeans would disapprove of such customs. 'But it is very good to remove the bad blood' she immediately added. She explained that people who have high blood pressure or suffer recurring headaches, and people who have been ill, feel much better after a scarification treatment. Fatiha has her ankles and wrists scarified every year in Shaban. If she does not do so, she becomes ill, her ankles become swollen and she feels as if she will burst.[10]

10. Legey (1926: 219–20) reports on women in Marrakech who organised bloodletting parties to which a *šerrâta* was invited. Generally, such *šerrâta*s were women related to a saint. The women who wanted to be scarified would dress up in their finest clothes and present their forearms and ankles to the *šerrâta* who would make many superficial cuts with a small sharp knife until a fine pattern of bleeding lines was formed around the wrists and ankles. Children could also be treated. On young girls, only the insides of her wrists and ankles would be cut. If they were cut all around their forearms and ankles like married women, it was believed that they would not bleed at the moment of their defloration. After the scarifications had been made, the cuts were rinsed and smeared with a tincture of safran, henna or *ᶜakr,* traditional rouge (Legey 1926: 220). At the time Legey lived in Marrakech (1913–26), scarification parties were held once or twice a year: in Shaban and in the hottest part of summer. The bloodletting was employed both to remove all ailments that one carries in one's body and to protect oneself against the Evil Eye.

Purifying the Psyche

Just as physical illnesses may be treated in Shaban by bloodletting, mental disturbances are also specifically tended to during this month. In the old cities of Fes, Rabat, Salé, and especially Marrakech this is done during nights of trance-dancing, which are called *lîla* or *derdeba*. *Lîla* comes from the standard Arabic *laila* and literally means 'night'. I have not been able to identify the word *derdeba* with any standard Arabic root. To Marrakchis, the words are synonymous.[11]

The trance performances are organised by members of the religious order of the Gnawa. For a better understanding of the religious context in which the *lilas* which are described in the second half of this section take place, I will first provide some information on the Gnawa and their conceptions of spirit possession.

The Gnawa and Spirit Possession

The Gnawa are spread all over Morocco, but there is a concentration of Gnawa teams in Marrakech. The Gnawa belong to what have been called the more popular orders. French scholars and better-educated and orthodox Moroccans tend to view the popular orders as degenerate forms of the theologically more sophisticated Sufi orders, 'corrupted by the base imagination of *le peuple*, by survivals from the ancient religions of the circum-Mediterranean cul-

Besides these scarification parties, during which small cuts are made on the wrists and ankles as a general protective and curative measure, the scarification of certain other parts of the body is believed to cure some specific illnesses. Akhmisse (1985: 84) lists some complaints and the corresponding spots on the body to be scarified:

Symptom	Scarification spot
lumbar pains	foot
pains in the legs	ankle
failing eyesight	temporal
pelvic pains	knee
headaches\dizziness\ headnoises	nape of the neck

According to Akhmisse, barbers, who also perform the circumcisions, apply these scarifications (ibid.). However, it might well be that although he does not mention it, this refers specifically to men, since I have heard women speak only about *šerrâtas*. Akhmisse also mentions some contra-indications; scarifications should not be applied immediately after having eaten a meal, and not on Fridays and during summer (ibid.). This last restriction contradicts Legey's observations regarding the scarification parties in Marrakech.

11. I have the impression that *derdeba* is more often used by people who themselves are involved in the trance rituals, whereas outsiders tend to refer to them more often as *lîlas*. Also, *lîlas* can be referred to with an indefinite article or in the plural ('a trance night' or 'trance nights'), whereas *derdeba* is only used in its singular form and always with the definite article ('the trance night'). Therefore, *lîla* may refer more closely to the phenomenon of trance rituals in general, while *derdeba* refers to a specific trance night which the speaker has in mind.

ture area, and by pagan influences from sub-Saharan Africa' (Crapanzano 1973: 1).

The Gnawa themselves do not perceive the combination of being a Gnawa-adept and a member of the orthodox Islamic community as problematic. To them, what outsiders would define as heterodox elements in their beliefs and practices are not contradictory to the five pillars of Islam, around which they try to arrange their lives as much as any other practising Muslim. In Marrakech, for example, I have heard some of the more active members of the order being addressed as *al-ḥajj* or *al-ḥajja,* the honorific title bestowed on a man or woman who has undertaken the pilgrimage to Mecca.

In the eyes of the Gnawa, the state of trance that they may enter is caused by a *jinn,* a spirit, who takes possession of the body. For this reason, orthodox Moroccans disparagingly call the Gnawa *ṭîfat š-šitân,* order or teams of Satan (Legey 1926: 15). Spirits are believed to live underground. But they are known to be fond of any dark, damp or wet place such as drains, public baths, toilets, and rivers. They may also live in grottos or trees. When in the vicinity of such places, people take precautions to keep the spirits at a distance, particularly after the *ᶜaṣr,* the time of the afternoon prayers when they are especially active. Moroccans fear spirits because, although not ill-natured as such, the *jnûn* are highly whimsical, easily insulted and vengeful. Especially those people who are angry or frightened are likely to be attacked by the spirits, as are people during the liminal phases of their lives, when passing from one social status to another, such as couples about to be married, pregnant women, newborn babies, and boys about to be circumcised.[12]

People find out that they have been attacked by a spirit if they fall ill or have dreams or visions in which the spirits talk to them. In other cases, they may suspect having fallen victim to *siḥr,* magic. When someone fears she has been attacked, she visits a Gnawa *mqeddem* or *mqeddma,* a male or female leader of a Gnawa

12. Several authors have asked what kind of people become possessed: cf. Jansen 1987 and Maher 1974. Both authors concentrated on female victims and concluded that, according to the dominant ideology, these women fail their gender. Crapanzano's analysis of men who are involved in trance rituals in Meknes suggests that the same holds true for male patients (Crapanzano 1973: 213).

Unfortunately, I did not have the chance to study systematically the backgrounds of all people who entered the trance at the two *lîla*s I attended during my own research. However, in the few cases in which I was able to learn more about the dancers, they all fit well in the categories mentioned above; one of the *mqeddma*s is herself a divorcee. Among her clients were a woman who had recently been deserted by her husband, a woman who only after five years of marriage had given birth after making a sacrifice and dancing at a *lîla,* and several girls who were anxious about finding a husband or had problems with their boyfriends. The man who assisted the *mqeddma* during her *lîla* was ridiculed behind his back for being entangled in very serious problems with his two wives.

team.[13] Through her contact with the spirits, the *mqeddma* will make a diagnosis by determining what spirit has attacked her client.

Complete recovery, through exorcism of the spirit, is rare. In most cases, treatment consists of creating a lifelong working relationship with the *jinn* who has taken possession of its victim.[14] After a first attack, the spirit may demand that the affected person organise a *lîla*, a trance night or ceremony, in its honour. Such a curative *lîla* is supposed to bring immediate improvement to the situation of the patient, and should take place as soon as possible after the attack.[15] To keep the spirit satisfied, it is necessary that the patient continues to acknowledge its power over her by making a small sacrifice such as a chicken, or dancing in trance at subsequent *lîla*s.

More women than men are involved in trance-dancing. Of all the people present at the two *lîla*s I attended, about 75 per cent were women, and the percentage of women who entered in trance compared to men, according to my estimation, was over ninety.[16]

The Trance Nights during Shaban

There are two occasions for *lîla*s organised to honour and reconfirm the bond with the spirits. One of them is the week following the *mulûd* or birthday of the Prophet. The *lîla*s organised by Gnawa adepts living in Marrakech then take place during the *mûsems*, annual pilgrimages to the shrines of the saints at Tamsluht and Mulay Ibrahim. These *mûsems* will be further discussed in chapter 7. The other time during which preventive *lîla*s are organised is the month of Shaban.

The trance nights in Shaban are more specifically referred to as farewell parties for the spirits who will be locked away during Ramadan.[17] Lest the *jnûn* become angry about being imprisoned and, on the 27th of Ramadan, be ill-tempered upon release, the

13. In practice there are more female leaders and patients than male ones. Therefore, to maintain the readability of this text, I shall from now on speak about *mqeddma*s and female patients only. Unless specifically mentioned, what is said about them also applies to their male counterparts.

14. The inescapable fate of the possessed has even led to its recognition within the practice of Moroccan Family Law; some fifty years ago, the marriage contracts of women known to be possessed contained explicit clauses obliging the husband to allow his wife to leave the house any time she wanted to attend a *lîla* (Boughali 1988: 223).

15. This kind of *lîla* has been described for Salé by Reysoo (1988: 68–74). Since I have not had a chance to attend a curative *lîla* myself, I do not know whether the differences between the ritual as described by Reysoo and the one to be described here below are due to regional variations or differences in character between the curative *lîla*s, immediately following an attack by spirits, and the annually organised *lîla*s in Shaban, held as a preventive measure.

16. The preponderance of women in trance cults will be discussed in ch. 7.

17. My informants held different opinions as to where the spirits are located during Ramadan. Some were convinced that they are imprisoned in a corner of Paradise, others stated that they remain on earth. Yet others had no idea. The informants obviously did not share my interest in the whereabouts of the spirits. To them, what matters most is that they are rendered harmless by being chained up.

Gnawa perform their *lîla*s with the intention of placating them beforehand. It should be noted that these trance rituals are by no means preparations for Ramadan made by Moroccans or Marrakchis in general. As far as I know, no statistics exist regarding the number of people engaged in trance-dancing, but I estimate the number of people who visit a *lîla* during Shaban to be approximately 7,100. This constitutes about 2 per cent of the adult population of Marrakech, which means that 6 per cent of the families are involved in the trance ritual.[18]

A *lîla* is composed of three parts: (1) the *ḏbîḥa*, the sacrifice; (2) the actual *derdeba*, the trance night; and (3) the *tefrâq l-mîda* or *tefrâq ṭ-ṭbîqa*, the distribution of (the contents of) the table or breadbasket, which is also referred to as the *dlâla*, the auction. Each one of these three parts is a self-contained unit. Unless people have travelled very far, after the performance of one of the rituals they return home to devote themselves to their everyday tasks, only to come back some time before they expect the next part to begin. Yet, one part cannot be performed without also performing the other parts, which are clearly rites within a ritual. Moreover, the sequence in which the rituals are to be performed cannot be altered. There is some variation in the lapse of time allowed between the three parts, but once the *mqeddma*, the team leader, has opted for one alternative, she must adhere to it in any *lîla* she organises in future. Changing her routine would not only nullify

18. The number of people attending *lîla*s is based on the following information: according to several Gnawa musicians and a *mqeddma*, 'many' *lîla*s are organised during Shaban, especially from the 15th of the month onwards. During the first two weeks, the musicians claimed to have performed at *lîla*s twice or three times a week. From the 15th onwards, they were engaged every night. The number of Gnawa groups active in Marrakech were estimated to fluctuate between five and ten groups. (This is due to changes in the composition of groups. Musicians who usually play as regular members of a group may at times act as temporary *mqeddem*s and gather others around them.) Of the two *lîla*s I attended, one was labelled a 'large' *lîla* and was attended by some 90 to 100 people. The other *lîla* was a 'small' one, during which I counted about 70 to 80 people. (The minor difference in numbers cannot account for the different evaluation of the two *lîla*s. This discrimination had much more to do with prestige differences between the *mqeddma*s.) In order to determine the minimum number of people involved in the trance rituals, the following calculation was made:

first two weeks:		
1 *lîla* per night:	14 × 85 people	= 1,190
last two weeks:		
5 *lîla*s per night:	70 × 85 people	= 5,950
	Total:	7,140

The figure of the total population of Marrakech is based on data from 1982, adjusted by calculating a population growth of 3% per year (Annuaire Statistique 1989). It was assumed that 60% of the population consisted of adults and that families generally consist of 6 members.

the effects of the whole performance but also cause her to fall ill or go mad. Although the *lîla*s that are held in Shaban basically follow the same pattern, variations occur with each performance. I describe here a specific *lîla* which I attended on 25 March (17 Shaban) in 1989.

Several parallels can be drawn between the sequence of events and kind of activities which make up a *lîla*, and those of a wedding. Like a bride, the *mqeddma* goes to the *ḥammâm*, the public bath, the day before the sacrifice, and has her hands and feet decorated with henna afterwards. The day preceding the night during which a marriage is consummated, there is a party for the relatives and friends of the bride. This resembles the sacrificial ceremony which the *mqeddma* performs in the presence of close clients, relatives and friends in the afternoon before the actual trance night. Like a wedding night, the trance ritual, which is attended by a large number of people, lasts an entire night. As in the case of a bride, this night is followed the next day by a ceremony for which the *mqeddma* invites only her 'close ones' (*qurâb*). Also like a bride, she does not leave the house for three to seven days after the sacrifice. This behaviour may indicate that the relation between the *mqeddma* and the spirits is conceived of as a marriage bond.[19] In my description of a *lîla* I will follow this tripartite structure in which the trance ceremony resembles a wedding.

1. The Sacrifice The *ḏbîḥa* or sacrifice can be performed either on the day the actual trance night will take place, or one day in advance. It must always take place after the *ᶜaṣr* prayers, which are around four o'clock. The *mqeddma* is dressed up for the sacrifice in the white dress which is associated with the spirits who descend from the Prophet. Like His human descendants, these spirits are called *šurfa* (singular: *srîf*). From the moment that the sacrificial animals are brought in, the *mqeddma* should not talk and should keep her head bent down. Her face remains hidden beneath a white veil. This appearance and chaste behaviour makes her look like a bride.

Among the sacrificial animals, a white sheep and a black goat, associated respectively with the respectful *šurfa* and the *wlâd l-ġâba*, the sons of the forest, the most feared spirits, should always be present. The sacrifice of these two animals is indispensable for the trance ritual. Not only would it have no effect without them, but the absence of these sacrificial animals would also have dangerous implications for the well-being of the *mqeddma*.

19. In his study on the Hamadsha, Crapanzano (1973: 144) mentions that in some cases the bond between the possessed and the spirits is indeed perceived as a kind of marriage.

The slaughtering of the white sheep is a crucial and spectacular part of the sacrificial rite. By drinking the warm blood of the sheep the *mqeddma* enters the state of trance. To this purpose, the male leader of the Gnawa musicians catches the blood in a bowl. At one of the *lîla*s I attended, however, before he had the time to do so, he was brusquely pushed aside by the *mqeddma*. Until then she had been very composed and modest, but now she suddenly fell forward. She bent over the agonised sheep and drank straight from the spout of blood that gushed up from its throat, thus splattering her formerly spotless white dress with blood. The state of trance brought about by drinking the sacrificial blood is brought to a climax by dancing to the music played by the musical leader on his three-stringed guitar, called *sentîr* or *gumbri*. By this time the *mqeddma* is joined by other women who are called by the rhythm of the *šrîf*.

After having collapsed, she is carried away and laid down on a mattress behind the *mqaṭa^{c}a,* the area behind a sheet where nobody but she and her close assistants are allowed. This is the part of the sacrificial rite that the clients of the *mqeddma* have been waiting for anxiously, because now the spirits begin to speak through the voice of the still unconscious *mqeddma*. One by one, the most important guests are called to the sheet, from behind which the spirits whisper in their ears whatever they want to say to them before they are locked up during Ramadan.

After the spirits have finished conveying messages, the *mqeddma* 'wakes up' and devotes herself to a rite called the *^{c}emmer ṭ-ṭbîqa*, the filling of the basket with different kinds of food and drinks, each associated with its own spirit. The basket will not be opened until the concluding ritual following the day after the trance night. The filling of the basket concludes the sacrificial ritual.

2. The Trance Night The trance night begins after nine o'clock, when the *^{c}šâ'*, the last prayers of the day, have ended. The performance is opened by the Gnawa musicians singing songs in which they pay tribute to their patron saint Sidi Bulal and other saints of (regional) importance, among them Mulay Ibrahim and the Seven Patron Saints of Marrakech, whose protection and blessings are implored.[20]

Around midnight the leader of the musicians begins to make preparations for the *^{c}âda*, the rite in which the spirits are invited to be escorted to the courtyard where the *lîla* is taking place. The musicians lead a procession of young virgins, all carrying a burning

20. The patron saints of Marrakech will be further discussed in chapters 4 and 7. The *mûsem* or annual pilgrimage to Mulay Ibrahim will also be discussed in ch. 7.

candle in each hand, to the street outside the house. There they form a circle and the girls repeat a welcoming song to the spirits several times.

The meaning of the ^{c}*âda* was explained to me as *l-*^{c}*arâḍa lîl-mulûk*, the invitation to the owners, the spirits. This invitation is another example of the resemblances between *lîla*s and weddings: in the general Moroccan use of the word, ^{c}*arâḍa* does not indicate just any invitation, but more specifically denotes the rite of two women visiting all the homes of people who are invited to a wedding.

The ^{c}*âda* is one of the most dangerous moments of the *lîla*; the spirits enter the house, but have not yet settled in their place in front of the Gnawa musicians. To welcome them in their midst, the musicians eat a date and drink a spoonful of milk with a *mġurfa*, the wooden spoon also used to drink the Ramadan soup. In this respect, the *lîla* reinforces the parallel with a wedding once more, since the consumption of milk and dates is a recurring event in any wedding ceremony. In the milk which is consumed during the *lîla*, grains of incense, representing the spirits, have been diluted. All the men present are also offered milk and dates, but the women have to wait half an hour. This is said to be necessary because women are not as strong as men. Therefore, during the dangerous moment of the entrance of the spirits, they should not call attention to themselves, but wait to welcome the *jnûn* until these have taken their place in front of the musicians.

The first rhythm that is played after the ^{c}*âda* belongs to the *šurfa*, the spirits related to the Prophet. They are the highest in the hierarchy of *jnûn*. The people who dance 'to them' (^{c}*lî-hum*) must wear white, the colour that symbolises purity in Islam. The most important *šrîf* is Sidi al-Jilali. One of the *mqeddma*s whose *lîla* I visited, works for this spirit. She assured me that the *šrîf* is such a good and religious spirit that he is not locked up during Ramadan like the other spirits. This allows her to continue to work during Ramadan, unlike some other *mqeddma*s whose spirits are locked up and are therefore powerless during the fasting month.[21]

From the moment the rhythm of the *šurfa* is performed, the musicians continue to play the whole night. I could not distinguish between one rhythm and another, but the changing of the coloured dresses representing different spirits, and the different attributes, made it clear whenever another spirit had entered the floor.

The spirits demand some dancers to perform rather spetacular acts: the *šurfa* (white) entices them to cut themselves without

21. It is significant that the few men who trance dance, do so mainly or exclusively in honour of these highest-ranking spirits.

bleeding, Sidi Buhali (green) forces them to drink boiling water without burning their mouths, the Musawi (blue) allow them to dance with a bowl filled with water on their head without dropping it, and the Gnawa (black) have them hold candles under their arms and faces without causing burns. Besides these demonstrations of extraordinary skills, the spirits may also require the dancers to engage in very humiliating acts resembling those of animals. Sidi Huma (red) causes a dancer to hang out his tongue, moving it rapidly from left to right until saliva runs down his chin. In this state small children must be hidden, because the dancer would attack them and eat them raw, as he does the slices of raw meat cut from the sacrificial black goat. Next to Aisha Qandisha (black), the *wlâd l-ġâba* (black) are the most feared spirits. The trance of the people who dance to them may last as long as an hour. These 'sons of the forest' are said to originate from a large forest in the interiors of Africa. The dancers who dance to these spirits behave like savage animals; with their hands on their backs and moving their heads forward and backward with each step, as some bird species do, they circle around a plate of *zemmîṭa*, a dish made of flour roasted from fresh grains which looks like sand. All dancers cast glances at the plate, but it takes a while before one of them suddenly dares to jump out of the circle and grasp it. She leans over the plate to make sure nobody will succeed in an attempt to sneak it away. To keep the others at a distance, the dancer glares and snarls at them before sniffing the *zemmîṭa* and licking it up with her mouth, leaving traces of the 'sand' on her face. The dancer then collapses and is taken away. Then the same procedure begins again until all dancers have licked from the dish of *zemmîṭa*.

It must be noted that only a few dancers with much experience engage in acts which so clearly deviate from the highly regarded norms and values of Moroccans. Aside from the *mqeddma*s and their assistants, it is mostly men who give such performances. Most women only use their bodies to dance and do not call extra attention to themselves.

There are several ways in which someone may enter into a trance. Some people seem to faint on the spot where they are. In this case, the person sitting next to her will call one of the assistants who makes her sniff from a pot of incense and holds her wrists and ankles over it. This quickens the speed with which the spirit takes possession of the body of the person who then gets up to dance. Possession may also announce itself more suddenly, as when a woman shrieks out and crawls or rolls forward to the dance floor, making sounds that resemble those of low-status animals such as dogs, pigs or monkeys. Already moving violently to and fro, she is persuaded to inhale the incense. Next, a kerchief, in the colour of the spirit whose rhythm is being played, is thrown over her head. All dancers must wear such a kerchief. When someone is expected to dance for a long time, the assistants pull a dress of the same colour over her body.

It is said that trance dancers do not realise what they undergo. When asked afterwards what they felt during the trance, they do not seem to remember what had happened, other than that they passed out and woke up feeling very tired. Once a dancer has entered the state of trance, she is believed to be no longer in control of her body, which is completely taken over by the spirit who possesses her.

Because trance dancers are thought not to be in command of themselves, they must be closely watched to be protected against hurting either themselves or others. Therefore, there should always be someone close at hand ready to catch anyone who is about to fall, or to readjust the kerchiefs that are continuously slipping off the dancers. The assistants take a place behind particularly wild dancers to make sure they will not hit anybody. They may also hold the dancers by an extra kerchief, tied around the waist, to prevent them from falling. When there are more people dancing than the assistants can possibly keep an eye on, somebody from the audience is expected to get up to protect the dancers from hurting themselves and others. Since hardly anyone comes to a *lîla* on her own, most dancers are assisted by a close friend or relative.

When, for example, at one of the *lîla*s I attended, a dancer risked strangling herself by pulling the kerchief too tight around her neck, a bystander rose to release her from it. When another woman collapsed, somebody caught her just in time. A dancer who tried to leave the house and run away was noticed by someone who, again just in time, blocked the way to the door.

The Gnawa have good reason to keep up the appearance that the dancers are totally out of control and do not know what they are doing. In terms of everyday norms, their behaviour is shameful. If they were held responsible for their deeds, it would pose too great a threat to their reputation. Apparently some realise this themselves; when I asked a *mqeddma* if dancers know what they do or whether they remember what they have done while in trance, she replied: 'That is impossible, did you see that girl dance in her tight skirt in front of all those men? How could she have done that if she had known what she was doing?'

Yet, a closer look at what happened to dancers who for a moment escaped the attention of the assistants suggests that the dancers never lose total control over themselves. Even in cases where they were momentarily out from under the eye of the assistants, no accidents occurred. A dancer who was frantically stomping her feet, each time just missed the unconscious woman lying beside her on the floor. One man dancing to the rhythm of Sidi Huma, a cannibalistic spirit who is particularly fond of children, never noticed the small boy playing in a corner of the courtyard until the boy had reached the door of a room and was about to enter it. Only then did the dancer dart at him, again, just a few seconds too late to catch the boy before the door was closed behind him. Also, those dancers who collapsed without warning never hit their head straight on the cement floor. They either landed on their arms or in the laps of spectators sitting along the sides of the dance floor.

Therefore, contrary to the descriptions of the trance supplied by the Gnawa, I would argue that the dancers are never completely lacking self-control. They let themselves go only to a certain point. This may be far removed from the composure demanded in everyday life, but a minor degree of self-control is never given up.[22] Paradoxically, the trance appears to be a restrained form of losing control. Trance dancers may be possessed by the spirits, but once they have agreed to enter into a working relationship with them and live up to the rules and obligations involved, the boundaries within which the spirits can rule them are clearly defined. The situation of being possessed can eventually be handled. Once the obligations entailed by the bond with the spirits are met, not only do the trance dancers work for their *mlûk* or owners, but in turn, the spirits may also work for them. This is best expressed in the concluding part of the trance ritual, which is mostly referred to as the *dlâla* or auction.

3. The Auction The afternoon following the trance night, the rite called *tefrâq l-mîda* or *tefrâq t-ṭbîqa*, the distribution of the contents of the table or of the breadbasket, is performed. Many people, however, refer to the rite simply as the *dlâla*, the auction. This rite is attended only by those people who have close ties with the *mqeddma* and her spirits. Two big breadbaskets are brought from behind the sheet which hides the *mqâṭa*ᶜ*a* and put in front of the guests. From that moment onwards nobody should talk any more. First, one basket containing bottles with different drinks, each representing a different spirit, is opened. One after another, the drinks are poured into glasses which are passed among the guests who all take a sip. The meaning of sharing these drinks is *bâs nšekru l-mlûk*, to thank the spirits.

22. I think this can be compared to hypnosis. It is widely known that people under hypnosis will obey commands only to a certain point. They cannot be forced to perform acts that strongly contradict any highly regarded value they hold or might threaten their life.

When all the drinks are finished, an assistant opens the second basket. It is filled with foodstuffs representing the special powers of spirits to solve particular problems. These foodstuffs are then auctioned off on behalf of the *mqeddma*. Those who are interested are willing to buy at very high prices.[23] Others go home empty-handed.

After all items have been auctioned off, the prohibition on talking is lifted, marking the completion of the trance ritual.

The Shaban Trance Ritual and the Advent of Ramadan

When the trance ritual is seen in the light of the advent of Ramadan, it becomes clear that the possession of the dancers by the spirits expressed is diametrically opposed to the self-possession of people during Ramadan. Expressing the one emphasises the importance of the other. In fact, the whole Gnawa performance of the trance ritual during Shaban may be viewed as a play upon being in control, an exercise in being in or out of control. When the rite of distributing the breadbasket has been performed, the sense of being in control prevails.

The theme of control that is acted out marks the boundaries between life during the sacred month of Ramadan, in which self-control plays such a crucial role, and life during the other months of the year.

The henna on the hands of the *mqeddma* and the drinks and foodstuffs that are consumed during the sacrificial rite are elements with highly symbolic potential which feature in the fast as well as in many other rituals.[24] They are part of the general Moroccan ritual language and mark ritual settings. I would argue that these ritual attributes derive their *baraka* or supernatural power from their presence on the stage upon which many forms of ritualised behaviour are acted out.

23. To give a few examples, a sugarloaf, believed to come from Sidi Bulal, the *šrîf*, and to bring good health, was sold for 950 riyal (approximately $4.70), while a similar sugarloaf at the grocer's costs 160 riyal ($0.80). A bowl with six eggs coming from Lalla Mira was sold for 2,000 riyal ($10) to a woman who desperately needed its power to reconcile family members who lived a cat-and-dog life. Normally eggs cost 20 riyal each. A soupbowl with *slîlu*, roasted flour with ground nuts coming from the Gnawa, was sold for 1,000 riyal ($5) to a repudiated woman who was hoping this might make her husband return to her.

24. For example, in Marrakech not only brides but also the mother of a boy undergoing circumcision applies henna on her hands and feet. She must keep silent and cast her eyes down lest the barber be diverted by her and mutilate his patient. The boy himself is also decorated with henna and must drink milk and eat an egg to guarantee his fertility. Dates and nuts are eaten during almost any ritual such as circumcision ceremonies, on *ᶜâšûrâ'*, the tenth day of the Muslim New Year (cf. ch. 8). *Slîlu*, roasted flour with ground nuts and anice seeds, is eaten on *usbûᶜ*s, name-giving parties seven days after the birth of a child. Bread and sugar are taken home from most *mûsem*s or Saints festivals.

The trance ritual is the most extreme form of ritualised behaviour that occurs during Shaban. In this chapter, it has been shown that preparing oneself for Ramadan also consists of performing rather practical tasks. These preparations allow people to complete whatever activities they are still involved in and to purge themselves in order to make a fresh start at Ramadan. Almost without exception, everybody makes these preparations. In the view of Marrakechis one cannot, properly speaking, begin Ramadan without having taken these measures. Therefore, practical or 'instrumental' (cf. Leach 1968: 524) as these preparations may seem, they contain expressive aspects as well and are examples of the ritualisation of behaviour which characterises the preliminal phase of the fasting ritual. This preliminal phase leads people away from their everyday life into the liminal time and space of Ramadan.

three

Living Ramadan

During the last few days of Shaban, conjecturing about when Ramadan will begin is a favourite subject of discussion among Marrakechis. 'Have they started fasting yet in Saudi Arabia?', 'Do you think we will eat or fast on Friday?' Questions like these are starting points for lively conversations about when and how Ramadan will be this year. One of my informants stated: 'Friday with doubt, Saturday without doubt'. On Thursday afternoon the same woman predicted: 'Today at night the trumpetplayer will call'. The trumpetplayer is so closely related to the Ramadan activities, that she assumed that I would immediately understand her words to mean that Ramadan would begin that night. That same day, she turned on her television set earlier than usual so that she would not miss hearing the news about the new moon.

In this chapter I will describe the activities and the events which take place once 'the new moon' of Ramadan has been spotted, so that the reader will have an idea of the course everyday life takes during Ramadan before I analyse the meanings of the fast in the remainder of the book. I begin where the preceding chapter left off, and proceed to follow the ritual structure of the fast by describing the activities which mark the beginning of Ramadan. These initial activities are followed by an intermediate period of time during which specific fasting activities are repeated on a daily basis. This repetitive pattern is described in the second section. The third section focuses on the 15th and the 27th of Ramadan, which are two special occasions on which extra activities alter the regular fasting pattern. In the concluding section I describe the feast which marks the end of Ramadan.

Welcoming Ramadan

My informant who had predicted that Ramadan would begin on the day that I talked to her had been right. Around eight o'clock p.m. the beginning of Ramadan was announced on television. A few minutes later, the town's siren could be heard, informing the inhabitants of Marrakech that the new moon had also been seen over their city. This news was welcomed by many women in the medina by loudly giving *zeg̃gerets*, ululations, to express their happiness about the beginning of the blessed month. Many left their houses to congratulate their neighbours, saying: *mebrûk ᶜlîk ṛemḍân*, 'blessings be upon you this Ramadan'. The reply to this formula is *llâh ibârak fîk*, 'God bless you'.[1] In an excited mood, children gathered to march from alley to alley, beating their drums and singing special Ramadan chants. One of them went as follows:

> papa Ramadan is my Ramadan
> and to you I sell my trousers[2]

These lyrics, I was told, mean that Ramadan is so precious that one would even sell the very trousers one is wearing in order to have some money to buy the special foodstuffs for Ramadan. While in daily life children are expected to show respect for adults, the first night of Ramadan they are allowed to tease and taunt grown-ups with the following chants:

> Hey, you kif-smokers, throw away your pipes
> papa Ramadan is coming
>
> papa Ramadan lives
> and the smoking of kif is abolished
>
> enough of the whisky,
> the mosque weeps [for those who drink][3]

1. In former days, it was a custom to bring along dates on such congratulatory visits. In fact, everybody would present their friends with dates for the first evening of Ramadan. This was believed to ease the fasting. At the beginning of the twentieth century when the Sultan was in Marrakech during Ramadan, the Pasha would offer him a *hdîya* consisting of dates (Legey 1926: 177).

2. The Arabic text of this song is:
bâbâ ṛemḍân, ṛemḍânî
u ᶜlîk nbîᶜ serwâlî

3. In Arabic:
hâ, l-keyyâfa hezzû sqâfkum
bâbâ ṛemḍân jaykum

yhay bâbâ ṛemḍân
u yesqet l-keyâfa

baraka men l-wiski
u l-jmîᶜ tayebki

Legey wrote down some variations on these songs and mentions that not only were kif-smokers not allowed to show anger about being jeered at, but they were even supposed to give the singing children some coins (1926: 117–18).

In chapter 8 we will see how the children's parades through the alleys mark the first instance of the many inversions that occur during Ramadan to express the liminal character of the month. The singing of the children continues until early morning. Some of their mothers would not come home until the time for a last meal before the fasting begins. So, on the very first evening of Ramadan there was dense social traffic in the streets of the medina, quite different from normal when women go out as little as possible after dark and men tend to come home around ten.

This applies to life in the medina of Marrakech only. In the squatter areas outside the city wall, there is no electricity and apart from a few very small grocery stores there are no shops to keep open during Ramadan nights. Although people in this area visit their neighbours on the first night of Ramadan, no marked change to a more intensive street life occurs. In the *ville nouvelle* Gueliz the signs of the beginning of Ramadan are even less tangible outside the private homes of people. The town's siren cannot be heard there and in most cases contact with neighbours is reduced to a minimum. People in Gueliz tend to lead withdrawn lives within their European-style houses surrounded by big, walled gardens. They do their shopping in the French *marché* and other shops along the Mohammed V Avenue and few enter the medina at all. Consequently, many people are not aware of the fact that several of the festive Ramadan traditions are still performed within the old city walls.

When I told a young woman who was born in Gueliz about my experiences on the first night of Ramadan in the old city, the account seemed so remote to her that I might have been talking about a town far away from Marrakech. Overhearing our conversation, her mother produced a melancholic smile and remarked that she recognised much of the description from her own childhood in the medina. She even recalled some of the chants that children sing. However, like her daughter, she was surprised to hear that such practices were still observed in the medina. She explained that in her house, the only way to know that Ramadan is beginning is to watch television. In Gueliz people would laugh if she would ululate. Besides, it was no use going over to any of the neighbours to congratulate them on the coming of the fasting month; they were all *neṣrânîs*, a term which literally means Christian but is used by Moroccans to refer to Europeans.

During the night preceding the first fasting day, many Marrakchis stay awake or get up to have a light meal. Because the body is not yet used to the different eating pattern, one would feel very hungry the first day if this meal were skipped. In the days to follow, this feeling gradually diminishes, only to return towards the end of Ramadan. By then, the initial enthusiasm and reserves have drained away so that an appeal must be made to one's *ṣabr*, patience or endurance, to accomplish the fast.

This experience is shared by many people, and expressed in the Marrakchi saying: 'The first ten are for the youth, the second ten are for the middle-aged and the last ten are for the elderly'. This means that the first ten days are easy and can be accomplished by everybody, the second ten days are more difficult and require the experience of adult life, and only the elderly have enough patience to accomplish the whole fast without problems.[4]

Everyday Life during Ramadan

Once Ramadan has begun, the fast proceeds according to a pattern which is repeated on a daily basis. The characteristics of this pattern are the subject of this section.

A Relaxed Start

For most Marrakchis a fasting day begins by sleeping late. All government institutions and most shops have adjusted working hours, allowing their personnel to catch up on the sleep missed due to getting up for the nocturnal meal. Women, most of whom do not have regular jobs, may sleep until nine or ten o'clock. Some wake up briefly to see their children off to school and then lie down again for a while. A male informant commented that fasting is much easier for women who sleep late and spend the whole day in leisure. He did not realise that while women sleep longer in the morning, they also get up at night to prepare the nocturnal meal when the other members of the family are still asleep. This man's remark is but one illustration of how the fasting performance of women is not taken as seriously as that of men. It is an expression of symbolic male dominance in the Moroccan world-view, according to which women are tacitly presumed to be second-best Muslims (cf. chapters 5 and 6).

4. In Arabic:
l-ᶜešr l-lewwel lîs-sġâr
l-ᶜešr t-tâni lîl-mutawaṣṣit
u l-ᶜešr l-âḵir lîl-kbâr
In Rabat, Buskens (personal communication) noted another version of this saying:
the first ten days are of the flesh
and the second ten days are of the fat
and the third ten days are of the bones.

ᶜešr iyyâm l-ewwla dyal l-lḥem
u ᶜešr iyyâm t-tânya dyal š-šeḥm
u ᶜešr iyyâm l-âḵira dyal l-ᶜedem

Admittedly, there is some truth in the young man's statement: just like men, whose working hours are reduced during the fasting month, women take it easier during Ramadan. For instance, normally they get up early to prepare the dough for the bread that is consumed with the lunch, which is the main meal. During Ramadan, children who do not yet fast are served the leftovers from the night before for lunch, and preparing the dough is postponed until late afternoon. Also, I was told that there are women who do not wash 'from the first [call of the trumpet] until the trumpet of the feast'. Of course few people have enough clothes to last a whole month without washing, and women with small children have to do some washing every day.

Sleeping in Daytime

In the afternoon women are busy, so many take a nap at noon. In Marrakech, sleeping during the fasting day is not frowned upon, as long as it is not done excessively. Actually, people were a little surprised when I asked if sleeping was allowed during the fast. Women may sleep around noon. Men do so when they come home from their jobs. Once I even came upon a shopkeeper who had fallen asleep on the floor behind his counter during working hours. When awoken by my entrance to the shop, he did not adopt the apologetic demeanour of somebody being 'caught', but in contrast made it quite clear that I had disturbed his sleep.

In the family in which I spent Ramadan in Berkane, sleeping during a fasting day was valued differently. Although I was assured that it was not *ḥarâm*, forbidden to sleep, it was more highly valued if one could summon the 'courage' to stay awake and show the patience to endure the long fasting days. Yet, when somebody had fallen asleep, he or she was not woken up but was covered with a blanket. However, upon waking up the person was teased by the other family members for having given in to his or her weakness. More often than not, the *mater familias* would reprimand the sleepyhead and lecture us on the importance of displaying some 'strength' in accomplishing the fast. She herself also took a little nap quite often, but excused herself by saying that she was an old woman. On visits she denied this weakness. To the ever recurring question 'How is Ramadan?' (*kî dayra m^{c}a ṛemḍân?*), she replied that the fasting was not difficult at all and that she hardly slept during daytime.

The issue of sleeping during the fasting days was also discussed on television in 1988. In the special Ramadan series broadcast that year, one of the programmes showed a sketch of a man who remained in bed the whole fasting day. Whenever he was disturbed in his sleep by his wife or children he howled at them 'after sunset', and pulled the blankets over his head. The sketch was concluded by a shot of the wife, who turned to the camera and posed the question whether the fast of her husband would be *meqbûl*, accepted. This question was then discussed by a panel of Koran scholars. They reached the conclusion that sleeping the whole fasting day is not *ḥarâm*, forbidden, but does not yield any *ajr*, religious merit, either. They added that for people who are irritable, as in the case of those who have withdrawal symptoms through not drinking alcohol or smoking, it is even better to spend the day in bed, because quarrelling while fasting is more *makrûh*, reprehensible, than sleeping.

Preparing Food

The television sketch showed a man who was sleeping until he was woken up by his wife to break the fast. Most women cannot indulge in such luxuries. They spend the larger part of the afternoon preparing the food that will be consumed after sunset. In Berkane, women generally do not go to the market, but wait until their husbands or brothers bring home vegetables and meat. In all neighbourhoods, special Ramadan markets are set up so that people do not have to walk far with their heavy shopping bags while fasting.[5] In Marrakech, there are no such markets and shopping is done by women. Carrying home the heavy bags and preparing aromatic foodstuffs is not an easy task to perform on an empty stomach. They prepare not only the meal which is eaten immediately following sunset, but also make sure that the night meals only need to be warmed up, so that they are free to enjoy themselves in the evening.

The meal that is eaten to break the fast is called *l-fṭûr*, 'breakfast', a term which is usually associated with the meal eaten in the morning. As in English, the term properly speaking refers to the first meal one eats to 'break the fast'. The second daily meal during Ramadan is referred to as the *l-ᶜšâ'*, the same term which is used to denote the light meal that during the other months of the year is eaten at this time of night. During Ramadan, however, *l-ᶜšâ'* is a substantial meal. The food that is prepared for this meal is of the more sumptuous variety which, during the other months of the year, is eaten at midday. The last meal before daybreak begins is called *s-sḥûr*. It is usually a light meal, consisting of French toast, porridge or a sweet couscous.

5. Although these Ramadan markets relieve the burden of men who go shopping, they complicate matters for women who go out to visit friends. They sometimes have to make large detours to avoid passing the market. Being part of the men's domain, it is *ḥšûma* or shameful for a woman to be seen there.

With respect to the meals, three facts struck me: the quality of the food is better than usual, the amount of food is larger, and many women restore traditional cooking methods. Although during Ramadan the number of meals is reduced, both quantity and quality are increased. People may even have saved money in order to eat more sumptuously during Ramadan. Rich people, for instance, who are used to eating meat every day, improve the quality of their *tajîns*, stews prepared in earthenware cone-shaped pots, by adding extra olives or dried prunes and almonds. On their tables one can also find a large variety of Ramadan pastries. Poorer families, who normally eat little meat or can afford to do so only on Fridays, try to have meat, if not every day, then at least a few times a week during Ramadan. Equally, nearly all families I visited served at least some crumbs of the *s̆ebbakîya*s, the special Ramadan cookies.

In most cases, the amount of food prepared exceeds the quantity needed to fill the stomach. There should always be enough food to serve unexpected visitors their share of the lavish Ramadan meal. While this is also done in other months, during Ramadan being prepared to serve unexpected guests is of greater importance, since the chances that somebody will visit the house unexpectedly are greater. Another reason for preparing extra food is that during the fasting month, it is customary to send a share of one's own delicacies to neighbours, relatives or close friends every now and then.

Sharing lavish meals is a major preoccupation of Moroccans during Ramadan and women have the responsibility of making sure that the family can indulge in excessive consumption after sunset (*l-mġurb*). In preparing food they often employ traditional cooking methods. A few days before the beginning of Ramadan, one of my informants began to collect wood to burn under an old stove she almost exclusively uses during Ramadan. She usually cooks on a gas burner, but in her view, the *ḥrîra*, the special Ramadan soup, never tastes as good as when prepared on the old stove. Another example is the stew which during Ramadan is eaten for the *ᶜs̆â'*, supper, the meal that is consumed a few hours after 'breakfast'. Usually this stew is prepared in pressure cookers on gas burners. During Ramadan, however, many women use charcoal burners and cook in a *tajîn*. This takes much more time, but the better taste is considered ample compensation.

Tasting food is generally believed to be forbidden while fasting, so women have to rely on habit in measuring how much salt and spices must be added to the food. It is important for the *ḥrîra* to taste right the first day of Ramadan. If this is the case, women know that the soup will be tasty the whole month. Should, however, the *ḥrîra* be too salty or not spicy enough, then no matter how you try, the soup will not taste good the rest of the month.

Breaking the Fast

The last half hour before sunset is rush hour. Conflicts occur easily when hundreds of people, whose hunger by this time has made them irritated, try to push their way through the narrow alleys in the medina to get home, despite the fact that quarrelling during the fast is reprehensible.

Among those who elbow their way through the crowd are many young men who have been jogging during the last hour before sunset. Their faces show gratification and pride. They obviously enjoy demonstrating their excellent condition by accomplishing such performances on an empty stomach. People respond to these young sportsmen with respect for their strength. For the same reason, soccer games just before sunset are very popular. Almost every neighbourhood of the medina has its own soccer team and during Ramadan a competition is held between them, which attracts many male supporters. Special Ramadan soccer competition is also organised nationally between different towns.

At home, mothers or wives by this time have set the table for l-*fṭûr*, breakfast. In most families, this consists of at least a plate with boiled eggs and one with *šebbakîya*s. In richer families, additional pastries such as *beġrîr*, pancakes sprinkled with olive oil or honey, or *slîlu*, ground nuts mixed with roasted flour and spices, may be featured on the breakfast menu, together with different kinds of salads and drinks such as fresh orange juice or buttermilk. In the middle of the table of any family in Marrakech, Berkane and probably everywhere in Morocco, one finds the indispensable soup tureen with *ḥrîra*, the special Ramadan soup. The soup tureen is surrounded by bowls which each have a *mġurfa*, a wooden spoon, over them. This is another example of a tradition being restored during Ramadan. The restoration of old Moroccan traditions and, more particularly, the fact that everywhere in Morocco people break the fast by eating the same soup affirms the notion that Moroccans are one people.

This sense of communion is concretely experienced when all family members gather around the table at sunset to share 'breakfast'. The family ethos is strongly emphasised during Ramadan. Ideally, close relatives share breakfast at least twice a week. In my host family, one sister moved in with us for the duration of Ramadan and almost every day we were joined by one or two relatives for breakfast. Ramadan is also the time to invite friends over for breakfast. Such invitations render the host *ajr*. To a lesser extent the guests also achieve *ajr* for paying a visit.

A person invited for *l-fṭûr* lingers on to eat l-*ᶜšâ'* a few hours later. Meanwhile, the guest is served many glasses of tea or coffee – often both – with lots of cookies. Milk, costing 2.5 dirham per half litre, is considered expensive, but during Ramadan coffee is always prepared with extra milk. After *l-fṭûr*, some people go to the mosque to pray the *tarâwîḥ*, the Ramadan prayers. Among my informants in Marrakech there was no one who prayed the *tarâwîḥ* in the mosque. When women who pray their five daily prayers at home were asked why they did not go to the mosque for the *tarâwîḥ* or the Friday sermon, they answered that they did not feel at ease there. They considered the mosque more or less a men's place. One woman added defensively that there are also many men who do not go to the mosque.

Between *fṭûr* and *ᶜšâ'* older women mostly stay at home or visit neighbours and watch television, whereas men join their friends in the overcrowded pavement cafés. Young couples and youngsters love strolling along the avenues of Gueliz 'to let the *ḥrîra* sink in', as some young girls laughingly explained. Joining girls on their strolls, I noticed that watching and being watched plays as much a role as digesting the *ḥrîra*. Safely walking arm in arm, the girls dare look and smile at boys in a way they would not easily do outside Ramadan. Going out at night during Ramadan does not give them the reputation for being 'bad girls'. Normally, girls should behave modestly and not leave the house after sunset, which is equal to asking for trouble. Not so in Ramadan; once, when a boy followed a group of girls, a dignified older man dismounted his bicycle to reprimand him. He then hopped back on his bicycle and kept pedalling beside us, without talking or even looking at us, until the young man gave up and turned away.[6] On our Ramadan walks, I always saw many shy young couples stealing hugs and kisses in the park surrounding the Koutoubia mosque. Also, when my roommate and I once came across our next door neighbour in Gueliz, she confided that she could not come with us because she was on her way to see her boyfriend. Probably such secret encounters also take place at other times of the year, but I never experienced the same (semi)open atmosphere about it as during Ramadan. As will be argued in chapter 8, this blurring of, or even challenge to, normal moral standards is typical of the liminal character of Ramadan.

In the small town of Berkane things were different. Only in one rich family were the daughters allowed to leave the house after *l-fṭûr*, and were not to stroll along the shops situated on the main street, but to visit female friends. This happened secretly, that is, their mother allowed them to sneak in and out of the house when

6. This man possibly felt responsible and ashamed that a foreign woman was being hassled by one of his compatriots. At other times I noticed such protective behaviour only on the part of women, who in general seek and provide protection to one another from unwanted looks and conversations by men by joining any other woman who happens to be walking the same way.

their father was in the mosque praying the *tarâwîḥ*. Other families spoke disapprovingly of this practice and did not allow their daughters to go out, although I noticed in our alley that some neighbours visited each other. In Berkane, I knew many more people who prayed the *tarâwîḥ* than in Marrakech. In my host family, the mother went with friends to pray the *tarâwîḥ* in the mosque. The youngest son also visited the mosque, but his two brothers preferred watching soccer games or listening to the musical bands that play during Ramadan. The daughter had announced that she would also like to go to the mosque to pray the *tarâwîḥ*, but her mother would not hear of it. So, for her and her sister-in-law, the only entertainment that the Ramadan nights offered as a reward for having completed another fasting day was watching television and asking their brothers after they came home what was going on outside.

l-cšâ', the evening meal that is normally served between nine and ten o'clock in the evening, is consumed much later in Ramadan. Most families have *l-ᶜšâ'* between eleven and twelve o'clock at night. In order to be able to skip the nightly meal, s-*sḥûr*, some families even postpone *l-ᶜšâ'* until two o'clock in the morning and then go to bed, not to wake up until the morning. The inclination to share the meal with all family members is not as pronounced at *l-ᶜšâ'* as it is at *l-fṭûr*. Still, there is more sharing than during the rest of the year, when husbands and sons often do not bother to leave their friends in the cafés to come home and eat. The better quality of *l-ᶜšâ'* and additional meat during Ramadan may provide an incentive for them not to miss this meal. Also, because nobody is in a hurry to go to bed during the fasting month, very often the meal is not served until they have come home.

Having eaten *l-ᶜšâ'*, it is time to go to bed. By two o'clock in the morning stillness has come over Marrakech. The streets are deserted and most people are asleep. Not for long, however, because around three o'clock the oboists mount the minarets of the little mosques in the medina to wake people up, so that they can have the last meal before the dawn announces another fasting day.[7] Most people agree that it is difficult to get up and eat after barely two or three hours of sleep. The nights are cold and having eaten a rich *l-ᶜšâ'*, few have much of an appetite. Yet there is *ajr*, religious merit, in eating *s-sḥûr*, and many fear feelings of hunger during the day if they do not eat; so only a few, such as people who due to illness or their menses do not fast, skip *s-sḥûr*. In all families where I

7. The way in which Moroccans are woken up for *s-sḥûr* shows regional variations; in Berkane the oboist walks through the alleys of his living quarter, and in Fes a man with a kind of hammer knocks on the doors of all houses, while two trumpeters play on the minarets (cf. Chottin 1923: 283; 1927). Such customs are now vanishing, since most people no longer depend on these men but set their alarm clocks.

spent Ramadan nights, eating *s-sḥûr* was done quickly. Not much was said during the meal, and everybody went back to sleep as quickly as possible.

Not all households follow exactly the same daily routine during Ramadan as has been described above. Variations to this pattern occur. For instance, some families engage in more visiting and entertaining of guests than others do. Also, as the fasting month proceeds, some people get tired of eating *ḥrîra* every night and begin alternating this soup with other kinds of soups or porridges with medicinal herbs. Sleeping during the day increases as the month draws to its close.

Besides such variations, there are two occasions which prevent fasting from becoming a routine that might be performed more or less unthinkingly. These are 'the preferred days'.

The Preferred Days: the 15th and 27th of Ramadan

The 15th of Ramadan

The full Ramadan moon, when half of the fasting month is over, marks the first *fḍîla*, the preferred (day) or *weṣṭ ṛemḍân*, the middle of Ramadan. When asked why it is called the *fḍîla*, my informants answered that this did not refer to any religious prescription, but concerns a local custom to celebrate that Ramadan is half finished. Many Marrakchis even think that celebrating the 15th of Ramadan is typical for their town only. In Berkane, however, the 15th was also celebrated. On television, much attention was indeed paid to the way in which this *fḍîla* is celebrated in Marrakech, but impressions from other towns were also given.

Celebrating *weṣṭ ṛemḍân* includes giving presents to children and having chicken or rabbit for supper. Already a few days before the 15th toy-stalls appear on the square Jemaa al-Fna. Small shops all over the medina suddenly begin selling toys. The idea of giving toys to children, as explained to me, is to help children learn to love Ramadan so that by the time they begin fasting they will be happy to do so.

On the 15th, shops selling toys do very good business. The shopping area around the square Jemaa al-Fna is then crowded with mothers who combine buying toys for their children with buying a chicken or rabbit on ar-Rahba square. Many vendors of small stock are women. This is their chance to make good money selling the few animals, fed on leftovers of the family's meals, they raise on their roofs or in the storerooms. Prices increase due to the great demand; everybody wants a savoury supper prepared with chicken or rabbit for the 15th. Even the poorest families, who cannot afford to eat meat every night during Ramadan, make sure that, on the 15th, they have one of these animals on the menu. Around ar-Rahba small shops change into minuscule slaughterhouses. Although chicken and rabbit meat is available from the butcher's, women prefer to buy a live animal. As women themselves are forbidden to slaughter by Islamic Law, they have the animal slaughtered by a male member of the family.[8] Those with no man to hand stop at one of the temporary slaughterhouses on the way home.[9]

I participated in the celebration of the 15th of Ramadan twice, once in Berkane and once in Marrakech. Both experiences turned out somewhat disappointing. When in Berkane, on one of the first days of Ramadan, I wanted to take a picture of the breakfast table. I was advised to wait until the 15th, when the table would be even more abundantly set. I was told, with enthusiasm, how the streets would be full of vendors of chickens and rabbits and how good *l-ᶜṣâ'* was going to taste. However, on the 15th, the three brothers were entangled in an argument over whose turn it was to go shopping. They all stubbornly refused to go out. So, on the day when we should have been having the best meal of Ramadan, there was instead only some leftover bread, *ḥrîra*, and coffee prepared with powdermilk. The fact that it was the 15th was mentioned by no one.

Remembering this sad occasion, I was very much looking forward to the celebration of the 15th with my host family in Marrakech. Like the year before, long before the 15th was due, women began to volunteer information about it, basically describing it in the same manner as people had done in Berkane. Since I was often invited to share *l-fṭûr* with other families, I was only home every third or fourth night, but my hostess warned me not to accept any invitation for the *weṣṭ ṛemḍân*. It is considered shameful to eat outside the family circle on the 15th. To be sure, walking with her on the overcrowded squares ar-Rahba and Jemaa al-Fna on the morning of the 15th, selecting a fat rabbit and toys for the small ones, was exciting. Yet, like the celebration of the 15th in Berkane, the day ended in disappointment both for my hostess and myself. Her

8. In the absence of an adult male member, one of my informants in Berkane sidestepped this prohibition by letting her six-year-old grandson hold the knife under her hand while she slaughtered her rabbit.

9. The emphasis on buying a living animal and slaughtering it raises the question whether the notion of making a sacrifice implicitly plays a role. To God? A Thanksgiving for having accomplished half of the fasting so far without many problems? The fact that it was stressed that celebrating the 15th was not a religious activity contradicts this. A more practical motive could be that this way one can be sure that the meat is fresh. Yet, any other time of the year women are quite willing to buy rabbit straight from the butcher.

two sons and youngest sister, whom she had expected, did not show up.[10]

The 27th of Ramadan: laylat al-qadr

The second preferred day of Ramadan is *laylat al-qadr*, the Night of Measure.[11] In Moroccan Arabic, this night is more commonly referred to simply as *s-seb^{c}a u ^{c}ešrîn*, the 27th. Asking people to explain to me the significance of the 27th, I invariably received the same answers: *s-seb^{c}a u ^{c}ešrîn ḥsen men alf šhûr*, 'the 27th is better than a thousand months'; *nzel fîhâ l-qur'ân l-karîm*, 'in it the Holy Koran descended' [to earth]. These standard remarks refer to meanings which are closely related to the orthodox interpretation of the 27th of Ramadan. However, as we will see, there are meanings in the celebration of this holy night that are embedded in a popular Moroccan view of Islam. The celebration of the 27th serves as an example of how notions and performances of orthodox and popular Islam intermingle.

Children's First Fast Many children who have reached the age of eight or nine fast for the first time in their lives on the day preceding *laylat al-qadr*. When they accomplish the fast, in the evening there is a little party or at least an extra tasty breakfast for them. In some cases, girls are dressed up as brides towards sunset and break the fast by drinking a bit of milk and eating a date. One informant, a widowed woman in her forties, remembered having fasted several years on the 26th of Ramadan before she began to fast the whole of Ramadan. The first time, she had received a nice new dress and had felt very grown up.

Praying and Reciting the Koran The night between the 26th and the 27th of Ramadan is so sacred that many people spend it in prayer. The mosques are full that night, and on television one can watch a live broadcast from the mosque where the king attends a prayer meeting. Similar meetings with men of importance are organised all over Morocco. The next day, the newspapers report which notables attended which meeting and with how many other people.

During my first Ramadan in Marrakech, I was invited by Lalla Aisha, an elderly lady with three grown-up children and married to

10. These two experiences made me question whether it was pure coincidence that celebrations of the 15th in both families where I participated ended in a kind of failure, or if it is an indication of the slow waning of this tradition, giving way to a more purely religious performance of the fast.

11. In what follows, I shall translate *laylat al-qadr* into 'The Night of Measure', since this is more currently used than 'The Night of Power' as Arberry uses in his translation of the Koran (cf. ch. 1).

a tailor, to spend the 27th with her family. When I entered her house I found her husband and married daughter – who had come to her mother's house for the occasion of the 27th – watching television, which showed the king praying. Every time that the worshippers, in performing *rak*ᶜ*as* – bendings of the torso from an upright position, followed by two prostrations – pronounced the words *allâhu akbar*, 'God is great', Aisha's husband whispered the formula along with them. The *rak*ᶜ*as* were alternated with recitations from Bukari's compilation of Hadiths, read by the imam, and by two lines of prayers, which were repeated many times: 'Praise be to God the Powerful; Praise be to God the Merciful'. These are the same lines that are prayed when using prayer beads. In fact, Aisha's daughter was holding a string of beads in her hand and prayed along with the worshippers on television. Obviously proud of his daughter, her father commented that people who pray during the 27th are *fḍel llâh ktîr*, 'favourite to God very much'. He further explained that every time you pronounce these two lines, you earn yourself a plant or tree in Paradise. There is a lot of *ajr*, religious merit, in saying them, especially on the night of the 27th.

People who do not pray themselves can still earn much *ajr* by bringing couscous to the mosques. The food is shared by worshippers, who get hungry from praying the whole night, and by poor people who come to the mosque to eat this valuable *ṣadaqa* or alms-giving. Aisha explained to me that although any *ṣadaqa* handed out during Ramadan yields more *ajr* than during the rest of the year, the amount of *ajr* earned by sending couscous to the mosque exceeds all other forms of *ṣadaqa*. Clearly, the notions of *ajr* and *ṣadaqa,* which motivate and are expressed in many of the activities developed by people during Ramadan and which play an important role in making the fast a meaningful whole, reach their culmination during the *laylat al-qadr*.

As far as I know, none of my informants in Marrakech went to the mosque to pray on the 27th. When I asked about the praying, some women explained that they do not go to the mosque, but instead visit the tombs of the saints. A complete tour around the *seb*ᶜ*at rjâl*, the Seven Patrons of Marrakech, should be made on the night of the 27th.[12] This demands walking quite a distance, which is not very attractive so late at night, so many women settle for visiting only the most important saints.

Entering shrines is forbidden for non-Muslims, but Lalla Aisha and her daughter were prepared to take the risk and after having disguised me in a *jellâba*, a long overcoat, and a big headscarf, took me along with them on their tour to the saints. Although it was

12. For detailed information on the Seven Patrons of Marrakech, see Castries 1924.

past midnight, the streets were still full of people walking to and from the mosques, sometimes carrying big dishes of couscous on their heads. Many people, especially men, were wearing white *jellâbas*. We first entered the shrine of Sidi AbdelAziz. The women first kissed the corners of the saint's tomb and then sat down against the wall among the other visitors, mostly women, numbering about 40. After a while, Aisha got up and, facing the *miḥrâb* – a niche in the wall indicating the direction of Mecca – she began to pray.[13] We remained in the shrine approximately twenty minutes, and then left for the shrine of Sidi Ben Slimane. This shrine is adjacent to a large mosque. The shrine and the mosque share one entrance, and I noticed that some men who had visited the mosque also entered the shrine to salute the saint. All the women I observed went straight into the saint's shrine. The shrine of Sidi Ben Slimane was bigger and more luxuriously furnished than the one of Sidi Abdel-Aziz. Sidi Ben Slimane is believed to be a very powerful saint. According to Zainab, even the king visits him when he is in Marrakech. The good reputation of Sidi Ben Slimane and the location of his shrine may account for the fact that his shrine is visited by more men than that of Sidi AbdelAziz.

After Aisha and her daughter had prayed for a while at Sidi Ben Slimane's tomb, we went home. It was by now past one o'clock in the morning, the traffic in the alleys was decreasing and the lights were being extinguished. However, outside one building the sign *dâr al-qur'ân*, 'House of the Koran', was still illuminated by a string of light bulbs, and the alley was almost completely blocked by bicycles and motorbikes. Even from outside, men could clearly be heard reciting the Koran together. A complete reading of the Koran during Ramadan is considered to yield a lot of *ajr*. To this purpose, Moroccans follow the division of the book in sixty parts, of which they read two parts each night. Neither in Marrakech nor in Berkane did I meet people who actually read the Koran. However, many women watch and listen more or less attentively to the daily broadcasts of recitations on television. The seriousness of efforts to watch this programme became clear when, while visiting a family possessing a video-recorder, a son came home during the daily broadcast of Koran recitations and put in a videotape. Both his mother and his sister protested loudly and reprimanded him for not wanting to listen to the Koran.[14] Also, during Ramadan many

13. A woman who regularly performs the tour around the Seven Patrons later told me that one is supposed to recite the Sura *al-iḵlâs* (S.112) twelve times in each shrine. People who have not visited Koran school and do not know this Sura may pray whatever they think suitable. *Yṣelliw ben-nîya*, 'they pray through (their) intention'.

14. In fact, in many families, the television is turned on from the moment it starts broadcasting in the afternoon or early evening until midnight when the broadcasts have ended.

copies of the Koran are displayed for sale by street vendors and bookshops, and occasionally a shopkeeper can be seen reading the book. Like the banners bearing religious texts, which are put up over the entrances of the mosques, and the *tarâwîḥ* prayers said there at night, the reading of the Koran is an example of the intensified religiosity manifest during Ramadan. This religiosity reaches its climax on the night of the 27th Ramadan. Not only do a lot of people perform extra prayers that night at home, in the mosque, or in a saint's shrine, but in all towns there are meetings, such as in the *dâr al-qur'ân,* where men stay awake to recite together the whole Koran in one night.

Apart from those who prayed at the saint's shrines on the night of the 27th, I did not meet women in Marrakech who engaged in the extended prayer sessions either privately or collectively. This stands in marked contrast to the female participation in such performances in Berkane. As a rule, most Berkanis begin praying the five daily prayers at the same time as they begin to fast. This is from puberty onwards, which for boys is a few years later than for girls. Also praying the *tarâwîḥ* and the nightly prayer session on the 27th are more closely observed.

In the evening of the 27th, the female head of the family with whom I was staying was picked up by several friends to go to the mosque. When she had left, her daughter complained that it was such a pity that her mother had not allowed us to come with her. 'It is a pretty sight, the mosque is so full that people have to pray outside. That looks beautiful in the lights of all those lamps.' The pretty sight was not the only reason why Rahma would have liked to join her mother. She also would have liked to perform the prayers of the 27th. The two previous years Rahma had planned to perform the prayers, but nothing had come of it. Two years earlier, when she had only been sixteen years old, she had insisted on performing these nightly prayers on the roof. Like many Berkanis, she believes that every year some very pious Muslims, who pray fervently during the *laylat al-qadr,* can see the gate of Paradise open. Those witnessing may then formulate a wish which is granted by God immediately. Rahma explained that for this reason, many people perform the prayers on the roof of their houses, hoping to be one of the lucky few who will see the gate to Paradise. Rahma herself, however, had been so frightened on the dark roof that she descended within five minutes. Downstairs she met with her whole family, who laughed at her for fearing the darkness and for having overestimated herself; did she really think God would grant such a young girl the privilege of seeing the gate to Paradise? Convinced that she stood a chance, Rahma planned to try again the next year. However, when that year came, she happened to have her period in the week of the 27th of Ramadan. Her state of impurity forbade her to pray. By then, she understood that, indeed, God probably had found her too young to perform the prayers in the *laylat al-qadr*.

According to Warda, Rahma's sister-in-law, today very few people see the gate of Paradise, least of all in the city, where the city lights make it so much harder to scrutinise the sky. In the countryside it still occasionally happens, as was the case with Warda's own grandmother. Unfortunately, this woman had become so confused that she forgot to formulate a wish. A friend of hers had had more luck.[15]

The Return of the Spirits The gate of Paradise features in yet another sense in Moroccan religious beliefs concerning the 27th of Ramadan. Through it, the spirits who have been locked up during Ramadan are released on the 27th and return to earth. Their return is not without danger for human beings. One never knows in what mood the whimsical spirits will be, so precautions must be taken to avoid irritating them while they are trying to settle down again. In Marrakech and Berkane alike, many families keep all the lights in the house burning the night of the 27th. In this way, they hope that the spirits will find their way into the nooks and crannies they inhabit without bothering people. Lest the spirits should not feel welcome and become angry, different kinds of incense are burned to please them. Vendors who sell toys around the 15th, now sell incense. The incense should be burnt immediately following sunset before eating breakfast. A female member of the household walks from room to room holding a charcoal burner with incense. Without talking or otherwise communicating with other members of the family, she fumigates the corners of all the rooms and then leaves the burner in the courtyard. To convince me that the families sharing the courtyard were not the only ones who burn incense on the 27th, Zainab suggested I go out into the street. Indeed, the smell of incense was coming from the windows of almost every house and for some time the whole medina was enveloped in a cloud of incense.

That Zainab felt the need to convince me of the generality of performing this welcoming ritual for the spirits is significant. As was already mentioned in chapter 2, most informants were rather reserved or reluctant to discuss issues related to spirits. Fear that

15. This woman was standing in the doorway of her house when she suddenly noticed the gate of Paradise. Wishing for long hair, she uttered 'O Lord, give me a big head', that is, a head with strong beautiful hair. God, however, took the wish of the woman literally. Her head immediately grew so large that it got stuck in the casing so that the poor woman could not move to or fro. Realising her mistake she corrected herself: 'No, Lord, I did not mean a big head, but long hair.' The next moment her head was back to its original size and her hair grew so long that it dragged behind her over the floor.

talking about them might invoke them is one reason. Another reason is that many people are aware of the fact that the prominent role played by the spirits in their religious beliefs and practices is rejected by orthodox Muslims. Also, many know that Christians do not believe in spirits. By referring to the generality of the welcoming ritual for the spirits, I feel Zainab was trying to justify her own behaviour to me, whom she perceived to be a representative of those groups who reject such practices.

Upon arriving in Lalla Aisha's house after breakfast on the 27th, I commented on the smell of incense hanging over the medina, and asked why people burn incense on that day. Bending over slightly towards me, Lalla Aisha whispered: 'Because those people from under the earth come back, do you understand?' Her husband overheard us and angrily turned to Aisha. 'No, no, no, why do you tell her that? Do not tell her these bad things, tell her the true Islam [*l-islâm l-ḥaqîq*]. The incense is for the *malakiyyât*, the angels who are here during the night of the 27th.'

As with the performance of prayers on the night of the 27th, we see Lalla Aisha's husband relating more strictly to 'orthodox Islam', whereas Aisha herself integrates elements from what has been called 'popular Islam' in her ritual activities; she acknowledges the importance of praying, but chooses to do so in a saint's shrine where she feels more at home than in the mosque.[16] While she does not deny that incense should be burnt for the angels, in her view this does not conflict with, at the same time, paying homage to the spirits.

With the return of the spirits, magic regains its power. The incense burnt not only welcomes back the spirits, but also wards off any magic that might be performed against one during that night. For almost a month, gossip and stories about sorcery were practically unheard of, reaching a point at which people seemed to have forgotten all about their preoccupation with magic. With the coming of the 27th, the old fears come back in full force.

During my stay in Berkane, this fear for the powers of magic manifested itself in the great dismay caused by a sheep's head. On the 26th of Ramadan, while the *mater familias* and her sons were away from home, there was a knock on the door. An unknown boy handed over a plastic bag containing a sheep's head, with the message that the eldest son had sent it to be prepared for supper. Angrily, Rahma put the head in the refrigerator: preparing a sheep's head is a lot of work, and she was busy making cookies for the end of

16. Cf. Mernissi (1977) for an interesting account on how the shrines are more accessible to women and more compatible with their experiences than institutions such as mosques and hospitals.

Ramadan. When her brother came home she told him this. To her surprise he did not know anything about the sheep's head. We anxiously waited for the other brothers to return home. All of them claimed to have nothing to do with it. Who then did send the mysterious head? By this time the women were becoming alarmed. 'I will not eat any of it', Rahma exclaimed anxiously, 'We do not know who sent it and we do not know what has been done with it.' Warda refused to touch the head; this happened on the 26th of Ramadan. The day after would be the 27th, when all spirits and magical powers were to be released. Moreover, in Algeria, only twenty kilometres away from Berkane, it already was the 27th. For all she knew, the head might have come from there and was already bewitched. The next day, Rahma's mother left the house with the head. She knocked on every door in the neighbourhood to see if anybody knew more about it. As her youngest son had already suggested, it turned out that the head was meant for one of the neighbours but, being a stranger to the neighbourhood, the delivery boy had made a mistake. Afterwards, we could all laugh about the incident, but I will not easily forget the tense atmosphere that arose once the sheep's head was suspected to be associated with the fearful powers of magic that return on the 27th of Ramadan.[17]

Visiting the Dead The day following the night of the 27th is the *nhâr z-ziyâra*, 'the day of the visit' to the deceased. Early in the morning many Marrakchis, mostly women, go to the cemetery to visit their deceased relatives. On the way, they buy figs and dates to hand out as *ṣadaqa*, alms, to the children and poor people at the entrance to the cemetery. Some also buy palm leaves to sweep the tombs and *riḥân*, myrtle, to plant in or around the tomb to give it a nice smell. This is also considered giving *ṣadaqa*. In fact, women refer to the whole visit to the cemetery on the 27th Ramadan as *nṣedqu*, alms-giving (literally: 'we give alms').

One informant in her twenties invited me to come with her to the cemetery just outside the city wall to visit her mother. Still being a *bint*, an unmarried girl, she usually wears European-style clothes.[18] For our visit to the cemetery, however, she dressed in the

17. In a very vivid account of her life among women in Marrakech (1930–70), Peets describes similar examples of the suspicion and fears experienced by her Moroccan friends for the dangerous moments on the 27th of Ramadan, when the spirits, and with them the magical powers, return to earth (Peets, 1988: 101–65).

18. In Moroccan Arabic there are two terms to categorise people of the female sex; *bint* refers to girls, at the same time meaning a virgin, an unmarried female without sexual experience. *Mrâ'* refers to a married woman with sexual experience. This categorisation implies that unmarried females who may be in their forties or older are still referred to as a *bint*, a girl, whereas a fourteen-year-old female who is married is addressed as a *mrâ'*, a woman.

traditional *jellâba*, the long overcoat. I was to be disguised in one too; as an impure Christian I was not allowed in cemeteries. On our way, we were almost pushed over by dozens of small children begging and screaming for figs. In the cemetery other children were fighting to be chosen to collect the holy water from the well near the shrine of Sidi Sfaj, located at the rear end of the cemetery.[19] After Suad had pulled the weeds from her mother's grave, she washed it with the holy water and planted the myrtle on it. Myrtle contains *baraka*, divine power, she explained: 'It brings forgiveness from God'. She then sat down to think of her mother. With tears in her eyes, she told me how beautiful Ramadan had been when her mother had still been alive three years ago. She used to prepare wonderful meals and saw to it that the whole family celebrated the month together. Now the sisters had more or less drifted apart and did not share *l-fṭûr* more than two or three times a week.

We also talked about other people who had died in previous years. One of our neighbours had died only the day before. Suad called him a very lucky man. Having died in Ramadan, his soul would go straight to Paradise.[20] Not only did he die during the most blessed month of the year, but more particularly on a Friday, the blessed day. On top of that, it had been the 27th of Ramadan, the day which is better than a thousand months.[21] These were signs that our neighbour must have been a very good and pious man.

The Concluding Feast *ᶜîd al-fiṭr*

Once the 27th of Ramadan has passed, all attention is focused on the preparations for the *ᶜîd*, the feast, as the *ᶜîd al-fiṭr*, the Feast of Breaking the Ramadan Fast or Lesser Bairam is referred to in Morocco. The house is cleaned, albeit not as thoroughly as a few days preceding Ramadan. The public baths are once again overcrowded and the *mûl l-ferân*, the owner of the public oven, is working overtime to bake the hundreds of kilos of pastries and cookies that women have been making for the *ᶜîd*. In the old medinas shopping centre

19. Jemma (1971: 17), who mentions all the saints surrounding the cemetery, refers to Sidi Sfinj, the Fritter Saint. Many of my informants no longer possess much knowledge about the saints in their neighbourhood. However, those who do know the names of several saints insist on calling the saint in the cemetery Sidi Sfaj.

20. In an autobiographic novel, Oussaid (1988: 134) recalls how his mother tried to console him as a young boy when his father had died, using the same comforting thought: 'C'était son heure, me dit-elle, lui au moins a eu la chance de mourir le dix du mois sacré de Ramadan; dans la tribu ils savent tous qu'il est au paradis.'

21. Actually, Suad was manipulating reality here; the new day begins in the evening. The man had died early in the morning, which was, properly speaking, still the 26th of Ramadan. This detail was neglected by everyone whom I heard discussing the blessed moment of his death in the days that followed.

Semmarine, one has to push one's way through the crowd of women buying new clothes for their children, who should all be dressed in new on the ^{c}*îd*.

Two activities are central to the celebration of the *cîd*. The first is the handing out of the *zakât al-fiṭr*, the obligatory donation of food required at the end of Ramadan. In Moroccan Arabic, the handing out of these alms is referred to as *ḵerrej l-fiṭra*, taking out the *fiṭra*, the measure of wheat or barley constituting the donation. The second activity is sharing with family members and other beloved the first breakfast after Ramadan.

A week before the end of Ramadan, the selling of wheat, which is to be given away as the *fiṭra*, begins. Heaps of wheat are unloaded onto all the little squares in the medina. Every family buys at least one measure of wheat, or any other corn that they themselves have been using to bake bread during Ramadan, for each person living in the house, and often a few measures more. Moroccans consider the handing out of these *fiṭra*s to be very important. In their view, one's fasting is not valid until one has paid these obligatory alms, 'it remains hanging between Paradise and earth' (cf. Westermarck 1926: 100). The head of the household is responsible for handing out as many *fiṭra*s as there are residents in the house, including small children, servants, or, in the case of my host family, an anthropologist. These *fiṭra*s must preferably be handed out in the last few days before the ^{c}*îd*, so that poor people who receive them will have collected enough wheat to hand out their own *fiṭra* on the ^{c}*îd*. In any case, one should have handed out one's *fiṭra* before eating the first breakfast on the ^{c}*îd*. This applies to the *fiṭra* which is handed out on behalf of young children as well: Fatima, the sister of my hostess, came to spend the last night before the ^{c}*îd* with us. She handed out one *fiṭra* that evening, in case her baby daughter should wake up in the middle of the night and want her bottle.

Although there is a lot of *ajr* in eating the last *sḥur* or nightly meal, in my host family we did not get up until very early in the morning, when we were wakened by the music of the *ġeyyât*, the oboist, who was passing by.

The *ġeyyât* is one of the persons entitled to receive a *fiṭra* from each family in the neighbourhood of the mosque on top of which he has been playing his oboe during Ramadan. Other people who can come to the door to claim a *fiṭra* include first of all one's midwife. She should receive one measure for every child she has delivered. Next are the *gellâsa*s, the women who work in the public bath. Furthermore, the *mûl z-zbel*, the dustman, and the *beyyât*, the watchman who walks through the neighbourhood at night, are entitled to a fitra. In chapter 8 I will elaborate on the liminality of these personae who either deal with impure matter or are situated at the outskirts of the community, being awake and out of doors when others sleep.

Should there be *fiṭra*s left to be handed out when all these people have claimed their share, the remaining measures go to needy family members or other poor people. This *fiṭra* contains much *baraka,* blessings. Therefore, the people who receive the wheat preferably save it until the Feast of Immolation two months later, so that they can eat the meat of the sacrificial animal with bread prepared from the *fiṭra*s.

In our alley, only the oboist and the bath-house workers came to the door. When the son of my hostess tried to empty one *fiṭra* in the bag held up before him by one of the women, some of the wheat fell on the floor. This caused great consternation, and all the women began to shout at him. The boy was strongly reprimanded by his mother. Carefully, one by one the grains were picked up again, and the floor was inspected several times to make sure that not one grain was left on it. Zainab later explained that no grains from the *fiṭra* should ever fall on the floor. For one thing, it contained *baraka,* blessings, and something containing *baraka* should never touch the floor. Furthermore, by spilling wheat, the *fiṭra* is not the exact measure it should be. Last of all, in a house where grains from the fitra are spilled, there will be a lot of fighting during the coming year. It even happens that people secretly throw a handful of *fiṭra* grains into the house of a neighbour or somebody else they do not like so that that person will constantly be engaged in quarrels and fights. The *fiṭra* can also be used in a positive way. It is customary to hand out one *fitra* more than there are household members. This is called the *fiṭra l-ḥlâqem*, the *fiṭra* of the tonsils. This extra *fiṭra* will protect the household members against inflammation of the tonsils. Handing out yet another *fiṭra* protects the wool in the mattresses from being eaten by moths in the next year.

Besides handing out *fiṭra*s to passers-by, my hostess gave some measures to her own aunt, who shares the same courtyard. Both women later regretted this. As it is *ḥarâm*, forbidden, to eat from the *fiṭra* one has handed out, for a whole month following the Feast of Immolation, we could not share meals with aunt Latifa; her bread contained our wheat. Since breadcrumbs inevitably fall into the sauce during the meal, unless she served us on a separate dish, we could not eat with her.

After all obligatory *fiṭra*s were handed out, we had a light breakfast of rice porridge. I was invited to the breakfast table with the words *kûli awwel fṭûr dyal l-ᶜâm j-jdîd*, 'eat the first breakfast of the new year'.[22] I was told that the traditional dish for the first break-

22. The notion of the *ᶜîd* marking the new year will be discussed in ch. 8.

fast is *herbel*, a porridge from pounded wheat with butter and honey. *Herbel* is an elaborate dish to prepare, so many families have now replaced it with another kind of porridge. According to Zainab, as long as the porridge is white, as when prepared with milk, it will ensure that the new year is a good one, with an abundance of food (cf. Legey 1926: 177). While we were still eating this first breakfast, one of the women went to the kitchen to prepare *ġaif*, a kind of pancake on which either olive oil or honey is sprinkled. She made enough for any guest who would pass by that day to have their share. Around nine o'clock, our neighbour entered with a dish of porridge, saying *kûlu fṭûrna*, 'eat our breakfast'. We in turn went over to the neighbours to give them their share of our breakfast. The rest of the day was spent exchanging breakfast with relatives and friends. Guests came in saying *mabrûk ᶜlîk l-ᶜîd*, 'blessed be upon you the feast', and were replied to with the words *llâh ibârak fîk*, 'may God bless you'. Whomever I visited, at whatever time of the day, each time I was presented with a plate of pancakes and pastries with the words *kûli ḥaqqek fṭûrna*, 'eat your part of our breakfast'. Visiting friends and relatives and sharing breakfast with them on the day of the *ᶜîd* is a way of earning *ajr*. As one woman said to me as she kissed me goodbye after my visit: *rejlîk jâbûk ajr bezzâf*, 'your feet have brought you a lot of religious merit'.

Following those feet on the day of the feast was a pleasure. Nearly all children dressed up in new clothes, men in spotless white *jellâba*s and women in their prettiest clothes, and everybody watched everybody else. Besides the day of the Immolation Feast, the feast concluding Ramadan is the only occasion in the year when one sees husbands and wives walking together. Ideally, the closest relatives of both parties must be visited on the first day of the *ᶜîd*. The whole week following it can be used to visit more distant relatives. Most men are only free from their work the first three days of the week.

Paying visits to relatives and friends is not the only way to earn *ajr* on the day of the feast. There is a lot of *ajr* in performing the great ablution before having breakfast.[23] Women can also earn *ajr* by painting their hands and feet with henna for the feast. *Bel-ḥenna nferḥu bel-ᶜîd* 'By (having applied) henna we celebrate the feast', I was told. Above all, there is *ajr* in attending the special prayers and sermon given in the mosques and, more importantly, on the *muṣallâ*, a kind of oratory in the open air. The *musallâ* is exclusively visited by men.[24]

23. Moroccans usually do not use the proper religious terms for the ablutions. That performing the great ritual purification yields religious merit was described in the following words: *nhâr l-ᶜîd, d-dûš fîhâ ajr bezzâf*, 'on the day of the feast, there is a lot of religious merit in taking a shower'.

24. Women should not be seen by men while praying.

Women are allowed to attend the service in the mosque, but in Marrakech apparently few do so; not one woman mentioned attending the service to me when enumerating the activities that give *ajr* on the day of the feast. Although the women in my host family also gave me a list of activities that yield *ajr*, they did not perform many themselves. During the day, they did visit and receive guests and exchange best wishes, but they had 'forgotten' to buy henna, and found the meritorious early morning washing too cold.

Once again, there were many differences in Berkane. The family with whom I lived did not hand out the *fiṭra* in kind, but in money. Also, they did not wait for people to come by to collect it, but the *mater familias* took the money with her to the mosque and gave it to the imam to distribute it among the needy. According to her, most people in Berkane pay their *fiṭra*s in this way.

On the night when Ramadan was proclaimed finished, we were busy applying henna to each other's hands and feet until very late in the night. Remembering that it takes months for the henna on the feet to wear off, I insisted that only my hands be decorated. Initially, Hadda would not hear of it; on the *ᶜîd* all women must wear henna. If someone does not do so, other people will wonder why; is she not happy? Does she have a reason for not celebrating? Did she perhaps not fast . . .? The idea that one can distinguish, on the basis of the happiness demonstrated by people at the feast, between those who have kept the fast and those who have not, was also explained by Hadda's brother. According to him, people who have not fasted properly can be recognised by their black faces on the *ᶜîd*. To them, the feast is like any other day, they have no reason to rejoice. On the other hand, people who have kept the fast have the *nûr allâh*, the light of God, in their eyes. Bekey also mentioned a proverb indicating the difference between those who have truly fasted and those who have not: 'Whoever ate (during) Ramadan, his bones have shrivelled'.[25]

At four-thirty in the morning of the *ᶜîd*, my Berkani hostess woke up and performed the great ritual ablution. Dressed up in a new white dress and a white *jellâba*, smelling strongly of the perfume her husband had brought her from his pilgrimage to Mecca, she later left the house to go to the mosque for the special service there.

The rest of the day, the house was filled with guests. Each time a new visitor entered the same formulas were exchanged between visitor, V, and host, H:

25. Chemoul (1936: 406) reports the same words being used by a group of people, which followed a person through the streets, mocking him for not fasting.

V: *^{c}îd mabrûk*, a blessed feast
H: *llâh ibârak fîk*, God bless you
V: *n^{c}îdu u n^{c}awdu in šâ llâh*, we celebrate and (will) repeat this if God is willing
H: *ana wiyâk*, I and you

As has been mentioned before, it is *makrûh*, objectionable, to be engaged in disputes during Ramadan. In any case, if one's fasting is to yield any *ajr*, disputes should be settled on the *^{c}îd*. Therefore, my Berkani hostess was overjoyed when her brother came in to congratulate her on the day of the feast. Due to disputes concerning their inheritance, they had not talked to one another for years. Now they embraced warmly and whispered words of forgiveness. As we will see in the next chapter, reconciliation on the *^{c}îd* also takes place on the level of international politics.

On the first day of the feast concluding Ramadan, most people only eat the pancakes, pastries and cookies that make up the breakfast. In fact, any food eaten that day is called breakfast. Only on the second day are meals with vegetables and meat once again prepared. Some people, however, resume fasting on the second day of Shawwal, the month succeeding Ramadan. They fast for six subsequent days. This voluntary fasting is called *ṣawm aṣ-ṣâbirîn*, 'the fasting of the patient (ones)'. Fasting the *ṣawm aṣ-ṣâbirîn* renders a lot of *ajr*. As with most voluntary fasting, this form of fast is observed mainly by older people who also perform the five daily prayers. In Berkane I met more people who performed the *ṣawm-aṣ ṣâbirîn* than I did in Marrakech. After the last fasting day, they have a small celebration similar to the one on the first day of the *^{c}îd*: they have an elaborate breakfast and dress up nicely, visit friends, etc. After the *usbû^{c} l-^{c}îd*, the week of the feast, has passed, Ramadan is definitely over. Normal life is resumed, and when people talk about the *^{c}îd*, the feast, more often than not they are already referring to the next coming feast, the Feast of Immolation (cf. chapter 7).

four

Unification of the *Umma*, the Muslim Community

In the preceding chapters, we have seen how people in Marrakech and Berkane prepare themselves for Ramadan and organise their lives during the fasting month. The next three chapters will deal with three key notions which make performance of the fast a meaningful act in the view of Moroccans. This chapter will be devoted to the notion of *umma,* which serves as an overall frame of reference without which the other notions do not make sense.

Umma is the Arabic word for the Islamic community. It is a religious concept, not referring to any geographic entity, political or religious institution, but rather to an ideal organisation of all Muslims, regardless of race, nationality or religious divisions. *Umma* denotes the community of believers who share the basic principles of Islam: the Koran, Sunna and the Sharia, including its five religious duties. The ideal of *umma* is closely associated with the historical community of Muslims founded by the Prophet Muhammed, the *umma muḥammadiyyah.* This original Islamic community is believed to have been characterised by strong cohesion, equality and solidarity among its members. The corporateness of the Islamic community is considered to have declined since early Islam (cf. de Bruijn 1984; Waardenburg 1984). Therefore, referring to the *umma* means appealing to the ideal of restoring the original Islamic community.

In the two opening sections, it will be argued that, more than the execution of other religious duties, fasting sets Muslims apart from non-Muslims, thus emphasising the boundaries of the Islamic community. In the third section, different levels of the Islamic community will be identified. It will be demonstrated that, in their performance of the fast, Moroccans refer to the *umma* as the larger context in which the Moroccan nation, which is more particularly emphasised, is situated. Intensified sociability between kin, friends and neighbours during Ramadan highlights the real-life level at which Moroccans experience their membership of the Islamic community. In the fourth section it will be demonstrated that the fasting activities of women focus predominantly on the level of the local community.

The Fast as a Religious Duty for Muslims

Of the five religious duties, the fast is best observed by Moroccans. To be sure, an exception must be made for the *šahâda*, the Muslim creed, which is pronounced almost unthinkingly so many times a day that it loses some of its special significance.[1] The other religious duties are more difficult to perform. The *ḥajj*, the pilgrimage to Mecca, is too expensive for most Moroccans to undertake. The *zakât*, alms-giving, is also associated with the well-to-do.[2] According to my informants, the *zakât* is almost exclusively handed out by merchants and other entrepreneurs. It is distributed on the *ᶜâšûrâ'*, the tenth day of the Islamic New Year, but as we will see in chapter 7, not much attention is focused on it. The *ṣalât*, the five daily prayers, are observed by more Moroccans. Except in the North, where children begin to pray around the same time as they begin to fast, which is at puberty, mainly older people perform the prayers regularly.[3] Being close to death, these people *tayḵâfû men llâh*, 'fear God', as one woman explained to me. Although everybody agrees that praying is very important and that one really should perform the *ṣalât*, most of my informants did not hesitate to admit that 'their time has not yet come', or, as one woman put it: 'the duty is not yet mine'. She assured me that God will forgive those who begin to pray for not having done so before and taught me a saying concerning the matter: 'People who do not yet pray, are like a donkey tied by the feet until the afternoon. Only then is it instructed its work.' Those who pray are respected for doing so, but nowhere in Morocco south of Berkane did I see disapproval of people who do not (yet) pray.

This stands in striking contrast to the attitude towards fasting. First of all, unlike neglecting the other religious duties, not keeping the fast is considered both a crime and a sin. More than once, I was proudly told that should someone be caught eating, he or she can be put in jail or be sentenced to beatings. Article 222 of the Penal Code reads:

1. For example, as an exclamation expressing astonishment, to underline the truth of a statement. The formula is also recited every night before falling asleep.

2. The *zakât* proper is not to be confused with the *zakât al-fiṭr*, mentioned in ch. 3, which is handed out at the end of Ramadan.

3. In Berkane, I observed that almost everyone, from the age of 12 for girls and 15 to 18 for boys, performed the daily prayers. Berkane is situated in the foothills of the Rif mountains, which are known among other Moroccans as an enclave of religious conservatism.

> Celui qui, notoirement connu pour son appartenance à la religion musulmane, rompt ostensiblement le jeûne dans un lieu public pendant le temps du Ramadan sans motif admis par cette religion, est puni de l'emprisonnement d'un à six mois et d'une amende de 12 à 120 DH. (Blanc 1977: 132)

Article 222 is cited in the article 'Délit de Ramadan'.[4] Maintaining that religion is an individual affair, the author of the article addresses the question whether the law should be allowed to deny individuals the liberty to decide for themselves whether or not to keep the fast. By closely analysing the conditions stated in Article 222, he reaches the conclusion that they leave enough room for the individual who chooses not to fast, thus distinguishing between committing a crime, that is, breaking the fast in public, and committing a sin: breaking the fast privately (Berrada 1988: 54–5). Although the view that religion is an individual affair is quite novel to Morocco, it is worth noting that the author is in line with most Moroccans in that not keeping the fast is viewed as a sin. I have not heard the neglect of the prayers or other religious duties referred to as *ḥarâm*, forbidden or sinful.

In any first conversation with someone on the subject of fasting, it is always maintained that every Muslim fasts. The only exceptions mentioned are the elites of Casablanca and Fes, who are suspected of neglecting their religious duties. Even when I got to know people better, very rarely did someone admit that they had not kept the fast. In fact, I only know three individuals who claim not to fast for no other reason than that it is too tiresome or difficult. All three of them, a married couple and a young man, had given up fasting in their college years while they were living away from home. In all cases, they told me of their negligence during conversations in which they were trying to show off their modern, European way of living. Significantly, none of them had told their parents about their views regarding the fast. In the presence of other family members they kept up appearances and fasted. In fact, the single man has taken up fasting since he moved in with his family again.[5]

In the case of people who cannot keep the fast due to illness, many proved to be reluctant about it. Hardly ever did someone volunteer information about his or her condition. Most often I learned from others that they did not fast. I even know cases of two women

4. The article appeared in *Kalima*, a progressive magazine now silenced for having dared to tackle issues such as abortion (no. 25, 1988) and male prostitution (no. 24, 1988).

5. Fallers noted the same strong community pressure for the Turkish town where he conducted fieldwork. Among those who dared defy it were many officials without local ties (Fallers 1974: 38).

who, the one having diabetes and the other being bilious, knowingly risked their health by fasting when their doctors had strongly advised them not to do so.

Judging from the seriousness and fervour with which the overwhelming majority of my informants talked about Ramadan, I am convinced that most of these people keep the fast. They would be shocked to hear that someone in their circle was not doing so without a valid reason.[6]

Fasting Sets 'Us' apart from 'Them'

Variations in the standard reply to my question about why people fast in Ramadan were, amongst others, 'in order to be Muslims', 'so that God knows who are Muslims', and 'this is the religion'.[7] In the eyes of Moroccans, fasting, more than anything else, 'makes' a Muslim. To be sure, other practices also accentuate the Muslim identity. Yet, these are never as general or convincing as is fasting; while men are marked as Muslims by circumcision, women are not. Observing food taboos, such as not eating pork, is also emphasised in distinguishing oneself as a Muslim (cf. chapter 7). There is an awareness, however, that both practices are also observed by Jews, although one of my informants proved to be surprised when she learned that Jewish people, who are extremely impure in the eyes of Moroccans, also practise circumcision.

When I summarised conversations with informants by using the statement 'fasting makes the Muslim', they immediately added that fasting alone is not enough, one should perform all religious duties. Differences in the observance of religious duties and in attitudes regarding such observances, however, make it clear that, despite the fact that people realise and emphasise how it should be, in practice, fasting Ramadan is tacitly assumed to be the crucial factor in assessing whether or not a person belongs to the Islamic community. In the words of one informant: the fast reveals who has the *nûr llâh*, 'the light of God', in his or her eyes and who does not (cf. chapter 3).

That the observance of the fast serves as the criterion for determining whether someone is a Muslim or a *kafir*, an infidel, can be illustrated by the confusion it caused when I, a European woman,

6. Apparently, the fast is not as closely observed in all Islamic countries. Contrary to my experience in Morocco, I found that in the Northern Yemeni town of Hodeidah, having to break the fast due to illness is not viewed as negatively as it is in Morocco. Several women frankly stated, even during the first contact, that they did not keep the fast, vaguely mentioning `general weakness' as a reason. Fallers (1974: 38) and Goitein (1966: 108) note for Turkey and Egypt that quite a number of people do not keep the fast. However, it must be taken into account that under the influence of the revivalism of Islam that has swept over the Muslim world since the mid-1970s' the situation in both countries may have changed considerably since these articles were published.

7. Cf. Buskens (1987: 20) who received similar replies in Larache.

observed the fast. From the very beginning of my research, I had declared that I had no intentions of becoming a Muslim and explained my fasting as a desire to share in the experiences of the people around me and find out what it actually feels like to fast. This puzzled people. Why should anyone want to fast if it does not yield her any *ajr*, religious merit? More importantly, more than once I noticed how surprised people were that I managed to fast the entire month of Ramadan. Moroccans are very proud of being able to fast a whole month and assume that non-Muslims would not have the strength to do so.[8] My accomplishment of the fast was interpreted as a sign that I have good *nîya*, (religious) intention. Word spread about my fasting, and soon I found that in the neighbourhoods I visited regularly, I had gained a reputation for being or becoming a converted Muslim. When, for example, I tried to tell off some small boys for throwing stones at me, one of them yelled at me: 'So you tell us what to do? You, a Christian, who does not even fast?' Then, one of his friends remembered rumours about me and hissed to the others: 'Stop it, don't you know she is a Muslim?' Also, I noticed how some informants would correct friends who referred to me as *n-neṣṛâniyya*, the Christian: *mâšî neṣṛâniyya; mselma*, 'she is not a Christian; a Muslim'. As time elapsed and Ramadan lay more and more behind us, my reputation as a (potential) Muslim waned; apparently, it had been closely associated with my participation in the fast.

Ramadan is the month in which the line is more sharply drawn between those who are and those who are not members of the Islamic community. The distinction between Muslims and non-Muslims becomes more visible and is emphasised or even played out, as the incident with the small boys illustrates. In the medina of Marrakech, during Ramadan, the street cafés are all closed in daytime, but in the former French quarter, Gueliz, some are open. One finds an occasional Moroccan there who has not ordered anything and has just sat down to kill time until sunset by chatting with a friend. Most seats, however, are occupied by non-Muslim tourists visiting Marrakech, who have taken refuge in these cafés as the only place where they will be served 'normally'. They do not demonstrate any shame for quenching their thirst publicly. Many looks of curiosity and disapproval are passed back and forth between the fasting Muslims and drinking tourists in Gueliz.

8. This can further be illustrated by an incident that occurred when I was wearing my new *jellâba*, overcoat, to bring the bread dough to the oven. The owner of the oven complimented me on my new Moroccan garment and asked whether it was true that I performed the fast. When I confirmed this he asked me if I was a Muslim. My denial surprised him; if I managed to perform the fast, it should be easy to become Muslim, shouldn't it? To explain his point he told me the story of a Jew who in Shaban decided to become a Muslim. When Ramadan came, however, he was so shocked to learn that he would have to fast thirty days in a row, that he quickly changed his mind and remained Jewish.

The contrast between Muslims and non-Muslims is further emphasised in dress. As has already been mentioned in chapter 3 in relation to cooking techniques, for Moroccans, Ramadan is a time for temporarily restoring traditions. This is also expressed in the way people dress. In Berkane, although some adolescent boys even in Ramadan will not part with their blue jeans, virtually all girls who, during the other months, dress European style wear Moroccan dresses, tie back their hair and upon leaving the house cover themselves with *jellâba*s. When the youngest daughter of my Berkani hostess and I once came across a girl wearing trousers, my companion commented with a disapproving look on her face that the girl had no shame (*mâ teḥšems̆*) to be walking around like that during Ramadan.

In Marrakech, opinions regarding dress are not quite as strong, but as in Berkane, more people can be seen wearing the traditional *jellâba* during Ramadan, especially among those who pray in the mosques. Women who continue to dress European style make sure that at least their appearance is 'decent', and do not wear clothes that leave the upper arms and legs uncovered.[9] Make-up and perfume are avoided by almost everyone; it is considered *makrûh*, objectionable, and by some even *ḥarâm*, forbidden, to use such products.

This way of dressing stands in sharp contrast to the 'holiday outfits' worn by most tourists. Many do not seem to realise that wearing shorts and tight or sleeveless shirts may affront Moroccans. The confrontation with scantily dressed foreign women, a problem for men who may fear that their fast is rendered invalid by such distractions, is not the only concern of Moroccans in their contacts with non-Muslims during Ramadan, however. One day, as a young unmarried informant and I were walking along in a small alley in the medina, we had to edge our way through a group of Spanish tourists, some of whom smelled strongly of perfume, while others were smoking. Casting a hostile glance at the group, my informant commented 'They make us break the fast by inhaling their perfume and smoke.' Actually, this was not the case, as she later admitted. If

9. Adjusting one's dress in Ramadan to fit Islamic standards is a more general tendency in the Islamic world. In Riyadh, Saudi Arabia, where I spent Ramadan in 1981, clothing rules for foreign women at the time were restricted to loose garments that left only the head, hands and feet uncovered. During Ramadan, however, this was not sufficient. The *muṭawwiᶜ*s, the 'religious police', mostly older men who volunteer to patrol in the streets of Riyadh to ensure the obeying of religious rules, sent home any foreign woman who was not wearing the black Saudi Arabian overcoat and did not have her hair covered. Even wearing a headscarf and the traditional overcoat, I was once forbidden entrance to the bazaar.

Also, in Jordan the anthropologist Driessen met a woman who decided to begin to wear the *ḥijâb*, the clothes concealing the women's figure as worn by Muslim Sisters, from Ramadan onwards (Driessen, personal communication).

we had deliberately inhaled the odours, this might have been objectionable or forbidden. This incident illustrates that the woman, by exaggerating the consequences of our encounter with the tourists, reinforced the distinction between 'them' as non-fasting foreigners and 'us' as fasting Muslims.

Fortunately for those Marrakchis who experience the confrontation with tourists as a disturbance to observing the fast, the number of foreigners visiting the town drops remarkably during Ramadan. Up to 800,000 tourists, a number larger than its own number of inhabitants, come to Marrakech each year, and their presence greatly influences the character of the town (Daoud 1988: 42).[10] Ramadan appears to be the only 'low season' for tourism. For this one month of the year, the Marrakchis have their town more or less to themselves, as they together perform the highly regarded religious duty of fasting. Without the thousands of tourists, Marrakech exudes an atmosphere of peace that agrees very well with the contemplative and devout character of Ramadan. The striking absence of tourists enhances the sense of togetherness derived from partaking in the Islamic community by the inhabitants.[11]

Evoking the *Umma*

Ramadan is the time *par excellence* in which the appeal to the unification of the *umma* can be given shape. Muslims everywhere in the world perform the fast, all of them roughly following the same rhythm of feeling hungry early in the day, restless and anxious towards sunset and joyful and satisfied during the night. Moreover, the notions of the *umma*, religiosity, harmony and solidarity, are repeated in the aspirations of those observing the fast. Living Ramadan can even be viewed as a way to approach the ideal Muslim community as closely as possible. According to one male informant, if all Muslims would perform the fast properly 'Ramadan would be Paradise on earth'.

This statement refers to two different instances of unification that the fast ideally establishes: the unification of all Muslims, and, as life on earth and life in Paradise merge, the unification with God. The Arabic word for unification, *tawḥîd*, is an important Islamic concept. It refers first and foremost to the unity of God, and is expressed in the first line of the *šahâda*, the Muslim 'creed' or doctrinal formula: 'There is no god than God.' Sufis seek unifica-

10. The hotels of Marrakech have a capacity of 12,000 beds (Daoud 1988: 42). New hotels are still being built.

11. It must be noted that nobody stated this feeling spontaneously. However, when I mentioned that I noticed relatively few tourists during the fasting month, this was confirmed. Some people smiled and commented that this made Ramadan even better.

tion with God through mystical practices (cf. Schimmel 1983). As Denny (1985: 64) explains, the experience of the unity of God is articulated and maintained in the ritual duties: '*Tawḥîd* is not merely a matter of theological propositions, but also a living realization: the "making one" of God by total submission and service.'

The meaning of *tawḥîd* in relation to fasting did not occur to me until, during my second visit to Marrakech a year after my main fieldwork, it was pointed out to me by an educated key informant while we were discussing the tentative outline of my book. She subscribed to my analysis of the meaning of the fast based on the three conceptual structures which I present in my study, but suggested the qualification that fasting establishes the *tawḥîd* of the *umma*. Going through my material, I found that the importance of unification can also be recognised in the action and statements of people in relation to the meanings of purity and religious merit (cf. chapters 5 and 6). When I presented this idea to the aforementioned informant, she replied that she had never looked at it in that way, but could agree with my analysis.

How, then, do Moroccans conceive of the *tawḥîd al-umma*, 'unification of the Islamic Community' during the fast? In the following sections, I will treat three different levels on which the notion of *umma* is expressed during Ramadan.

But first it must be noted that the words *umma* or *tawḥîd* are no part of the daily vocabulary of most Moroccans. However, this does not mean that, as notions, the Islamic Community and unification do not play a role in their world-view. *Umma* and *tawḥîd* are abstract terms that most people who have not received formal Islamic education are not familiar with.[12]

The Greater Umma

Despite their failure to mention the religious term *umma*, it is apparent that the notion of belonging to a greater Islamic community encompassing all Muslims plays a role in the practice of fasting among my informants in both Marrakech and Berkane, albeit not a prominent one. This is probably true for most Moroccans. The most clear expression of the sense of *umma* are the occasional references made to the cradle of Islam, Saudi Arabia. The declaration there that Ramadan has begun and ended, or the number of days the Saudis have fasted, do not escape the attention of many people. Exchanging information about these issues is a common

12. In this sense, the concepts can be compared to that of purity, which plays an important role in the lives of Moroccans. Yet, *ṭahâra*, the religious term for purity, is seldom used by common people (cf. Buitelaar 1985a).

topic of conversation during Ramadan. Also, the religious ties with Saudi Arabia, in turn linking Moroccans to other Muslims in the world, are underlined by the fact that during Ramadan a considerable number of (rich) people go on ^{c}*umra*, a voluntary minor pilgrimage to Mecca. The ^{c}*umra* can be performed any time of the year, but is mostly performed during Ramadan. One of my informants living in the rich quarter of Gueliz planned to go on ^{c}*umra* in Ramadan 1989. She and her husband had already been to Saudi Arabia twice before; the first time to perform the *ḥajj*, the pilgrimage proper, the second time for an ^{c}*umra*, which they had performed during Ramadan. Now widowed, she would this time be accompanied by her eldest son. When asked if there was any particular reason for performing the ^{c}*umra* in Ramadan, she replied that performing this voluntary pilgrimage during *š-šher l-mbârak*, the blessed month, yields a lot of *ajr*, religious merit. Furthermore, she recalled from her former visit what an impressive experience it had been to be fasting in the holy city of Mecca, amidst Muslims from all over the world, together waiting for the cannonshots which are discharged on a hill on the outskirts of Mecca to announce sunset.

Unlike the *ḥajj*, for which Royal Air Maroc has a monopoly on the transport of the thousands of pilgrims to Mecca at extremely high fares, the ^{c}*umra* can be made much more cheaply with bus trips, organised especially for this purpose during Ramadan. Shortly before Ramadan begins, posters advertising such trips appear everywhere on the walls and shop windows in Marrakech. The texts of these posters try to lure potential clients to book a reservation by assuring them that *ḥrîra*, the typically Moroccan Ramadan soup, will be served every night during the journey, both on the way to Mecca and in the holy city itself. Mention of this detail on the posters, insignificant as it may seem, is an illustration of the fact that however universal the religious duty of fasting among Muslims may be, in the eyes of Moroccans there is a specifically 'Moroccan way' of performing it.

The Moroccan Nation

Indeed, among the masses the notion of Islamic community is more manifest on the national than on the international level. In several ways, fasting reinforces the notion of belonging to *l-waṭan*, the home country or (Moroccan) nation. Eating *ḥrîra* is so closely associated with breaking the fast in Morocco, that this soup has become a national symbol for Ramadan. Cartoons in the newspapers depict people jumping into a bowl of *ḥrîra* or showering themselves with the soup, all to show the gratification this favourite Moroccan dish offers after a long day of fasting.

What makes *ḥrîra* so suitable as the national dish for breaking the fast is that the ingredients can easily be adjusted to meet any budget and family size. Rich families use chopped meat and kilos of fresh tomatoes, whereas poorer and very large families replace fresh tomatoes with tomato paste, meat with extra chickpeas and lentils and add more flour and water to make the volume of the soup meet the size of the family. Although each household has its own recipe, these are all variations on the famous Moroccan *ḥrîra*. The fact that nearly all people eat the same soup directly after sunset enhances a sense of communion; it stimulates the notion of establishing one Moroccan people of fasting Muslims. Restoring Moroccan traditions such as cooking in earthenware *tajîn*s on charcoal burners and wearing *jellâba*s also expresses the 'typical Moroccan way' of fasting.

The notion of constituting one Moroccan community of Muslims is strongly emphasised in the mass media. Especially during Ramadan, emphasis on *l-waṭan*, appealing to nationalist feelings, is stressed daily on television and in newspapers. When television broadcasts are interrupted each night by the call to prayer which announces sunset, images of famous Moroccan mosques such as the Hassan tower in Rabat and the Koutoubia in Marrakech fill the screen. Also, every night there is a broadcast of *al-Andalûs*, music brought to Morocco by Muslims fleeing from Spain at the time of the Reconquesta. Al-Andalûs has become the classical music of North Africa, although most Moroccans claim that it is specifically Moroccan. Furthermore, the popular Egyptian soap operas have to compete with plays and films in the Moroccan dialect, many more of which are broadcast in Ramadan than during the rest of the year. In the newspapers, Ramadan's ability to unite all Moroccan regions is expressed in articles with headlines such as 'Le jeûne dans la perle du Moyen-Atlas' (*Le Matin du Sahara*, 28.5.87: 16), 'Ramadan à Fes' (ibid., 25.5.87: 16), and 'Marrakech: Fidélité aux traditions et aux coutumes ancestrales' (ibid., 16.5.87: 12). Also, much attention is paid to the special Ramadan football competition among towns from all over Morocco.

Most topics on television and in newspapers appealing to *l-waṭan* highlight the image of the Moroccan nation as a cohesive Islamic community. This is most clearly seen in the way King Hassan II, skilfully employing television and the government paper *Le Matin du Sahara* as mouthpieces, presents himself as *amîr al-mu'minîn*, Commander of the Faithful. For centuries, general recognition for this honourable title of Morocco's ruling sultans, which is today formally decreed in the constitution, has served to unify the country religiously where it was divided politically into the *bled l-maḵzen* (literally country of the government), that part of the country where the sultan was politically acknowledged, and the *bled s-sîba* (literally country of the dissidence) where his administrative authority was challenged or rejected.[13]

In an attempt to meet demands of the nationalist movement after independence in 1956, Hassan's father, Muhammed V, strove to modernise the image of his authority by exchanging the title of sultan for that of king. Succeeding him after his death in 1961, Hassan II followed in his father's footsteps by presenting himself as head of a modern state. These days, when he appears on television to address the Moroccan people directly, the king is usually seated behind a huge writing desk, wearing a European suit.

Since the succession, however, cooperation between monarchy and the nationalist movement failed to be successful time and again and in the end was given up. Eventually the army became the only base for organised political support, while at the same time presenting the major threat to the existing political organisation. The king, therefore, distanced himself from this institution. Since 1973, only the isolated legitimacy and institution of the monarchy are left to support the system (Zartman 1987: 6).

Since the early 1980s, Hassan II has had to deal with a growing, albeit not yet significantly strong, opposition to his power from the militant Islamic movement. Slightly under 15 per cent of Moroccan university students are actively involved in this movement. A far greater number are sympathetic with militant Islamic ideas (Munson 1986: 275). Influenced by the events of the Iranian revolution (1978–79), many Moroccans now believe that religious discourse is directly related to politics. This shift in attitude has been met by an increased religious content and rhetoric in the royal discourse (Eickelman 1987: 89). Having proved its ability to unite power in the past, the monarch's identity as Commander of the Faithful is put forward as part of a strategy to appeal both to members of the different potentially political movements and to the majority of the politically less active Moroccans. The slogan *allâh, al-waṭan, al-malik* – God, the fatherland and the king – which is painted on walls and inscribed in mountains everywhere in Morocco, reminds the Moroccan people of the religious legitimacy of the king to rule the country.[14]

13. One of the useful criteria by which the *bled l-makzen* and *bled s-sîba* could be distinguished was the recognition of the sultan's right of taxation. Yet even within the *bled l-makzen* this claim was not always acknowledged (Claisse 1987: 52). This illustrates that the distinction between the *bled l-makzen* and *bled s-sîba* was not a static or unequivocal one. Rather it fluctuated along with the loyalties and coalitions of different Berber tribes.

14. As Eickelman (1987: 90) remarks, this (rural) majority has erroneously been depicted as apolitical: 'sufficiently pushed with violations of popularly accepted notions of social injustice and authority, it can create major political ruptures and test the limits of the effective use of force and repression'.

Ramadan is the pre-eminent month in which the monarch reminds his people of his role as Commander of the Faithful, on occasion skilfully referring to aspects of the Islam of the educated elite, while at other times appealing to notions of sainthood and *baraka*, blessing, which play a prominent role in popular beliefs. He does so by presenting himself both as representative of the Moroccan people within the greater Islamic community and as head of internal religious affairs in Morocco.

His role in representing the Moroccan people within the greater *umma* finds expression in the first week of Ramadan, when *Le Matin du Sahara* publishes a series of reports on the many congratulatory letters that the king has received from other Islamic countries. In 1988, in his own congratulations to Islamic leaders elsewhere, Hassan II explicitly referred to the ideal of *umma*:

> il M'est agréable de partager votre espoir de voir la Oumma islamique se ressaisir, dépasser ses dissensions et s'interdire la délapidation de ses ressources matérielles et humains.
>
> Nous vous renouvelons Notre ferme engagement à oeuvrer de concert pour unifier les rangs de la Oumma islamique, coordonner ses efforts jusqu' à la réalisation de ses aspirations à la prospérité pour devenir un facteur d'équilibre, de modération et de paix entre les peuples conformément à ce que Le Trés-Haut a dit dans Son Livre Saint . . . (*Le Matin du Sahara* 19.4.88: 1)

Another example of the way in which the Moroccan king emphasises his identity as *amîr al-mu'minîn* in the international perspective of formal Islam is by presiding over a series of lectures given by *ᶜulamâ'*, official religious leaders from different countries. These 'Conférences Religieuses du mois de Ramadan' are organised yearly in the royal palace in Rabat. They are attended by international religious scholars and prominent Moroccan figures. In 1988 Hassan II received, amongst others, Islamic scholars from China, the USSR and the United States. In *Le Matin du Sahara* nationalist feelings were boosted by praising Morocco for its conciliatory role in world politics by bringing together representatives of diverse regimes:

> Ces Ouléma et autres invités de différents régions du monde et de pays à régimes politiques et doctrines différents se trouvent, à l'occasion du mois sacré de Ramadan, dans notre pays, terre de rencontre du tous les Musulmans du monde et de tous ceux qui oeuvrent pour le triomphe et la grandeur de l'Islam et des causes décisives des Musulmans. Le Maroc est ainsi fier d'être en centre de rayonnement de l'Islam et un point de rencontre des Musulmans indifféremment e leur nationalités, de leur continents et des doctrines suivies dans leurs pays. (*Le Matin du Sahara* 30.4.88: 1)

The religious lectures cover subjects ranging from the relationship between science and religion, the Code for the Rights of Children in Islam, and Islam and peace (cf. *Conférences Réligieuses* 1988). All lectures are broadcast live on television. Many shots show Hassan II with his two sons at his side, all three of them dressed in the traditional white *jellâba* and intently listening to the lecture. Elaborate reports are published in the newspaper summarising these lectures. Such articles invariably open with a phrase underlining the religious and political leadership of Hassan II:

> S.M. le Roi Hassan II, Amir El Mouminine, entouré de S.A.R. le Prince Héritier Sidi Mohammed et de S.A.R. le Prince Moulay Rachid a présidé le [date of lecture] au Palais Royal de Rabat la [ordinal number] causerie religieuse du mois de Ramadan . . . (*Le Matin du Sahara,* April 1988)

A telling example of how Hassan II accentuates his combined political and religious authority was offered in Ramadan 1988. On 16 May, 29 Ramadan of that year, he made a move to restore political relations with the Algerian president Chadli Benjedid. The relations had been broken off twelve years earlier. It was no coincidence that the reconciliation between the neighbouring nations was announced on the first day of the feast concluding Ramadan (cf. *Le Matin du Sahara,* 17.5.88: 1). Such action is very much in line with the notion of forgiveness, which, according to popular perceptions of the fast, people should demonstrate on the day of the feast. Fasting entails more than refraining from eating, drinking and enjoying sexual contact. As one informant put it, 'fasting is everything with the mouth', which includes refraining from arguing. The first day of the concluding feast is considered to be the most proper occasion for conciliatory deeds. Referring to this notion of forgiveness on the feast, in *Le Matin du Sahara* (17.5.88: 1) it was commented that the king had been inspired by the sacredness of Ramadan in taking the decision to restore relations with Algeria. Thus, in his role as political leader, Hassan II was able to assert the legitimacy of his authority by presenting himself as a devout Muslim who observes the tradition of reconciling oneself with enemies on the occasion of the feast which concludes Ramadan.

Feeding popular notions of the monarch's legitimacy by adroitly linking political measures with religious beliefs has proven to be effective; during the month of Ramadan in 1987, the year preceding the reconciliation between King Hassan II and President Chadli, there had also been a summit meeting between the two leaders. Politically speaking, the encounter did not meet its desired goals (cf. Soudan 1987). However, Hassan II's attempt fostered goodwill among Moroccans. The opening of the meeting was broadcast live on television. In Berkane, members of my host family sat glued to the television to see who would arrive first at the tent where the negotiations were to take place. To their relief it was Hassan II. Obviously proud of their king, they commented that he would therefore gain the most *ajr,* religious merit.

The king appeals to popular conceptions of Ramadan in his endeavour to reaffirm his authority in yet another way. Every year, the day his father Muhammed V died is commemorated on the 10th of Ramadan, according to the lunar calendar employed in Islam. Since all other national days of commemoration follow the Gregorian calendar, one might wonder why an exception is made for the death of Muhammed V. Two motives play a role. Muhammed V is a powerful symbol of Moroccan nationalism. The French sent him into exile in 1953, but were forced to allow him to return in 1955. A year later he became the first ruler of independent Morocco. This made him the hero-leader of the struggle for independence (cf. Geertz 1968: 80–1). During the week of his commemoration, many articles appear in the papers applauding his part in liberating the country from the colonial yoke. Commemorating the death of this national hero in Ramadan has the advantage for Hassan II that the community feelings enhanced by collectively performing the fast can thus easily be focused on the throne. Moreover, the pervasive link between Islam and the Moroccan dynasty is reaffirmed. Hassan II belongs to the House of the Alawites, which traces its descent from the Prophet Muhammed. As members of this holy lineage, the Alawite rulers are endowed with a large amount of *baraka,* divine blessing. The *baraka* possessed by the Alawites is the main source of legitimacy for the king's dual authority as *amîr al-mu'minîn* (cf. Geertz 1968: 54; Combs-Schilling 1989).

Hassan II emphasises the sacredness of Prophetic descent by associating maraboutic elements with the veneration of Muhammed V's tomb. Its architecture is inspired by shrines, scattered across the country as the visible markers and centres of the saints cult which plays such an important role in Moroccan Islam. Commemorating the day of the death of the present king's father on the 10th of Ramadan enhances Muhammed V's reputation as a *ṣâleḥ,* a holy or pious man. As we have seen in chapter 3, in popular conceptions of Ramadan, if someone dies during this blessed month, it is a sign of his or her piety. This fits very well with the image of Muhammed V as a national hero with maraboutic features. This image is accentuated by the memorial services held in his honour in mosques all over the country. In 1988, the resemblance between the commemoration of Muhammed V's dying day and the veneration of traditional saints was further emphasised by a collective circumcision, organised by Hassan II on the 10th of Ramadan for three hundred boys from poor families on his account. Similar rites are part of many *mûsems*, annual pilgrimages to saints' tombs (cf. Reysoo 1988: 94–9).

Attempts to relate the royal cult to the saints cult have been successful. In a conversation about saints, I once asked a male informant how a person becomes a *ṣâleḥ*, a holy man. The man replied that such a person should have led an exemplary life as a good Muslim, so that after his death people visit his grave to partake in some of the *baraka* that surrounds him, until eventually he becomes a *ṣâleḥ*. He added: 'Take for example Muhammed V, the father of the king, may God have mercy on him. Now he is only dead, but in hundred, hundred fifty years time, if people continue to visit his grave he will become a *ṣâleḥ*.'

The recognition of the sacredness of Muhammed V also fortifies the religious legitimacy of Hassan II as his successor in the sacred dynasty of Moroccan rulers. The extent to which the present monarch is able to claim the right to act as Commander of the Faithful was demonstrated during Ramadan in 1988, when he put forth a *fatwâ*, a religious decree, exempting those engaged in the battle to control the plague of locusts in the south of Morocco from fasting. Exposure to extreme heat and toxic gases was considered too much to bear while fasting. For similar reasons, soldiers on patrol along the border with West Sahara were exempted from the fast (*Le Matin du Sahara*, 19.4.88: 1).

As far as I know, the claim that working in the service of the nation is more important than abiding by religious prescriptions was not questioned by any of my informants. In their eyes, as *amîr al-mu'minîn* the king has the right to take such decisions. The meaning of the concept *amîr al-mu'minîn*, was explained to me by relating it to images of Hassan II as captain of a ship carrying all Moroccans, skilfully steering his people along the way of Islam (*ṭarîq al-islâm*), or as headmaster of a school of ignorant children, or as the father of all Moroccans. As these examples demonstrate, the king's endeavours during Ramadan to promote nationalist feelings, by appealing to an *umma* of Faithful Moroccans, of which he is the Commander, are to some extent effective.

The Local Community

Despite all efforts to manipulate the implicit religious perceptions Moroccans have of Ramadan, the notion of community which is evoked and expressed by the collective fast is most clearly experienced on the local level, rather than the national or international.

The sense of oneness is most concretely felt and emphasised between those who are *qurâb* or close. The concept *qaraba* carries meanings which range from asserted and recognised ties of kinship to ties of patronage and clientship, and common bonds developed through neighbourliness (Eickelman 1976: 95–105). During Ramadan, communication between *qurâb*, that is, close friends, neighbours or family members, is intensified. For instance, ideally all family members gather around the breakfast table some time before sunset, and together wait for the call to prayer from the mosque or the town's siren, announcing *l-mġurb*. This contrasts sharply with behaviour outside Ramadan, when fathers and husbands may prefer to eat alone. Also, young men often do not bother to be home in time to eat together with the family but either eat in town or warm up food when they come home. In early Ramadan, however, family ethos is actualised. In most families, all members gather around the breakfast table to wait for l-*mġurb* together. Although some men retreat with their bowl of soup afterwards, most of them do not want to miss sharing the precious minutes immediately preceding and following the *l-mġurb* with other family members. At this time everyone is happy to have accomplished another fasting day and to be rewarded with a bowl of *ḥrîra* and other delicacies that are displayed on the table.

A person who is not able to be at home with his or her family during Ramadan is pitied. A few days before Ramadan, my hostess was visited by an illiterate friend who asked her to read the letter she had received from her son, who had left Marrakech to try his luck in finding a job elsewhere. She was too impatient to listen to the long greeting formulas and interrupted her friend by asking repeatedly 'Is he coming home?' When there was nothing in the letter about a homecoming, the disappointed woman began to cry and lament that she and her poor son would not be able to share the *l-fṭûr*, breakfast, that year.

Very often, the intensified sociability is extended to guests. Ramadan is the pre-eminent month for extending invitations to acquaintances and friends. During the other months of the year, anybody who enters the house and finds its inhabitants eating is asked to join in, but invitations to lunch are rarely offered, usually involving relatives and close friends only. Men invite their friends to their homes less than women do. The home is the 'sacred' private domain where other men have no business. During Ramadan, however, things are different. Women can go out at night without damaging their reputation, and men and women mix more freely during the fasting month. Therefore, Ramadan is a good occasion for a man to invite a friend to his home.

Moreover, inviting a casual acquaintance, or being invited by one, is less risky during Ramadan than in other months. As a rule, Moroccans do not trust strangers and will not easily enter their houses or invite them to their own. Many people fear being poisoned when eating the food of a stranger. Also, strangers who enter the house may have been sent by somebody who wants to bewitch the owner.[15] As the *jnûn* or spirits who work for sorcerers are locked away during Ramadan, witchcraft is harmless during that month. As a consequence, the occasion can be seized upon to invite a casual acquaintance for *l-fṭûr*. Thus a relative stranger can become a friend. Sharing food has the important ritual value of creating and stressing *communitas*. This is expressed in the proverb 'People who have shared food do not deceive one another', while disrespect of the mutual loyalty created by having shared a meal is condemned strongly, as in the proverb 'Cursed, son of a cursed one, is he who eats food and deceives' (Westermarck 1930: 104).

The notion of community is also enhanced by the many activities that take place everywhere in town during Ramadan. These vary from the soccer competition that is organised between the different quarters of the town, to the many events that are held during the famous Ramadan nights, such as open air pop concerts and the plays, recitals and films programmed under the title *Nuits de Ramadan* by the French cultural centre in Marrakech. Even for those who do not participate in such activities, just strolling along the overcrowded streets at night, enjoying the public entertainment on the square Jemaa al-Fna, watching and being watched by other elated Marrakchis, contribute to the experience of communal spirit.

The intensified sociability during Ramadan goes hand in hand with the performance of religious deeds to express the notion of local community. In fact, even sharing breakfast with friends has a religious flavour to it; it is believed to yield extra *ajr* to extend an invitation to friends during Ramadan. Furthermore, community feelings are enhanced by the *tarâwîḥ*, the collective Ramadan prayers performed in the mosques at night, as they are by the increased frequency with which *ṣadaqa*, alms, are distributed during Ramadan. The many dishes of couscous that are brought to the mosques during the *laylat al-qadr*, the Night of Power, are but one example of this. In general, mendicancy during Ramadan is met with a more generous response, thus allowing people to express

15. Westermarck (1930: 214) mentions some Moroccan proverbs which illustrate these fears:
Lâ tsârda b ḥạdd wä lá tsâkul ta^{c}*âm l-*^{c}*árta*
'Don't accept anybody's invitation, and don't eat the food of invitation'
^{c}*Andek ṭsâkul ṭa*^{c}*âm l-mṣâdfa*
'Take care not to eat food offered to you casually'.

solidarity with fellow community members.[16] The same is true for the handing out of the *zakât al-fiṭr*, the obligatory donation of food, towards the end of Ramadan. Those entitled to collect such donations are primarily people involved in community services such as attending deliveries, keeping the alleys and public baths clean, and informing people when it is time to eat or fast.

The intensified sociability among *qurâb* or close ones, the increase in collective religious performances and the solidarity expressed by alms-giving are all central to the concept of *umma*. The combination of activities that express these notions therefore evoke a kind of low-level *umma*.

Despite the emphasis which Moroccans put on unification of different levels of *umma*, I noted that differences that separate people cannot be overcome during Ramadan. Due to the intensified sociability among those who have a place and family where they belong, marginal people are more easy to identify. Mentally handicapped people who are seen eating during daytime are looked at with a mixture of pity and disapproval. Uprooted people who wander through the deserted streets at the time when most people have entered their homes and sit around the table to break the fast look more lost than ever, and the collection of homeless or isolated men who have gathered on the square Jemaa al-Fna to break the fast with a bowl of *ḥrîra* bought from a food-stall is a pitiful sight.

Umma Membership of Women

Expressing membership of the *umma* through fasting is of special significance to women. Together with their participation in the pilgrimage to Mecca – which, however, is only possible for a minority of Moroccans – women's participation in the fast is most 'visible' in comparison to other collective rites which focus on the *umma*, and digresses least from men's participation. In these other rites, men appear to be the leading actors: more men than women visit the mosque to say their prayers. Women who perform the *ṣalât* do so mainly in their homes. Those who visit the mosque to pray collectively take a place in the back of the mosque or in a room adjacent to the main hall, where they cannot be seen by men. Also, whereas men may pray out loud, this right is denied to women, who must perform their prayers in silence. Since most people consider mosques to be 'men's places', women's attendance at the special prayer meetings on the occasion of the commemoration of the

16. During my stay in Saudi Arabia, where at the time mendicancy was forbidden, an exception was made during Ramadan. Many (immigrant) mothers with small children then took to the street to claim the Islamic right to receive alms. Other sources confirm this image (cf. Antoun 1968; Fallers 1974; Roog 1988).

birth of the Prophet is limited compared to that of men. Lastly, women's participation in the sacrificial feast also mainly takes place 'backstage', after the most dramatic act, the ritual slaughtering, has been carried out by the male head of the household (cf. chapter 7).

Even during Ramadan women's opportunities to express allegiance to the *umma* are less abundant than those of men. Since the mosque is viewed as a man's place, very few women attend the *tarâwîḥ*, the communal Ramadan prayers, and the special prayers on the feast which concludes Ramadan. More importantly, during menstruation, women are impure. This renders their fast invalid. Menstruating women detach themselves from fasting people in order to eat or drink. They become temporary outsiders, who cannot meet the requirements which are demanded of members of the *umma*. Later in the year, women fast to compensate for missed days, but this does not counterbalance fasting during Ramadan, when the entire Islamic community is supposed to be fasting (cf. chapter 5). The notion of the greater *umma* is, therefore, less apparent in women's performance of the fast than in that of men.

Women's less visible participation in rituals that celebrate the *umma* has led some authors to conclude that women operate outside the *umma*. The Moroccan sociologist Mernissi (1975: 81) for example, distinguishes between the public universe of the *umma* and the domestic universe of sexuality. She argues that the *umma* consists primarily of male believers, and that women's position in it is ambiguous. She then goes on to argue that while in theory the domestic universe is shared by individuals of both sexes, in practice its members are primarily female.

A view in which the public face of the *umma* is rigorously seperated from the domestic domain, however, does not do justice to women's participation in religious activities. The *umma* does not stop at the front door. Like the men who pray in mosques, women who perform the *ṣalât* at home do so facing Mecca, the geographical centre of the *umma*. Also, many houses are decorated with reproductions of calligraphic religious citations or images of the Kaaba in Mecca.

I would therefore ague that the *umma* manifests itself at different community levels and that the participation of men and women may vary at each level. For example, many housewives take pride in preparing the special Ramadan soup which people everywhere in Morocco eat to break the fast. Since women watch a great deal of television, the notion of Moroccan nationhood which, as we have seen, receives much attention during Ramadan, also reaches them. Most of my informants have great respect for King Hassan II and are proud to see the monarch on television when he is surrounded by religious scholars from all over the world during the religious conferences which he organises during Ramadan. Yet, the king appeals more directly to men as collective representative and guardian of *l-waṭan*, since for them, in his authority as 'Father of the nation', as the title of *amîr al-mu'minîn* was often explained to me, the king acts as an identification model (cf. Combs-Schilling 1989).

Women's fasting activities focus most clearly on the local community. It is mostly women who maintain and intensify relations with the *qurâb* or close ones during Ramadan. They spend much time preparing the meals which, for once, are shared by all family members, and it is their responsibility to serve guests. The actions which women undertake to obtain religious merit also concentrate on the local community: they distribute bread to children in the street, offer mendicants a bowl of soup, prepare couscous for those who pray in the mosques during the Night of Measure and visit the cemetery on the following day.

So far, we have seen how fasting during Ramadan sets Muslims apart from non-Muslims, thus drawing the boundary of the *umma*, the Islamic community. At the same time, differentiation of the *umma* is elicited through emphasis on Moroccan nationhood, while the unifying quality of Ramadan is most concretely discernible within the confines of the local community. This is especially so in the case of women, who are largely absent in the collective religious performances, but are responsible for the intensification of contacts among 'close ones' during the fast.

In the next chapter, we will see how members of the Islamic community are more particularly set apart from non-Muslims as a result of the process of purification which is effected by the fast.

The trumpet player who plays from the minaret every night of Ramadan

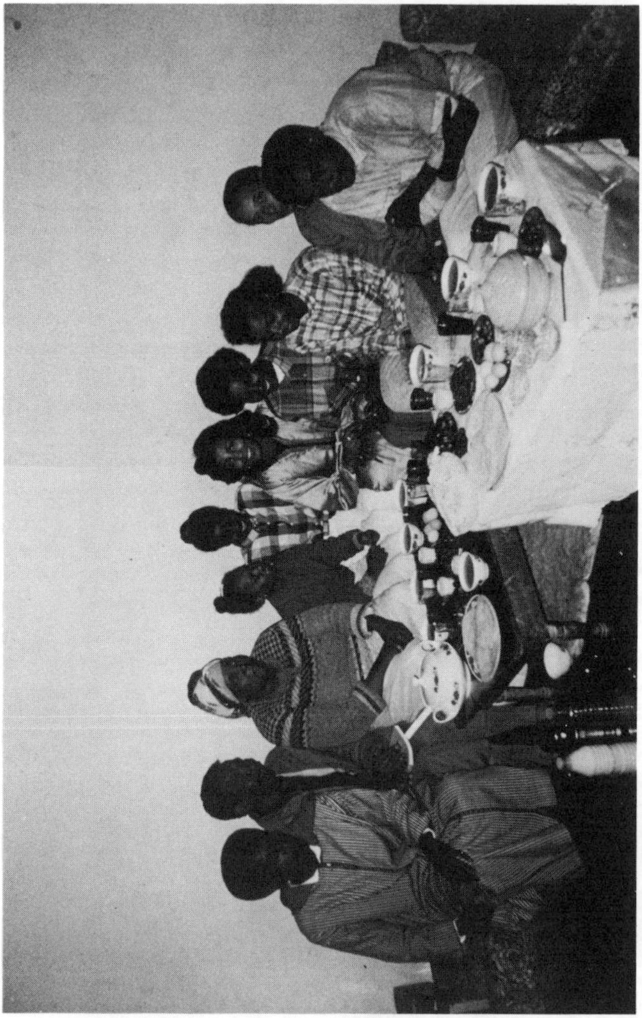

Family gathered around the table to break the fast

Handing out alms on the 27th Ramadan

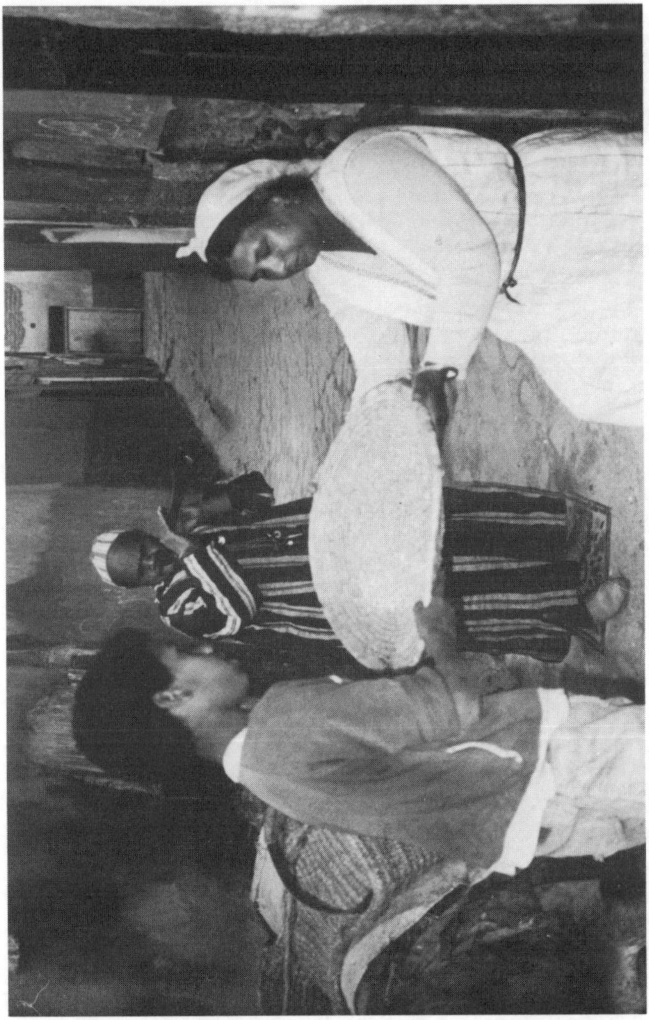

The obolst collects his share of the *Zakât al-fiṭr*

Men returning from the mosque on occasion of the end of Ramadan
(Courtesy of Léon Buskens)

five

'Ramadan Makes One Healthy': The Meaning of Purity

One of my most vivid recollections of fieldwork concerns a rather painful incident during my first Ramadan in Morocco. One week before the beginning of the fasting month, I was introduced to Aisha, a friend of my hostess in Berkane. Aisha immediately won my heart with her cordiality and spontaneously related stories about her life as a traditional midwife. I was therefore very pleased to meet her again on the second day of Ramadan. After my hostess had greeted her guest, I also bent forward to kiss and congratulate her with Ramadan. Unlike the week before, however, Aisha shrank from me, and instead of allowing me to kiss her only shook my hand. I was surprised; why would she be so reserved when she had been so warm-hearted only a week earlier? Fearing that I had said or done something wrong, I later asked my hostess about the change in Aisha's behaviour. Her answer puzzled me: 'She was afraid you are not *nqîya*, clean.' 'Why would I not be clean?', I pursued. 'Because you are a *neṣṛâniyya*, a Christian. You might have been wearing lipstick or something.' 'Then why was she not afraid of my uncleanliness last week?', I continued. 'She is fasting now', was the brisk reply of my hostess, who had clearly become irritated because of my failure to understand something so obvious to her.

In retrospect, the incident with Aisha was one of the best clues to help me grasp the meaning of purification and purity in the practice of fasting. If, in the eyes of Aisha, I was unclean because of being a Christian, obviously she was not thinking of uncleanliness in the physical sense of the word. Rather, I interpreted her statement to mean that as a Christian I was ritually impure according to Islamic principles. Normally, my impurity did not interfere much with our contacts; Aisha had not hesitated to kiss me the week before Ramadan. That she refused to do so once the fasting month had begun illustrates her preoccupation with purity during Ramadan.

In this chapter I will demonstrate that this heightened sensibility concerning purity is a central aspect of living Ramadan. After discussing the way purity is conceived of in Islamic law and Moroccan views of purity in the first two sections, the interpretation of fasting as a kind of purification is discussed in the third section, while the idea of the beneficial effect of this purification process to one's physical and mental health is looked at in the next section. The purificatory quality of fasting is believed to be less effective for women; this subject will be treated in the concluding section.

Purity in the Islamic Doctrine

In classical Arabic the proper religious term for purity is *ṭahâra*. *Ṭahâra* refers not only to purity but also to the process of purification in the technical sense of the word. *Ṭahâra* plays an important role in the Islamic doctrine. 'Purity is half the faith' is a saying attributed to the Prophet Muhammed (Tritton 1987: 608). It is a condition that renders the performance of religious duties such as the prayers and the fast valid. Purification must therefore always precede these activities. Elaborate rules are laid down for removal of various states of impurity. The main distinction is between major and minor impurity. One finds oneself in a state of major impurity after ejaculation, sexual intercourse (with or without ejaculation), menstruation, childbirth, before adopting Islam and at death. These conditions require the *gusl*, the major ritual ablution, which consists of washing the whole body three times, beginning with the limbs. Minor impurity is the result of contact with the following substances: any traces which are left after urination or defecation; dust or mud on the roads; soles of shoes; blood squashed out of a full-fed flea; blood or pus from a boil or pimple or from cupping (Tritton 1987: 609). The state of minor impurity must be alleviated by performing the *wuḍû'*, the minor ritual ablution. This consists of rinsing one's head and limbs three times.

Contact with the above-mentioned polluting substances cannot always be avoided. Besides these, there are impure substances and (visibly impure) bodies such as wine, pigs and dogs with which contact is *ḥarâm*, forbidden or taboo. On a more abstract level a distinction is made between material defilements and moral defilements as a result of sinning or having evil thoughts. The moral side of the purity complex is expressed by the fact that any purification ritual must not be performed mechanically, but should be preceded by the *nîya*, the intention to do so: by thinking of God and reciting special prayers. Islamic scholars have further developed the moral side of purification by distinguishing four stages in the purification process:

1. of the body from physical dirt
2. of the members from offences
3. of the heart from evil wishes
4. of the spirit from all that is not God (Tritton 1987: 608).

Moroccan Views on Purity

When my informants refer to the religious complex of purity, they do not use *ṭahâra* or other classical Arabic terms that people with a higher Islamic education would employ. They only use the word *ṭahâra* for a very special case of purification: the circumcision of boys. When referring to the purity complex, in general they use the same Moroccan Arabic terms that denote the profane distinction between 'clean' and 'dirty' (nqî – mwessek̲).

Not all prescriptions concerning purification receive equal attention. For example, from the age of puberty most people observe the prescriptions concerning the major ritual ablution, which always concludes the weekly visits to the public bath. The minor ritual ablution, however, is closely associated with the five daily prayers. People who do not pray do not perform it. Furthermore, according to orthodox Islam, consuming wine or pork is equally *ḥarâm* and polluting. Yet, many men and some categories of women drink wine.[1] Most women indulge their husband's drinking, considering it one of the vices of men. Both men and women consider eating pork much more objectionable and sinful than drinking wine or other alcoholic beverages.

Besides the fact that some purification prescriptions receive more attention than others, there exist some 'rules' in the Moroccan purification practices that strictly speaking are not prescribed by Islamic doctrine. That the left hand is considered to be more impure than the right hand is consistent with the official prescription to clean oneself with this hand after defecation. However, the fact that I as a left-handed person had a hard time washing the dishes in Berkane with my right hand, was a result of an interpretation of this purification rule on the part of my hostess that went beyond the official prescription. She was convinced that if I used my left hand the dishes would remain 'dirty'. Even within Morocco, notions concerning purity may differ regionally. In Marrakech, where people are generally less preoccupied with living 'strictly' by what they assume are the Islamic rules, nobody commented when I washed the dishes with my left hand.

1. Prostitutes and *sîk̲ât,* female dancers and singers in mixed musical groups, drink overtly.

Fasting and Purification

Especially during Ramadan, Moroccan perceptions concerning purity become manifest. Fasting is only valid when the conditions of purity are met. Performing the major ritual ablution before fasting would suffice. However, afraid that their fast will not be valid because of impurity, people take extra precautionary measures such as giving the house a thorough cleaning and visiting the public bath a few days before the beginning of Ramadan.

As the incident with Aisha shows, people continue to take extra measures to avoid polluting situations during Ramadan. That some women do not wash clothes 'From the first call of the trumpet to the trumpet of the *ᶜîd*' (cf. chapter 3) can also be interpreted in this light; saving enough clean clothes to last the entire month of Ramadan precludes having to deal with dirty laundry and the risk of being polluted by it. In Sidi Slimane, women told me that during Ramadan they visit the public bath twice or even more times a week. Ramadan is the only time of the year that their bath is open for women in the evenings, and they love to combine taking an extra bath and enjoying the special sociability of the Ramadan evenings.

During Ramadan, many married couples sleep in separate beds. I noticed that in many families either the husband or the wife sleeps on a couch, preferably in another room. Upon showing me her house, one woman giggled when she pointed out where she slept and where her husband, whispering 'You know why, don't you?' Her giggling increased when I told her I had no idea. 'Well', she explained, 'you do know we have to be clean during Ramadan? But if my husband and I sleep together, we are not clean, we must go to the public bath, but that is impossible at night, so our fasting would not be valid.' I told her that I had heard that purification could be postponed until the morning, and the fast of those who perform it then was accepted as long as the 'sleeping' together had taken place before sunrise. She acknowledged this, but in her view, it was no real solution to the problem of sleeping in one bed. 'What if my husband in his sleep turns over and accidentally touches my breasts after sunrise? Then we have both broken the fast without even having begun the new day!' Although not all my informants were quite as willing to speak openly about this subject, most confirmed that many women sleep apart from their husbands during Ramadan.

The fact that many married couples spend the Ramadan nights in separate beds and abstain from sexual contact even during the hours when formal prescriptions would allow it, is yet another example of the precautions against pollution that exceed the regulations laid down in the Islamic doctrine.

Except for such unfamiliar situations as when Aisha had to decide whether or not kissing a Christian would be polluting, taking these far-reaching measures is not simply a matter of choosing to be on the safe side in a situation when precise knowledge about the formal prescriptions concerning purity is lacking. The people with whom I spoke are convinced that not taking these precautions would devalue their fast.

To understand this we have to realise that in the Moroccan view purity is not just a matter of someone or something being either pure or impure. Rather, purity comes in degrees. Dogs and donkeys, for example, are impure animals, but not quite as much as pigs are. Urine is impure, but the urine of a woman's own children less so; the contact would not render the fast of the mother invalid. Cosmetics are attributed different degrees of purity. Kohl, the pounded antimony that women put on their eyelids, is considered a purifying substance. The purifying effect of henna, the natural red dye that women put on their hair and decorate their hands and feet with, is believed to be even more powerful. 'Henna comes from Paradise' and 'Henna contains a lot of *baraka*' women told me to explain their fondness of it. *Swâk*, a kind of bark which is used to clean the teeth and colour the gums red, is considered neither pure nor impure. Perfume oil allegedly imported from Muslim countries is pure. My hostess in Berkane used the perfume which her husband had brought her from Mecca only to visit the mosque on the concluding feast of Ramadan, attributing to it a high degree of purity because of the sacredness of its place of origin. On other occasions she would use European eau de cologne, which she considered neither pure nor impure. Other cosmetics which have been introduced by Westerners, such as eye shadow, lipstick and nail polish, on the contrary, are largely considered impure.

The remarks on henna and perfume oil from Mecca illustrate that purity and *baraka*, blessings or divine power, are closely related concepts. People who are close to God, such as the descendants of the Prophet and those who have performed the pilgrimage to Mecca, are considered to possess a lot of both *baraka* and purity (cf. Munson 1984: 35). Many people who performed the *ḥajj* express their purity by wearing white clothes, white being the colour that represents purity.

If, in the eyes of Moroccans, purity comes in degrees and is closely related to the blessedness of *baraka*, it is not surprising that during Ramadan, the most blessed month of the year, people do not feel content with strictly abiding to the formal prescriptions concerning purity. As I interpret their actions, people are preoccupied with purity in order to match the sacredness of Ramadan and gain as much as possible from the beneficial combination of these influences.

The Purifying Quality of Ramadan and Health

Physical Health

Fasting itself is conceived of as a form of purification. By abstaining from food and drink, the body is considered to come to a rest, allowing it to discharge waste products which have accumulated in it during the preceding year. This purification of the system is considered to have therapeutic effects. The meaning of the statement *ṛemḍân ta-yṣeḥḥeḥ*, 'Ramadan makes one healthy, strong', given as an answer to my question about why people fast, illustrates this point. In the verb *ta-yṣeḥḥeḥ* several shades of 'making healthy' are united. *ta-yṣeḥḥeḥ* comes from the root Ṣ.Ḥ.Ḥ. and is closely related to the word *ṣḥîḥ*. I have heard Moroccans use this word in several ways. When something or someone has been made healthy they refer to the result as being *ṣḥîḥ*. In Moroccan Arabic, *ṣḥîḥ* refers to 'vitality', 'health' and 'strength'. It may also be used to refer to the quality of being intact, not broken (down) or rotten. It may also mean 'pure' in the sense of a pure substance, not mixed with substances of lesser value or quality; when, for example, the alloy of a bracelet contains mainly silver it is praised for being *ṣḥîḥ*.

Ṣḥîḥ does not only designate the aforementioned qualities as such, but also refers to the process of increasing and strengthening them. As Rabinow (1975: 65) puts it: 'To be *ṣḥîḥ* has a double connotation: the presence of this vitality and its increase and deepening.' In a broader sense, then, I would argue that the meaning of *ta-yṣeḥḥeḥ* is to replenish vitality, to render perfect or complete.[2]

Ramadan is considered to render a person 'healthy' in an all-embracing way. In Islam, the believers are commanded to surrender themselves to God as complete persons; the *tawḥîd* or unity of the body and the mind is presupposed in the performance of religious duties, which entails both physical and spiritual exercise. The ritual ablutions consist of a spiritual component: pronouncing the *nîya* or intention to purify and to discard sinful thoughts; and a physical component: rinsing the body with water. The unity of the body and the mind also finds expression in the way reciting religious formulas and prostrations are combined in the prayers. Fasting is the most telling example of how having 'surrendered to God', which is the literal meaning of the word *muslim*, is both a physical and a spiritual affair. To perform the religious duties is considered beneficial for both the body and the mind.

2. The close relationship between the concepts *ṣḥîḥ*, purity, and *baraka* conforms with Douglas's (1966: 70–3) theory on 'purity and danger': completeness is a quality that defines the purity of an object (substance/person) and, by setting it apart, its sacredness protects it against contamination.

My informants are well aware of the 'healthy' aspects of their religious practices. After *s-sḥûr*, the meal eaten in the middle of the night during Ramadan, my hostess in Berkane often advised me to climb the stairs to the roof. 'Saying prayers is our kind of sport, but you should do some other physical exercise to digest the meal before returning to sleep, otherwise you will get ill.' Likewise, there is a close connection between performing the ritual ablutions and health; when someone has just returned from a visit to the public bath, he or she is greeted with the phrase 'To your health', the response to which is 'May God give you health'.

Despite this widespread belief in the beneficial influence of fasting on health in general, once the initial enthusiasm to fast has faded, people acknowledge that fasting may be accompanied by minor bodily disorders. Especially when Ramadan draws to its close, the inevitable question *kî dayra m*^{c}*a ṛemḍân?*, 'How is Ramadan treating you?', with which one is greeted in the street, is answered by mentioning headaches, dizziness or constipation or by diplomatically stating *šwîya*, 'not too bad' (literally: a little).

Yet, the idea that fasting is good for the body is generally shared; it cleans the stomach and allows all vital organs to come to a rest. As a result, the body grows stronger. The man who told me that Ramadan makes you healthy clenched his fingers into a fist to give his words more emphasis. The young men who play soccer and go jogging every late afternoon during Ramadan thus demonstrate the strength that is gained by fasting. One of Buskens' (1987: 57) informants claimed that the headaches he suffered due to a car accident were relieved by fasting.

The notion that fasting promotes health is so pervasive that one of my informants, who is bilious, refused to accept the idea that in her condition fasting was dangerous, and continued to fast until the day of her operation. It also partly explains why the vast majority of Moroccan women continue to fast during pregnancy. People feel that, in most cases, fasting does not interfere with illness, although taking medicine constitutes a problem. I was told that most people who need medicine adjust the times and dosages they take to fit fasting prescriptions. However, there was some doubt about the consequences of drug use for the validity of the fast if the medicine is still active in the body during fasting hours.[3]

The purifiying effect of fasting is affirmed in the mass media. In the Moroccan schoolbook *Instruction Islamique* for students in their

3. Cf. Aslam and Assad (1986), who found that of the 325 outpatients studied in Kuwaiti hospitals, more than 65% changed the way in which they took their medicine during Ramadan. Of those who did not change their pattern, 14% were already on a single drug dosage, which did not interfere with their fast. Particularly in elderly patients, changing drug-taking habits could lead to potentially serious drug interaction and toxic side-effects.

second year of secondary school several 'hygienic virtues' of fasting are mentioned:

> Il a été prouvé médicalement que le jeûne est utile dans le traitement de nombreuses maladies et qu'il est même l'unique traitement dans certaines d'entre elles. Bien plus, il allége l'appareil digestif et nettoie l'estomac des dépôts alimentaires qui y persistent après leur assimilation et s'entassent pendant une année entière, provoquant ainsi beaucoup de maux au corps. Ajoutez à cela qu'il aide à combattre l'hypertension artérielle, le diabète, l'embonpoint, ainsi que les maladies cutanées et autres . . . (*Instruction Islamique* 1984, II: 94)

During Ramadan, newspaper articles appear with headlines such as 'Les effets bénéfiques du jeûne' (*Le Matin du Sahara*, 5.5.87), 'Les vertus thérapeutiques du jeûne' (*Le Matin du Sahara*, 23.4.88: 5) and 'Ramadan et la santé' (*L'Opinion*, 25.4.88: 7).[4] In such articles, Ramadan is praised as a *période de purification* and the fast is described as *purificateur de l'esprit et de l'organisme* (*Le Matin du Sahara Magazine*, 1–8 May 1988: 30).[5]

In most cases when the Moroccan newspapers refer to scientific research on fasting, they fail to mention that the outcome of these studies do not refer to the Islamic practice of fasting but rather to fasting continuously over an extended period of time in the form of abstaining from eating but not from drinking (cf. Ben Yusif 1990). Only Alami (1988: 3) cites a Western scholar who denounces 'la pratique primitive' (*sic*!) of fasting in daytime and feasting at nighttime, as is done by Muslims. Alami comments that this practice

4. In almost all these articles, the authors cite American and European scientists – albeit not always in combination with booktitles – who have done research on fasting (among others Carrington: *Vitality, Fasting and Nutrition*, Dewey: *Chronic Alcoholism* Jackson:, Mac Fadden: *Encyclopedia of Physical Culture*, Shelton: no title).

I have come across similar instances in which informants adopted Western scientific discourse to validate Islamic principles. A university student majoring in Islam, for example, told me about an experiment which was carried out in a laboratory to find out whether the Islamic prescription of washing seven times a plate from which a dog has eaten before using it again was scientifically justifiable. Scrutinising the plate through a microscope, the experiment proved that, indeed, the bacteria transmitted by the dog's tongue had been completely removed only after seven washings. In the eyes of my informant, this proved the superiority of Islam which possessed knowledge of bacteria centuries before the Western scientific discovery. In the same vein, I have heard people legitimate the Islamic prohibition to eat pork by referring to research which had proven that this meat contains substances that are detrimental to the body. Buskens (1987: 56) rightly remarks that such rationalisations are examples of the cultural dominance of Western culture. Somehow, the explanations offered by non-Western cultures for comprehending the world do not seem completely valid any longer in the eyes of their own members, but need to be affirmed according to Western standards.

5. Apparently, similar articles occur in Algerian newspapers during Ramadan. Benkheira (1986: 40) cites a quotation of the Algerian Minister of Religious Affairs in *El-Moudjahid* (6.7.82): 'le ramadan n'est autre qu'une école dans laquelle sont éduquées les âmes, une clinique dans laquelle sont soignés les corps quelles que soient les maladies.'

only concerns 'le jeûne de certains Musulmans de notre époque', referring to the fasting of the elite. One of the article's conclusions is that the excesses of rich people contradict the Islamic prescriptions. The main theme of the article is that biology and medicine have proven the merits of the Islamic way of fasting, which, thanks to its moral and spiritual principles, involves not merely a physical abstinence but has an individual and collective educational character as well (ibid.).

Moral and Societal Health

As fasting has both physical and spiritual aspects it can be seen as an exercise in the *tawḥîd* or unification of the body and the mind. Comparing the three degrees of fasting as distinguished by al-Ghazali (1955: 81) to the four stages of purification mentioned in this chapter, we may conclude that the spiritual requirements of the two practices largely overlap. All sinful thoughts should be abandoned and be replaced by meditation on God. In the daily fasting practice of most people, such total concentration on God is hardly possible. Despite the special character of Ramadan, they continue to work and coordinate family life. I have seen shopkeepers read the Koran when not attending to clients and noticed that people eagerly watch the religious programmes that are broadcast more frequently during the fasting month, but, for the majority of my informants, the spiritual side of fasting consists of trying to avoid sinful thoughts. In Berkane, this was more pronounced than in Marrakech. One of the reasons why sleeping during daytime is disapproved of is that people are afraid they might have sinful dreams. When there was tension between two persons, they would often try to avert an argument by saying 'I am fasting', and turning away. In Marrakech, I noticed this kind of mental exercise less often. There, mainly older people, who were reputed for their piety, acted in this way. Their behaviour was in stark contrast to that of many young men, who do not give up their habit of looking and sometimes whistling at girls during Ramadan.[6]

Although very few people are able to meet the high requirements for spiritual purification in the way these are formulated by theologians, most Moroccans consider the physical process of purification through fasting spiritually purifying as well. Fasting is believed to atone for past wrongdoings. On the banner which is suspended over the entrance of the mosque in the central square in Marrakech

6. Buskens (1987: 65) noticed the same behaviour of young men in Larache. They excused themselves by joking that the Prophet had stated that the first glance cast at someone does not matter; to avoid first glances one would have to walk around with closed eyes, which is impossible. Only a second look renders the fast invalid. The solution was to prolong the first look!

during Ramadan, the following Ḥadith-excerpt, or tradition of the Prophet, is cited: 'The sins of him who fasts during Ramadan in faith and sacrifice will be forgiven.'

In the eyes of Moroccans, purity influences people's morals. For instance, the impurity of Christians is thought to be one of the causes of the decadence that is believed to characterise modern Western society. As an educated girl stated, the divorce rates in European countries are extremely high because Europeans eat pork. She explained that pork kills the soul and thus the capacity to feel compassion for others. Although nobody articulated the connection, this example illustrates how, in the Moroccan world-view, the concepts of the Muslim community and purity are related. Purity is a mark of Islamic civilisation. People who deliberately pollute themselves by consuming impure foodstuffs and drinks are not able to develop a lifestyle consistent with the harmonious and wholesome society envisaged in the concept of *umma*. Striving to attain or maintain purity enhances the morals needed to achieve the ideal of *umma*. Women often remarked that Ramadan is the best time of the year because men do not drink alcohol. Hence, women feel much safer during Ramadan; fewer domestic quarrels occur and they do not risk coming across drunken men in the streets at night.[7] To further attain the ideal of *umma*, Moroccan cities are 'cleaned' of deviant elements during Ramadan. The newspapers report more police raids on prostitutes and drugs dealers during the fasting month than during the other months of the year (cf. *L'Opinion*, 15.5.87: 6).

The link that people make between the purifying quality of fasting and its alleged effect of upgrading society aptly illustrates Douglas's contention that pollution beliefs and moral codes are closely connected (cf. Douglas 1966; 1970). She argues that rites of bodily manipulation enable people to know their own society. The functions of the body afford a source of symbols for other complex structures: 'The rituals enact the form of social relations and in giving these relations visible expression they enable people to know their own society' (Douglas 1966: 128). In the Moroccan case, the physical experience of the body gradually undergoing purification during Ramadan sustains the view of the wholesome Islamic community.

The purificatory climax is achieved on the day of the *ᶜîd*, the concluding feast of Ramadan. The night before this feast, most women apply (purifying) henna to their hands and feet, and in the early morning of the *ᶜîd*, many people perform the major ritual ablution, which is believed to yield much religious merit. To

7. It would be interesting to know whether safety is a feature of Ramadan that is particularly experienced and expressed by women or whether this notion also plays a role in men's views.

express the condition of purity achieved by having fasted a whole month, on the day of the ᶜîd, most people preferably put on new, or at least clean, clothes. Similar to the purification activities before Ramadan, which mark the transition from normal time and space to the sacredness of Ramadan, performing the ritual ablution and putting on new clothes at the end of Ramadan mark the transition from the liminality of the sacred month back to life in the everyday world, albeit a transformed life (cf. chapter 7). After Ramadan, people are not quite the same; the fast has cleansed them from their former sins. The end of Ramadan marks a new beginning. When there is not enough money to buy new clothes for all members of the family to express this new beginning, children, who by virtue of their innocent age are pure by definition, are given priority. Men come next. On the day of the concluding feast, most men wear a spotless white *jellâba*, thus expressing their purity. Some older women may be dressed in the same colour symbolising purity, but most women wear colourful dresses.[8] This explicit difference in dress between men and women suggests that women have not completed the process of purification as effectively as men have.

Purity and Women

Women are believed to complete the process of purification less thoroughly than men because they are in an impure state more often. This condition renders their fast invalid. A woman who has given birth remains impure for forty days. Should she have the misfortune to give birth just before Ramadan begins, she will not be able to fast at all. More importantly, women in the fertile years have to cope with six or seven days each Ramadan during which they may not fast because of menstruation. They experience this as a failure, and their fasting is generally assumed to be less valuable than that of men.

Menstruation is one of the reasons why girls begin to fast at an earlier age than boys do, namely at menarche. Informants told me that learning to fast is less difficult for girls than for boys; girls have to break the fast for at least six days during Ramadan, while boys have to fast the whole month once they begin. One woman explained that for women to have fasted as many Ramadan days as men have by the end of their life, they have to begin at an earlier age to make up for all the fasting days missed due to menstruation.

The notion that the fasting performance of women is inferior to that of men also finds expression in the discrediting of the practice

8. Abu-Lughod (1986: 132) describes the same symbolic association of men with purity in the wearing of white for the Awlad 'Ali, Bedouins living in the Western Desert of Egypt.

of making up for missed fasting days later in the year. 'It is not the same thing', as the aforementioned Berkani woman remarked. That is, fasting during the other months of the year does not render the same amount of *ajr*, religious merit, as fasting during the sacred month of Ramadan. That women may choose to fast on the days most suitable to them devalues the days they fast in compensation. It is believed that some women are so cunning as to select the short and cold winter days to complete their fasting obligations (Dwyer 1978a: 108).

The depreciation of women's fasting activities appears to be shared generally. Even women themselves do not seem to realise that fasting on regular days, when they have to wake up at an early hour to prepare meals for other family members, may be more difficult than fasting during Ramadan. In my view, without the stimulating presence of other fasting people and the promising prospect of *šebbakîya*s or other Ramadan pastries at night, fasting to compensate for missed days must be less satisfying than fasting during Ramadan.

Not only are the days that women must fast outside Ramadan depreciated, men even suspect that women do not fulfil their obligations as they should. During Ramadan, everybody is preoccupied with fasting and one can actually 'see' others fast. It is much harder to keep watch on women's fasting practices outside Ramadan. Consequently, some men assume that women do not follow the prescriptions but continue the fast during their menses and do not make up for missed days later in the year (cf. Buskens 1987: 65). This assumption is wrong but understandable. A woman considers it *ḥšûma*, shameful and improper, if a man notices that she is menstruating. Most menstruating women therefore try to conceal their condition. They do not eat or drink in the presence of men and, in Berkane, the women in my host family even withdraw from the company of other women to break the fast. When nobody is looking, they drink some water or warm up last night's coffee, and hide in the most concealed corner of the kitchen, behind the door, to retrieve a chunk of bread from under their clothes.

Menstruating women do not use their condition as an excuse to prepare themselves good meals. They mostly eat the leftovers from the night before. In Berkane, most women I know even limit themselves to the absolute minimum: a glass of water and a small piece of bread. In general, women do not feel relieved that they are 'excused' to eat during their menstruation days. On the contrary, many women believe that they are obliged to eat during menstruation, which they experience as a restriction on their fasting. As I interpet it, drinking a sip of water and eating only a mouthful of bread is a form of symbolically breaking the fast. In the view of these women, eating and drinking until they are satisfied is *ḥarâm*, forbidden.

Both in Berkane and in Marrakech, women told me a story about Fatima, the daughter of the Prophet, to explain why fasting during menstruation is *ḥarâm:*

> On a journey through the desert Fatima had her period. Her Father ordered her to eat, but she refused. Then the camel she was riding refused to continue and lay down. Once again the Prophet commanded his daughter to eat. She persisted in her refusal, arguing that there was no food or drinks left. For the third time Muhammed insisted she eat, if only sand of the desert. Fatima ate a handful of sand, whereupon her camel rose to its feet and the journey could be continued.

In Berkane, this is where the story ended. In the Marrakchi version, Fatima had not been riding a camel but a mare. Because Fatima was too ashamed (*ḥešmet*) to admit her condition, and hence tried to hide it by continuing to fast, the mare she was riding became barren. 'We must do like the daughter of the Prophet', an uneducated married woman in her thirties commented after telling the story. 'Because her father made her eat, we must eat as well. Had she not been ordered to eat, we would not have to eat either'. My informants interpret the fact that the mare became barren as a warning to women that the same might happen to them if they are so ashamed of menstruation that they continue to fast.

Like those of the Prophet, the traditions on the conduct of Fatima serve as a guiding principle for Muslim women. I have not been able to trace the above-mentioned story in Bukari's compilation of traditions, and suspect it is a Moroccan folk story. Its popularity among Moroccan women is obvious, since the story bears close resemblance to the way Moroccan women themselves feel about being obliged to break the fast when they have their period. Fatima shows the willpower to keep the fast as men do. She only breaks the fast, reluctantly, after having been ordered three times to do so. She does not use her condition as an excuse to treat herself to a good meal but only breaks the fast symbolically by eating sand. The story reminds people of the fact that the 'prescription' of breaking the fast during menstruation is not an excuse concocted by clever women to escape the fasting regulations, but was imposed on them against their will.

If they had a choice, many women would prefer to keep the fast. They do not state this openly, which would be interpreted as a blasphemous criticism of God's will. These days, many women use birth-control pills, which makes it possible to postpone menstruation until Ramadan has passed. When, at a gathering of neighbours just before Ramadan, women were calculating which week of the fasting month they would be menstruating, one woman suggested this manner of postponement. One of her friends, however, remembered, having learned from the religious television programme *rukn al-muftî*, that this is *ḥarâm*; it is God's will that women should bleed once a month.

That women would prefer to fast all days of Ramadan is expressed in the proud statement of some women that they had fasted throughout Ramadan during their pregnancies. In fact, none of my informants could produce the name of a woman who had not done so. With a broad smile on her face, one woman told me about the early years of her marriage, when, for five successive years, she had managed to fast the whole of Ramadan because of being pregnant: *ṣemt nîšân*, 'I fasted straight', she added proudly. The word *nîšân* encompasses meanings such as 'straight', 'along the straight and narrow path', 'sincere', 'sound' and 'in the proper way'. All these meanings are positively valued. Hence, the remark *ṣemt nîšân* implies that in the eyes of my informant, women, most of whom have to break the fast due to menstruation, do not fast in the most proper or best way, that is, fasting the whole of Ramadan as men do.

The idea that the fasting performance of women is not as 'sound' as that of men is confirmed in the folk story about Lalla ^{c}Uda. The name Lalla ^{c}Uda is derived from Lalla Mas^{c}uda, who was the mother of the Saadian Sultan al-Mansur (1578–1603). The folk story as related by story tellers on the square Jemaa al-Fna runs as follows:

> Once upon a time during Ramadan, the pregnant Lalla ^{c}Uda was strolling through the park that surrounds the Koutoubia mosque. A large nice-smelling peach so appealed to her that, without thinking, she picked it from the tree and ate it. Only then did she realise that it was Ramadan and that she had broken the fast. She went to a Koran scholar for advice. He told her she could atone for her sin by performing *ṣadaqa*, alms-giving. Lalla ^{c}Uda brought all her jewellery to the goldsmith, who melted it down and transformed it into the three golden balls that still decorate the minaret of the Koutoubia mosque. Also, as a warning to the Marrakchis that they should not make the same mistake, she paid the oboists and trumpet player of the town to play a song every evening about Lalla ^{c}Uda who ate during Ramadan.[9]

9. See Morsy (1983: 109–10) for an early version of the same legend as recorded by Thomas Pellow, who visited Marrakech at the beginning of the eighteenth century.

Children in the medina still sing this song during Ramadan:

Lalla ^{c}Uda ate during Ramadan
a peach and a pomegranate
may The Merciful forgive her[10]

It is fascinating that Lalla ^{c}Uda's conduct is interpreted as sinful. According to the prescriptions, a pregnant woman may break the fast if she fears fasting might be detrimental to her baby. In the story, Lalla ^{c}Uda was not thinking about her baby but ate because she fancied a peach. Normally, however, during the first three months of her pregnancy, a woman is said to *ta-tweḥḥeb*: she might suddenly develop an appetite for something. If this is the case, she must immediately eat whatever she is craving. Not satisfying her appetite is believed to be dangerous for the child. Therefore, traditionally, when a woman whose neighbour is pregnant prepares a good meal, she will bring a portion of it to the pregnant mother to make sure that, if the smell of the food whets her appetite, she will eat and avoid endangering the baby. It is possible that Lalla ^{c}Uda's pregnancy had progressed beyond the third month. Nobody with whom I discussed the folk story suggested that her circumstances might have excused her. All condemned her conduct as morally wrong.

The tale of Lalla ^{c}Uda eating a peach and a pomegranate whilst she should have been fasting is analogous to the story of Eve's desire for the taste of the forbidden fruit. Dwyer (1978a) mentions similar Moroccan folktales in which women's behaviour resembles that of Eve. As in the folktale about Lalla ^{c}Uda, the overriding message of these tales is that women are morally inferior to men.[11] This idea is in accordance with the negative view of women's conduct during Ramadan in comparison to men.

According to Islamic law, if women make up for the fasting days missed during Ramadan, their fasting is equally valuable to that of men. Likewise, although women may be in an impure condition more often than men, according to Islamic law impurity is not a quality more inherent to women than to men. In the Moroccan interpretation of Islam, however, cultural dominance of men finds expression in the belief that, no matter how strong a woman's faith might be, her performance of the fast is always inferior to that of men, who are not restricted by physiological encumbrances. Hence,

10. In Arabic:
Lalla ^{c}ûda klât ṛemḍân
bel-ḵûḵa u r-rumân
yesmeḥ lîhâ r-raḥmân

11. It must be noted that the Koran does not mention Eve being tempted by Satan or eating the forbidden fruit sooner than Adam (cf. Sura 20: 116–21).

the purifying aspect of fasting is more pronounced in men than in women. Due to menstruation and procreation, women are generally considered to be more impure than men.[12] This impurity influences women's religious (and moral) worth, which is believed to be inferior to that of men. Put in the words of a male vegetable seller interviewed by Eickelman (1976: 133): 'They [women] don't know Islam like men do; they even have tricks to avoid fasting.' Clearly, this is a typical male perspective on the religious practices of women.

The perception that since the religious practices of men are not hampered by uncontrollable bodily processes they are the rightful holders of sacred accomplishment seems to reinforce Ortner's argument (1974) on the propensity for societies to associate men more with culture and civilisation and women more with nature. Ortner suggests that this association is derived from the fact that women involuntarily bleed each month and give birth to children in an involuntary act of nature (Ortner 1974: 74–5). Ortner has been criticised for assuming that the categories 'nature' and 'culture' are pan-cultural notions rather than the products of a Western intellectual tradition, and for assuming a cultural unity which leaves no room for the fact that different groups in society may have different views and experiences (cf. MacCormack 1980; Moore 1988: 13–21). Dwyer has shown for Morocco that each gender is involved in both 'nature' and 'culture', but that in the course of their lives women are believed to move from the cultural to the natural, while men move from the natural to the cultural (Dwyer 1978a: 174). She also demonstrates that women's symbolic models often differ from men's: women tend to value themselves more highly than men value them, while they tend to value men less than men value themselves (ibid.: 178). Women's valuation of their own fasting practice sustains this view. Although many women share the view with men that their fasting is found wanting, they do not view menstruation or post-partum impurity as an excuse concocted by clever women in order to evade fasting prescriptions. Instead, they experience their failure as the result of an inescapable fate and would not think of inventing 'tricks' to avoid fasting.

In the next chapter, I will return to this issue and describe how women develop their own strategies to make up for their shortcomings by performing religious acts that render *ajr,* religious merit.

12. Cf. Faithorn (1975: 138) who points to the fact that biased Western anthropologists working in the Highlands of Papua New Guinea have focused on women as polluting agents rather than on the substances and circumstances which can be polluting.

six

Pathway to Paradise

Nearly every Friday of Ramadan, after coming home from the Friday sermon in the mosque, Laila, my hostess in Berkane, untied her headscarf and produced some sweets, figs or lumps of bread or sugar. These foodstuffs had been handed out as alms in the mosque by someone who thus hoped to gain *ajr,* religious merit. When the time to break the fast drew near, Laila put a bowl with the alms on the table. After sunset she distributed its contents among the family members with the words *kûlu l-baraka,* 'eat the blessings'. Before Ramadan she had also come home with alms occasionally, but the frequency of receiving alms increased considerably during Ramadan. Laila also handed out alms during the fasting month, besides striving to gain *ajr* in various other ways.

In this chapter we will have a closer look at the notion of *ajr* and its meaning in the practice of fasting. The first section on *ajr* in Islamic doctrine is followed by two sections in which Moroccan conceptions of *ajr* and its counterpart blessings (*baraka*) are analysed in relation to the image of God. The remaining sections focus on the various ways Moroccans collect *ajr* during Ramadan, and the particular importance of religious merit for women.

The Concept of *Ajr* in Islamic Doctrine

According to Islamic doctrine, the term *ajr* has two meanings. As a juridical term, *ajr* is associated with the first Muslim community, where it denoted wage or pay. In the Koran *ajr* also refers to the *mahr,* the bride price paid by husbands to their wives and the money they must pay to divorced wives who raise the children. As a religious term, *ajr* means the spiritual reward for pious acts, the accumulation of which yields admittance to Paradise (Schacht 1969: 209). According to Sura 6: 160, pious acts will be credited, although the term *ajr* is not specifically mentioned: 'Whoso brings a good deed shall have ten the like of it, and whoso brings an evil deed shall only be recompensed the like of it; they shall not be wronged' (Arberry 1955, I: 169). Well-intended yet imperfect performances of the religious duties render a single reward, while successful performances are rewarded twice or more (Schacht 1969: 209).

Moroccan Views on *Ajr*

Given the preoccupation of my informants in both Berkane and Marrakech with collecting *ajr*, it is surprising that in Moroccan ethnography little attention has been paid to the subject. In the indexes of their books, most authors give several entries to the closely related notion of *baraka*, blessings, but almost none to *ajr* or its English translations spiritual reward and religious merit.[1]

Contemplating why these authors fail to pay attention to the concept of *ajr*, I think two factors may have played a role. First of all, I suspect that collecting *ajr* is predominantly a preoccupation of women, while the anthropologists mapping the cultural and social landscape of Morocco have mainly been men, who had little access to the domains of women. However, among female researchers only Maher (1974) pays attention to *ajr*, while Dwyer (1978a) and Davis (1983) fail to mention it. To explain this, we must turn to a second and more fundamental factor; the notion of *ajr* may well have been neglected in favour of the notion of *baraka* or blessings. The latter offers many examples of 'local' interpretations of Islam, whereas the former seems to concern religious activities which are closely associated with 'formal Islam'. Fascination with the exotic may have led researchers to neglect what they presumed to be familiar aspects of religious beliefs, much in the same vein as the study of maraboutism, which has received far more attention from anthropologists than the performances of official Islamic feasts such as Ramadan.[2] Only Munson (1984) lists an entry on *ajr*, but in the text *ajr* merely appears in a quotation of an informant and is not further analysed. Although Maher (1974: 98) has not entered *ajr* in her index, she is the only author I could find who mentions some cases of collecting *ajr* in her description of the 'signs of salvation' which poor people seek for want of any material sign of favour from God.

When my informants speak of *ajr*, they do so mainly in the religious sense of the term, although its association of a payment for rendered services is not altogether absent. For example, in return for her assistance with delivery, women usually pay the midwife a small sum of money besides offering her ritual presents, such as washing powder and soap, to purify herself after the defilement of the delivery, and a cone of sugar, containing a lot of *baraka*. Some-

1. See among others, Crapanzano (1973), Davis (1983), D. Dwyer (1978a), K. Dwyer (1982), Eickelman (1976), Geertz (1968), Geertz, Geertz and Rosen (1979), Maher (1974), Munson (1984), Rabinow (1975), Westermarck (1926).

2. Cf. Keesing (1989) who argues that reward structures, criteria of publishability, and theoretical premises of our discipline make anthropologists 'dealers in exotica' who seek the exotic and ignore the mundane and unremarkable. Through this filtering process, a view of cultural relativism and radical diversity is sustained by way of which Otherness is characterised and essentialised.

times, however, the midwife does not receive anything, as was the case with one of my informants who assisted her neighbour twice in delivering a baby: 'She wanted to give me something for it, but I refused. For me, it is *ajr* to do such a thing.'

Jansen (1987: 156–7), who describes similar cases in Algeria, gives an interesting account of the advantages to midwives in renouncing money for their services and claiming to work for *ajr*. In this way, the midwife develops multi-stranded, long-term personal relationships which offer both parties more trust and security, while avoiding the disgrace of having to work for money in the public domain. This enables the midwife to earn a living while at the same time living up to the Maghrebian world-view, according to which women are provided for by husbands and fathers and remain in the private domain.

Moroccans distinguish between religious acts that are *mafrûḍ*, obligatory, which involve religious duties such as the five daily prayers and the fast, and *ḥasanât*, acts that are Sunna, which in classical Arabic refers to the tradition of the Prophet, but in daily discourse means 'recommendable'. Performing the religious duties may yield *ajr*, but a significant amount only if the basic prescriptions have been exceeded. For example, one girl stated that 'performing the prayers at home gives you 1 *ajr*, but performing them in the mosque gives you 27 *ajr*'. In general, people do not calculate *ajr* in such precise figures. Most informants speak about 'a little' or 'much' *ajr*. In particular, deeds that are believed to be recommended by the Sunna, such as voluntary fasting or performing the major ritual ablution on Fridays, are considered to yield much *ajr*.

Strictly speaking, one can only obtain *ajr* for such pious acts after having met the basic requirements of the religious duties.[3] To explain this, a male informant made a comparison between performing religious deeds and paying money: 'When you have purchased something on credit, what do you do first? Pay the person to whom you owe money or give it away to someone else as alms? Of course you must pay back what you owe first!' To substantiate his point he told the following story:

> One day a man visited a Koran scholar and posed the question which of the Seven Heavens is the most difficult to enter. Instead of replying, the *fqi* asked him whether he performed the daily prayers and the fast. When his visitor denied this, he stated 'do what is near before you want what is far away'.

3. The Iranian peasants among whom Loeffler (1988: 85) conducted his fieldwork held a different opinion. One of his informants told him the following story: '600,000 people made the pilgrimage to Mecca, but God approved of no one's. He did, however, approve of the pilgrimage of a man who never made it. This man had given all his money he had set aside for the pilgrimage to a poor woman . . . merits are earned by serving other people, by helping them, not simply by fulfilling religious obligations like saying the prayers.'

Because voluntary religious practices are only merited when the obligatory duties are fulfilled, it is more specifically the elderly who perform deeds that render *ajr*. One informant offered an additional explanation: 'Of course older people want more *ajr:* they are closer to death and fear God. Young people do not think. They say: "what am I going to do with *ajr*?".'

Each deed performed for *ajr* brings one one step closer to Paradise. In this way, *ajr* establishes a kind of *tawḥîd* or unification between life on earth and life in Paradise. This is, of course, a comforting thought for old people for whom death is close. In practice, however, I have also seen younger women who do not fulfil all religious duties, but perform acts for *ajr* all the same. It was explained that their religious merit may not be valid now, but will be credited to them once they begin to observe the duties.

Ajr is believed to be written down in an account-book. Every person has an angel on each shoulder. Each day the angel on the left shoulder writes down in the account-book whatever sins one has committed that day, whereas the angel on the right shoulder keeps a record of the good deeds.[4] On Judgement Day all Muslims must queue up in front of the archangel Gabriel (Jibril) and present their account-books. If one's *ajr* exceeds one's sins, one may enter Paradise. If the number of sins is larger, then one is directed to Hell. Most informants agreed that *ajr* may compensate for sins which have been committed but will never annul them. One woman, however, was convinced that by collecting religious merit one's sins can be cancelled: 'When you have a lot of *ajr,* this is as good as having performed the pilgrimage to Mecca; your sins will be forgiven.'

According to Marrakchi traditions, *ajr* earned by one person can be passed on to others. Women who, on their way to the cemetery, distribute dates and figs believe that they obtain *ajr* on behalf of both themselves and the deceased whom they are going to visit. Also, young children who fast one day during Ramadan may give away the merit thus earned to one of their parents. My hostess recalled how, as a child, she had always given the *ajr,* religious merit, which she had earned by fasting, to her mother: *ṣemt ᶜlâ ḥsâb ummî,* 'I fasted on account of my mother.' The view that *ajr* may be transmitted to others contradicts the opinion propounded by the Moroccan religious establishment: watching the television

4. In the chapter on purity we have seen that the right hand is associated with purity, and the left hand with impurity. The association of the left shoulder with the record of one's sinful deeds and the right shoulder with that of one's meritorious deeds is part and parcel of the same right-left opposition. The superiority of the right over the left is general to the Middle East and finds expression both in the Koran and the Hadith. In the Koran, e.g., it is stated that the elect are on the right of God and the damned on His left (Sura 56: 9). According to a tradition God has two right hands (cf. Chelhod 1973: 240 for these and other examples).

programme *qadîyât ramaḍân* on Friday night, we learned that the custom of children fasting for their parents was not valid. According to the presenter, *ajr* is purely personal and cannot be given away. A *wîlî, a wîlî*, 'oh dear, oh dear', the woman exclaimed while watching the programme. 'Do you remember I told you I fasted for my mother? So the poor woman never received the *ajr* I earned for her.' She almost had a fit of laughter about her childlike *naïveté*.

The *ajr* earned by performing some specific religious acts is believed to be transformed into material forms in Paradise. For example, I was told that each time Muslims finish praying a string of prayer beads, God will plant a tree for them in their garden in Paradise. Also, for the *ajr* earned by pouring holy water over the grave of relatives during visits to the cemetery, an angel with a mug of water will stand beside the grave of the person who did so until the Day of Resurrection to give her or him to drink whenever she or he is thirsty.[5]

Ajr is closely related to the notion of the Islamic community. Earning religious merit is associated with living up to high moral standards, which Moroccans perceive to be Islamic principles rather than universal human values. This may be illustrated by citing one of Munson's (1984: 118) informants: 'A Muslim must help his brother. We are not like the Christians. We help each other . . . Brotherhood is neither sold nor bought . . . The Muslim who gives to his brother has much *ajr*.'

According to some informants, the woman who told me that my feet had brought me *ajr* for visiting her on the day of the concluding feast of Ramadan was mistaken. In the view of my informants, non-Muslims do not go to Paradise and therefore cannot earn *ajr*. Other informants were more lenient; they suggested that the religious merit I had earned by fasting would be credited to me retroactively once I converted to Islam.

The concept of *ajr* is connected with the concept of *baraka*. In the most general sense of the word, *baraka* is 'the manifestation of God's grace on earth' (Rabinow 1975: 25). This supernatural power can take many forms: it is a concrete quality which may refer to the blessedness of states, such as fasting or performing the pilgrimage to Mecca; of things, such as bread, water and henna; of persons, such as the descendants of the Prophet and saints; or of places, such as mosques, shrines and wells (cf. Westermarck 1926, who men-

5. Apparently, Iranian peasants have similar views on the possibility of religious merit (*savab* in Persian) to be transformed into concrete form. For example, Loeffler (1988: 146) cites one man saying: 'If I had all the gold of this world, I couldn't take a bit of it with me when I die. But if I give it away to others, it earns merit – 100% it does. If I help the unfortunate, the poor, the destitute, the hungry, naked, weak, old or blind either with my health or my actions – my pockets will be full on the Last Day.'

tions hundreds of examples of *baraka*, many of which are still in force in contemporary Morocco).

Both *ajr* and *baraka* are essential to leading a successful life as a Muslim. As an uneducated divorcee stated: *ḵessek baraka fî ḥeyatek u ajr ᶜend llâh* 'you need blessings in your life and religious merit with God'. The power of *baraka* helps a person to cope with problems and makes life on earth easier, while *ajr* facilitates the entrance to Paradise, and mainly concerns the afterlife.

The ways to obtain these divine forces, however, differ. *Baraka* is there for the taking. Basically, all one has to do is to expose oneself to its power. To be true, this may take quite an effort, as I experienced while climbing up a very steep mountain with a barren informant in order to reach the shrine of a saint whose blessings we sought. Yet, *baraka* can be collected by anyone. In the form of henna or incense one can even buy it and take it home and share it with others. *Baraka* is diffuse divine energy which is contagious. It can be passed on from person to person.

According to most uneducated informants, *ajr* can also be transmitted. Yet, more than is the case with *baraka*, it is stressed that each individual must actively achieve *ajr* by performing religious acts her- or himself. To collect *ajr*, a conscious effort must be made. Any action to gain *ajr* must be preceded by proclaiming the *nîya*, the intention. This is not necessarily the case with *baraka*, which may be obtained unconsciously, as when traversing sacred ground.

Secondly, in alms-giving *ajr* and *baraka* are two sides of the same coin. The person who hands out alms thereby earns religious merit. Because they are alms, the items that are distributed contain a lot of *baraka*. Also, the distribution of certain foodstuffs or other things in which *baraka* inheres, yields more *ajr* for the donor than the offering of other gifts. In Marrakech a vanishing tradition among women consists of inviting children who are playing in the street into the house on Friday and serving them couscous for *ajr*. Before the children go home, the hostess smears their heads with henna, which is said to contain so much *baraka* that it is called 'one of the blessings of God'. Sometimes, *ajr* and *baraka* are interwoven to such an extent that informants view them as identical terms. In a discussion on the relation between *ajr* and *baraka*, an educated informant initially stated: '*Ajr* and *baraka* are really one and the same thing.' However, after giving some examples of cases in which one may obtain *ajr* and others in which one may obtain *baraka*, she qualified this statement, saying: 'There is no *baraka* without *ajr*.' Confusion about the two notions also arose in a discussion with another, uneducated informant when I asked her to expain why children, during their Friday treat of couscous, have their heads smeared with henna. The woman replied: 'Henna is *ajr*, just like bread, wheat and sugar.' Suspecting that she had skipped a link, namely that these items only produce *ajr* once they are given away as alms, I later confronted her with her own enumeration and asked her what these items have in common. This time she replied that they all contain *baraka*.

The tradition of serving children couscous is an illustration of yet another way in which religious merit and blessedness are linked; it takes place on Friday, *l-yawm l-mbârak*, the blessed day. It yields more *ajr* to perform religious acts on blessed days than it does on other days of the year. Hence, it is not surprising that most entries about *ajr* in my fieldnotes concern activities during Ramadan, the blessed month. Before we turn to this, however, I will, in the next section, reflect on what the relationship between *baraka* and *ajr* can tell us about the Moroccan image of God.

Blessings, Religious Merit and the Image of God

As a pair, the concepts of *baraka* and *ajr* provide an interesting insight into the image that Moroccans have of God. The idea that blessings must be counterbalanced by 'earning' *ajr*, through the performance of religious acts, reflects a rather transactionalist and pragmatic attitude towards the divine. It suggests the image of God as an accountant, who keeps records of *ajr* and *baraka* as receipts and expenditure.

Informants often referred to the performance of religious deeds as a kind of payment. Women call fasting a compensation for the days missed during Ramadan, a way of 'paying back' these days. The male informant who maintained that *ajr* can only be obtained after the requirements of the religious duties are met, likewise compared the performance of religious deeds to paying money. The image of two angels who keep a record of good and bad deeds also confirms the image of careful calculation.

Watt (1970: 31–2) describes the same bookkeeping idiom in the Koran. In his view, this may be accounted for by the experience of the Prophet Muhammed as a merchant (cf. Buskens 1987: 44). The Tappers (1987: 83), who in Turkey found a similar attitude towards religious activities, mention that this calculating approach is fostered by the religious establishment, and note that it fits with the capitalist ethic of contemporary Turkey.

Although the calculating attitude may be compatible with capitalism, it is not solely characteristic of this form of socio-economic organisation. The valuable element of the view forwarded by the Tappers is that it compares the way people relate to each other with the way they relate to God. As Christian (1989: 168) argues: 'The different ways of communicating with the divine and making bargains with the divine are related to the ways that people arrange transactions with each other' (cf. Eickelman 1976: 160).

The notion of reciprocity implied by the pair *baraka–ajr* by which Moroccans perceive their relation to God, also underlies the way they organise relations between themselves. In any relationship, communication is interpreted in terms of favours paid and favours received. At an early age, children learn that 'You don't get owt for nowt'. Mothers, for example, persuade their children to run errands by allowing them to keep the change.

The idea that any need for a service requires bargaining over the favours that will be exchanged in this connection, permeates all interaction. Someone who wants to apply for a passport, for example, in most cases will not go directly to the town hall and fill in a form, but rather first seeks contact with an influential person who is willing to accept personal favours. She or he will try to create a bond of obligations with such a person who then feels compelled to employ her or his influence in procuring a passport. Likewise, people have little confidence in the free treatments by doctors from public hospitals. The large fee charged by private doctors is felt to offer more likelihood of fair treatment.

Even relations among close kin are measured by reciprocity. A woman who has received a dress from her richer sister will be sure to return the favour by doing the washing or going shopping for her sister. Consistent with Mauss's essay on the gift (Mauss 1970), any form of gift exchange establishes new relationships or confirms existing ones. Declining gifts or an invitation to a meal equals denying the existence of a relationship.[6] In the rare case that an offer cannot possibly be accepted, the wronged party will declare *fik l-ḥaqq*, 'the judgement is on you', meaning 'you owe me one'. For example, I was invited by a family to attend the 15th of Ramadan in their home, but I had already promised to spend that evening with my host family. Since it is customary to spend the 15th at home, the lady who had invited me was ready to excuse me, but still, she teased me by repeating *fik l-ḥaqq* several times during our conversation. Indeed, among friends, the formula is usually used as if it were a joke, but more often than not, the offender subsequently organises a dinner party in her home for the woman whose offer she refused.

The more intimate the relationship, the more time is allowed or even expected to elapse before a favour granted must be returned. Indeed, friendship is proven by the extent to which postponement of reciprocity is tolerated. This I learned the hard way. I once need-

6. Cf. Mauss's account on the 'total prestation of gift-exchange' which involves:
i. the obligation to give
ii. the obligation to receive
iii. the obligation to repay (Mauss 1970: 11).

ed money urgently. Since the banks were closed, a friend offered to lend me some money, insisting that *nti k̲tî, âna wiyâk, bḥâl bḥâl,* 'you are my sister, you and I, we are the same'. Having been brought up with the notion that borrowing money is improper, the next morning I went to the bank and returned the money to the woman. She was very upset by my behaviour. Once again she emphasised that I was her sister and insisted that I keep the money for some time. I had clearly insulted her by so quickly trying to sever the bond of obligation by which I was tied to her.

Christian (1989) describes the same mechanism of reciprocity in Spain. He arranges the secular transactions of exchange on a continuum from strict reciprocity to a kind of family communism and compares this to the way transactions with the divine are organised. He then goes on to argue that there is a kind of equivalence between the forms of reciprocity appropriate to different levels of intimacy between human beings, and those related to the different degrees of intimacy with divine figures. The strict reciprocity appropriate in the authoritarian relation between God and His people appears to be mediated by relations with the Mother Mary and the local saints, which allow for a more diluted reciprocity in the form of making promises at shrines (Christian 1989: 168–87).

This analysis also applies to the Moroccan ways of dealing with the divine. As has been shown in this chapter, much attention is focused on the way God's blessings must be repaid by performing religious deeds for *ajr*. In maraboutism, *baraka*, mediated by the saints, plays a more important role than *ajr*. As in relations to close friends, the intimate and informal relations with saints imply that one need not worry about settling debts promptly. Moreover, relations with the saints are conditional: people visit shrines to ask for a favour and promise to make a sacrifice once the favour has been granted. Ultimately, however, God's blessings can only be acquired by regularly performing pious deeds for *ajr*s.

Ajr during Ramadan

Ramadan is the pre-eminent month for performing *ḥasanât* or good deeds. During this blessed month, the spiritual reward for good deeds is believed to be higher than during the other months of the year. Jokingly, using the dual form in order to make her statement sound more sophisticated, an educated young woman stated: *fî ṛemḍân, kull šî ajrayn,* 'during Ramadan everything is two *ajr*s.[7]

7. Standard Arabic distinguishes between the singular, the dual, and the plural form. Although in Moroccan Arabic the dual exists, the suffix is often replaced by the plural form of the noun, preceded by the numeral 'two'. The religious discourse of Koran scholars is in Standard Arabic. By imitating the style of Koran scholars – who to date are invariably men – while being a woman herself, my informant indeed made quite a joke.

In the preceding chapters, numerous examples of activities which people undertake during Ramadan to obtain merit have already been mentioned. Some of these are social, such as inviting friends for breakfast in the evening, settling disputes before the end of Ramadan, and visiting relatives on the day of the Feast. Other deeds relate to more person-orientated expressions of piety or *nîya*, intention, such as reading the Koran or listening to its recitation, praying with a string of beads, performing the great ritual ablution on the day of the concluding feast, and fasting the first six days of the month succeeding Ramadan.

These religious acts may be performed by both women and men. However, some religious deeds are more gender-specific. Men in particular pray the *tarâwîḥ*, the special Ramadan prayers, in the mosque every night and spend the night of the 27th in the mosque reciting the Koran. Visiting the *muṣallâ* on the feast concluding Ramadan is an exclusively male privilege. These are all public activities, which are considered more proper for men than for women. More importantly, a successful performance of these activities demands at least some formal education, which women lack more often than men.[8]

Women employ other strategies to earn religious merit. Preparing couscous for those who pray in the mosque on the night of the 27th of Ramadan and applying henna on the hands and feet for the concluding feast of Ramadan are *ajr*-generating activities performed especially by women. It would be wrong to conclude that female pious acts consist of mainly local practices which deviate more from the formal prescriptions than the special prayers said by men in the mosque. Like many other activities undertaken by women during Ramadan, these religious deeds are examples of alms-giving, and patience or endurance. Both concepts play a significant role in the Islamic doctrine.

Alms-giving for Religious Merit

It is recommended that *ṣadaqa* or alms-giving be performed during the fasting month. In Bukari's compilation of traditions it is said that during Ramadan the Prophet Muhammed was 'more generous than the rain-bringing wind' (Jeffery 1962: 92). In general, women are more actively involved in giving alms than men (cf. Buskens 1987: 39; Maher 1974: 99). Having less money at their disposal than men, they do so mainly in kind. A woman may give away one of her dresses to a poor neighbour or relative, offer a chunk of bread or a bowl of soup to a passing beggar, or distribute *šebbakîyas*, Ramadan cookies, among children who are playing in the street.

8. In 1980, 54% of Morocco's urban population over the age of 10 was illiterate. Of the 200,000 pupils in primary school, 64% were boys and 36% girls (Lentjes 1981: 216).

The dates and figs that women hand out to poor people and children whom they encounter on their way to the cemetery on the 27th of Ramadan are alms, and some women described the ritual of visiting the dead on that day as a deed of *ṣadaqa*. As the opening anecdote of this chapter demonstrated, the alms are not necessarily distributed to the poor only. I have also seen children who were sent out by their mothers, with a basket filled with small pieces of bread, to hand these out to any passer-by who would accept it. Especially during Ramadan, people are keen to receive such alms, since they contain much *baraka*. According to women in Berkane, because of this divine quality *ṣadaqa*-food remains in the stomach for forty days before it is digested. Consequently, eating such nutritious foodstuffs helps one to better endure the fast.

Some alms render more *ajr* than others. This is not only the case with goods containing *baraka*, but also with things that the benefactor finds it hard to part with, for example when a woman gives away a dress which she is fond of wearing herself. More than once I was told that giving away something that is of no importance to oneself is, properly speaking, no *ṣadaqa* but merely a present. The word *kadû*, coming from the French *cadeau*, was used here rather than its more traditional Arabic equivalent *hdîya*, thus connoting the non-Islamic nature of such a gift.

Therefore, performing *ṣadaqa* may require a considerable effort and sacrifice on the side of the benefactor. An incident in my host family in Berkane during the second week of Ramadan illustrates how difficult this can be. One night my hostess Laila had a bad dream. Early next morning she sat down next to me to tell what had happened in her nightmare:

> Coming home from shopping she was met by two beggars at her door. She ordered her daughter-in-law to give the women some flour. Instead of doing this, the young woman offered them a large amount of the valuable grain harvested from Laila's own land in the countryside. With love she had washed and sorted the grain and had saved it for family use during Ramadan. She made a remark about this to her daughter-in-law but received an impudent reply in return. As it is improper to argue during Ramadan, Laila kept silent. Then she saw herself confronted with a second problem: the mendicants would not leave. They complained that they preferred sugar and cooking oil instead of flour or grain. Now Laila panicked. What was she to do? Although a row had to be avoided, she could not think of an alternative that would send the two ungrateful women away.

At this point she woke from this upsetting dream.

Like all religious deeds that render *ajr*, performing *ṣadaqa* paves the way to Paradise, as well as reinforcing and enhancing one's social status on earth. This means that, in order to live up to expectations, people may feel compelled to give. Beggars make clever use of this by appealing to the sacredness of Ramadan. More than in any other month of the year, large numbers of beggars sit at the entrances of mosques and shrines. They remind passers-by of their religious duty to give alms with formulas such as *fî sabîl llâh*, 'on behalf of God' *llâh yḵellîk*, 'may God protect you', and *llâh yerḥem wâlidîk*, 'may God have mercy on your parents'.

Indeed, Laila's story suggests that alms-giving may not always be quite as voluntary as it seems. As an older woman, who is head of the family and visits the mosque regularly, it is more or less expected of Laila that she show her worth as a Muslim by way of giving *ṣadaqa*.

In her dream, Laila clearly felt trapped. She was angry both with her daughter-in-law and with the audacious beggars. Yet because it was Ramadan, she wanted to refrain from arguing. Her struggle for self-mastery is an example of what was described to me as *ajr bel-fumm*, 'religious merit by means of the mouth'.

The Female Virtue of Patience

It is not surprising that during Ramadan, when people are preoccupied with the mouth as the principal boundary marker between what is allowed and what is not allowed, one can also obtain religious merit through the mouth. *Ajr bel-fumm* implies refraining from lying, gossiping, and, emphasised most by women, arguing.

As in many Moroccan families, my Berkani hostess and her daughter-in-law did not get along very well. At the beginning of Ramadan both had tried their best to reduce the tension for the duration of the sacred month, but by the end of the first week Laila could no longer hide her feelings. When she was irritated, she warned her daughter-in-law by stating *mâ nqûl lîkš, âna ṣayma*, 'I won't say anything to you: I'm fasting'. A few days later, the bickering between the two women began again. The discrepancy between what was considered proper fasting behaviour and their actual feelings proved to be too large. Despite their good intentions, before Ramadan was over they were scolding each other as much as before. I did not realise the extent to which Laila had suffered as she tried to restrain herself until a few days after the *ᶜîd* when she had literally had a 'fit' of anger. A seemingly inane incident with her daughter-in-law's mother triggered such overwhelming emotions that she began to shout and shake vehemently, eventually falling on the floor and losing consciousness.

Trying to avoid arguments is closely related to the emphasis that women place on the virtue of showing *ṣabr*, patience, during Ramadan. *Ṣabr* is an important concept in Islamic doctrine. In many pericopes of the Koran, *ṣabr* is mentioned, for instance:

> Peace be upon you, for that you were patient. Fair is the Ultimate Abode. (S13: 24)

> Now today I have recompensed them for their patient endurance; they are triumphant. (S23: 111)

In the Koran, *ṣabr* covers meanings such as patience in general, as well as endurance or tenacity, particularly in relation to the *jihâd*, the fight against infidelity, and resignation. Sometimes it refers to fasting, as in *šahr aṣ-ṣabr*, 'the month of *ṣabr*', that is, Ramadan (Ruska 1987: 25). The high value of *ṣabr* is illustrated by the fact that As-Sabur is one of the beautiful names of God. Two kinds of *ṣabr* are distinguished: the endurance of physical ills, whether actively, as in performing difficult tasks, or passively, as in suffering blows, and spiritual endurance, in the sense of renunciating natural impulses. In general, the salutary effect of *ṣabr* consists of all that strengthens the religious impulse and weakens the passionate one (Ruska 1987: 27).

In Moroccan Arabic, *ṣabr* covers both physical and spiritual aspects, and refers to a set of meanings which vary from patience and endurance to perseverance and self-possession. 'To learn to be patient' was a common theme in the answers provided by informants to questions about why they fast. *Ṣabr* includes several practices associated with the fast: the special dish of couscous eaten during Shaban to celebrate the coming of Ramadan is called *gassa ṣ-ṣâbirîn*, 'the dish of the enduring people' (cf. chapter 2). Displaying the *ṣabr* to endure the hunger implied by the fasting process without becoming irritated or getting involved in arguments is an important means of collecting *ajr*. Also, the voluntary fast during the first week of Shawwal, the month succeeding Ramadan, is called *ṣawm aṣ-ṣâbirîn*, 'the fast of the enduring people' (cf. chapter 3).

Apparently, men also emphasise the importance of *ṣabr* during Ramadan (Buskens 1987: 72). However, my female informants proudly state that *ṣabr* is primarily a virtue of women. 'Of course women have more patience than men', a recently divorced young woman exclaimed, while laughing about my obviously silly question concerning the distribution of patience between men and women. 'Haven't you heard that my ex-husband has remarried already? He does not have the patience to take his time and search properly. I am not in a hurry, I can wait.' What my informant was alluding to is that she has more control over sexual desires than her ex-husband. This contradicts the view generally expounded by men that they are less ruled by flesh-centred desires and tensions (*nefs*) than women (Dwyer 1978a: 152). The divorced woman's view reinforces Dwyer's argument that women's valuation of themselves is less negative than men's, while they qualify the high valuation men have of themselves (ibid.: 178).

Women attribute their superiority in exercising *ṣabr* to the confined space within which they spend their lives. Unlike men, they do not leave the house, seeking distraction out of doors to forget their sorrows. Instead of running away from their problems, women remain calm and come to terms with them.

Not only do my informants claim that women have more *ṣabr* than men, they also consider girls to develop *ṣabr* at an earlier age than boys. They do not play and fight outside like their brothers, but spend much time in the house with their mother, who teaches them *ṣabr*. Indeed, one often hears a mother order her daughter: *ṣebberi*, 'control yourself', for example when the girl is nagging about a sweet or a dress she wants to wear. The early development of *ṣabr* in girls plays a role in their participation in the fast; it was explicitly mentioned as one of the reasons why girls are capable of fasting Ramadan at an earlier age than boys.

Davis (1983: V) and Dwyer (1978a: 153) also found that Moroccan women laud *ṣabr* as a specifically female quality. Davis warns her Western readers that the patience of women is not merely to be understood as a passive attitude of resignation, but rather as a female means of exercising power:

> I often heard women say 'I'll be patient' or 'women are patient' but after I became more familiar with the culture I realized that this meant much more than just enduring whatever came their way . . . women's patience is not merely passive, but rather involves holding their power to check until the right moment to act. (Davis 1983: v)

While I agree with this view, it should be added that *ṣabr* is power of the less powerful: acting within the realm of patience involves, in most cases, influencing the views and decisions of others, which allows little room for initiating action independently.

The *ṣabr* that women develop within the confinement of their homes and neighbourhood is wedded to another highly valued quality in the Moroccan code of conduct: *ᶜaql*, reason. In the Moroccan context, reason signifies adroitness or cleverness more than a capacity for dealing with abstract rational phenomena (Eickelman 1981: 181). Contrary to *ṣabr, ᶜaql* is considered to develop as one acquires more autonomy in the social world. Men expound the view that reason is likely to be more developed in men than in women (Dwyer 1978a: 153; Eickelman 1976: 132). Eickelman describes *ᶜaql* as a key metaphor by which men can discipline their desires: 'Men's capacity to follow the divine model [the assumed Islamic code of conduct of which *ᶜaql* forms a part] reaffirms that they are not bound by their passions to live in a totally anarchic world.' Arguing that fasting symbolises most intensely people's capability to discipline their desires, Eickelman (1976: 137) concludes that 'For most Moroccans, the celebration of Ramadan distinguishes men with reason'.

According to Dwyer, women downplay the importance of ^{c}*aql* in men: men may acquire more reason than women, but only at an older age (Dwyer 1978a: 153). Probably because ^{c}*aql* is a male-related concept, I have not heard my female informants mention it often. When I asked women to give their view about the distribution of ^{c}*aql* between men and women, they did not deny that women possess less ^{c}*aql* than men. According to an educated young woman with whom I discussed the issue, it is written in the Koran or in the Hadith – she could not remember which – that 'Women remain wanting in reason as well as in religion'. 'But do you know why?', she added, 'Because a woman gives birth. Towards her children, she uses her kindness more than her reason; when she hears her child cry in the street, she does not think but immediately forgets whatever she is doing and runs to her child to comfort it.'

The Moroccan view that a mother's natural tie to her children stands in the way of her religiosity is also described by Combs-Schilling (1989: 240). According to her informants, if God had asked Hajar, the mother of Ismail, to sacrifice her child, unlike Ibrahim (Abraham), she would have refused to fulfil His command. The perception of women being more subject to their animal nature confirms the aforementioned argument developed by Ortner (1974) that it is a pan-human tendency to associate the female more with nature and the male more with that which lies beyond: culture and civilisation. Combs-Schilling follows up on this argument by stating that since in Islam, as in Christianity and Judaism, God is stepped out of nature and elevated beyond this world, women are excluded from ultimate sanctity and the power of transcendence into eternal life because of their association with nature. They can only achieve eternal life through men. Women give birth to what is temporal, whereas men give birth to what is durable (Combs-Schilling 1989: 256–7).

My data on the collection of *ajr* by Moroccan women suggest that this statement must be qualified. Women can attain eternal life without mediation by men, but they have to work harder for it and the pathway to Paradise is longer. In the view of some of my informants, women can even give away religious merit and thus help others to achieve eternal life.

It is worth noting that women may cast their natural tie to children in religious terms. The informant who explained to me why women have less reason than men suggested women's kindness as a counterbalance to the fact that their reason and religiosity remain wanting. The term which she used for kindness was *laṭâfa*. In Modern Standard Arabic, *laṭâfa* is common speech and denotes kindness. In the Moroccan Arabic dialect, the usage of *laṭâfa* is restricted and has strong religious connotations. *Laṭâfa* is one of the qualities attributed to God, while Al-Latif is one of His ninety-nine names. By emphasising kindness where they lack reason, my informant thus attributed another highly valued Islamic virtue to women.

More importantly, we have seen that women clearly maintain that men are not the sole possessors of self-control over natural passions. They closely associate the female quality of *ṣabr* with self-possession as well. Hence, if the core meaning of Ramadan is putting to the test the self-control of Muslims, as Eickelman rightly argues, then *ṣabr* may be considered the female counterpart of *ᶜaql*. Therefore, the following rephrasing of Eickelman's argument represents more closely the views of most Moroccans: 'The celebration of Ramadan distinguishes men with reason and women with endurance.'

Women's Models in a Men's World

In the chapter on purity, we have seen how in the male-dominated Moroccan world-view women's lack of self-mastery over the bodily processes of menstruation and procreation devalues their performance of the fast. The emphasis that women during Ramadan put on the female virtue of *ṣabr* as an alternative form of self-possession shows that they do not completely acquiesce in the male-held symbolic conceptions of the worth of women's fasting practices but put forward their own representations. To put this in terms as formulated by E. Ardener (1972; 1975) and S. Ardener (1975): although, within Moroccan society, women constitute a 'muted' group, whose self-perceptions are largely influenced by the way they are represented in the dominant world-view, they have developed a partial countermodel. As is characteristic of muted groups, the articulation of this countermodel remains largely within the women's world (cf. Dwyer 1978a: 178).

Women's preoccupation with *ajr* can also be interpreted in the light of a female countermodel. In the male-dominated view, women's religious esteem is considered to be less prestigious than that of men. Not only does their frequent state of impurity hamper performance of the religious duties, equally important is the invisibility of many of their religious practices, more particularly those that are most directly inspired by the doctrinal prescriptions and recommendations. For example, although women may contribute to the purchase of the sheep that in almost every family is slaughtered during the Feast of Immolation, they are not allowed to perform the ritual slaughtering themselves. Also, the majority of women who perform the five daily prayers do so within their homes instead of going to the mosque. Moreover, it is considered improper for women to call attention to their prayers. It is forbidden for women to pray out loud and, unlike those of men, women's prostrations never result in a *zbîb*, a 'raisin', a spot of darkened tissue on the forehead due to keratinisation. *Zbîb*s are developed by touching the floor during prayer, and are recognised as a physical sign of someone's religiosity.

Jansen interprets the performance of activities that yield *ajr* as a particularly female survival strategy. She argues that women who perform tasks for *ajr* instead of money do not try to appear more religious but rather refer to *ajr* to turn a work relation into a kinship bond and a public job into a private one. By creating substitute kin ties they also obtain substitute support, thus being able to earn a living without defying the cultural value that women should not operate within the economic realm (Jansen 1987: 157). I agree that women put more effort into performing deeds that render *ajr* than men do. However, in cases where women prefer to claim *ajr* where they might have accepted money for their services, although this may indeed be a survival strategy, the possibility that women thus want to express piety should not be discarded. Moreover, an analysis in terms of survival strategies may account for this particular way of working for *ajr*, which is the realm to which Jansen restricted her analysis, but it does not explain many other instances where women act to obtain *ajr*.

For a better understanding of these activities, another line of reasoning may be adopted. Maher (1974) and Loeffler (1988) associate the importance of earning religious merit with poor farmers who due to their workload cannot meet the requirements of the religious duties. To these rural people who generally lack any formal Islamic education, performing deeds for *ajr* is a strategy to compensate for their shortcomings with respect to the official prescriptions. Similarly, as women's reputations in the dominant Moroccan world-view are considered to be inferior to those of men as a result of their having more difficulties in meeting the requirements of the religious duties, performing acts for *ajr* may be a strategy for women to compensate for their religious shortcomings.[9] In doing so, they construct a more favourable religious self-representation to counterbalance male-dominated views of female religiosity.

9. Cf. Tapper and Tapper (1987: 76) some of whose female informants stated that they need to be more religious than men because they have been told (by the religious establishment) that they are more sinful than men. The services which these Turkish women organise to commemorate the birth of the Prophet are more elaborate and more emotional than the services held by men.

seven

A Cycle of Celebrations

When, in 1987, I visited Morocco for three months in order to do preliminary research on Ramadan, my Berkani informants objected to my plans to leave before the Feast of Immolation, which was to take place a month after my departure. They told me about the Great Feast with enthusiasm. The celebrations of the tenth day of the Islamic New Year, and the birthday of the Prophet, were touched upon as well. It was not until the next year, when I had an opportunity to attend these rituals in Marrakech, that I fully realised how right my Berkani informants had been in stressing that I participate in the other celebrations as well. Participation in the complete cycle of Islamic rituals helped me to elicit the meaning of the specific combination of key concepts in the celebration of Ramadan.

In this chapter I will briefly describe the other celebrations of the ritual cycle in order to assess to what extent the central notions of different levels of *umma*, the Islamic community, *ṭahâra*, purity, *ajr*, religious merit, and *baraka*, blessings, recur in the other feasts. I will also compare the stringency of the regulations of the feasts and the extent to which the feasts are recognised by the Moroccan religious establishment. Adopting this approach, it is impossible to do justice to the rich and specific character of each of the celebrations described. Since these descriptions focus only on themes related to Ramadan, they must necessarily remain incomplete.

Descriptions of the Other Feasts of the Islamic Cycle

The Feast of Immolation

The Feast of Immolation or 'Great Feast' (*l-^{c}îd l-kabîr*), in the Islamic doctrine called *^{c}îd al-aḍḥâ*, is on the tenth day of the twelfth month of the Islamic year, *ḏû al-ḥijja* (see chapter 8, p.171 for an overview of the Islamic calendar). This is the month during which the Pilgrimage to Mecca takes place. The ritual slaughtering of a ram, to commemorate Ibrahim's willingness to obey God's command and sacrifice his son Ismail, is a rite that is performed not only by the pilgrims in Mecca, but ideally by all Muslims.

Two weeks before the feast, the waste land outside the city walls of Marrakech, near Bab Aghmat, is transformed into a big marketplace where farmers from the larger area flock together to sell their sheep to the townspeople.

In the view of my female informants it is incumbent upon the male head of the household to provide the family with a sacrificial animal. 'Why did I marry if my husband does not bring me a ram?' one woman replied when I asked her who was going to buy the sacrificial animal in her family. However, many women have to find ways to earn money for the animal as well, since their husbands do not earn enough to buy a whole ram. The few women who go to the sheep market are mostly women without men.

The week before the sacrificial feast women are very busy with preparations. Like the week before Ramadan, the house is given a thorough cleaning. Men go to the public bath the day before the feast, because they have to be in a pure state when they slaughter the ram. Fewer women go to the public bath. When I asked my hostess about this, she laughed: 'On the day of the feast you will see why.'

Voluntary fasting is recommended the day before the ritual sacrifice. This day corresponds with the standing on Mount Arafat during the Pilgrimage. Some people also refrain from eating or drinking on the morning of the feast, and do not eat until the first meat of the slaughtered ram is prepared much later that day. The breakfast of those who do eat should consist of a white porridge. After breakfast men may go to the special prayer meeting held on the *muṣallâ*. Those who stay at home watch television, which broadcasts a similar prayer meeting in Rabat attended by the king. Dressed in a white *jellâba,* Hassan II is shown praying. Afterwards he accepts congratulations from Muslim ambassadors and other high Muslim officials. Then the king proceeds to the courtyard of the mosque where he sacrifices a ram on behalf of the Moroccan people. The spectators are anxious to witness this scene, because it is generally believed that one should not slaughter one's ram before the king has sacrificed.

In many male-headed urban families the ritual cutting of the throat is done by the oldest male member, and the butcher is called

1. The tasks a person should carry out depend on her or his position within the family. As I had seen in Sidi Slimane in 1984, the woman who occupies the lowest position in the hierarchy, i.e. the adult daughter who is not yet married, carries out the dirtiest part: she has to burn the head over a fire, which is accompanied by heavy smoke production. She also empties the paunch, but because this task should be carried out very carefully, usually an experienced older woman cleans and prepares the tripe, as well as the delicate organs, which in the family in Sidi Slimane is prepared the same day in a big stew. It is a Marrakchi tradition, on the other hand, to cut them to pieces and leave them in a spicy marinate overnight. The next day, pieces of paunch are filled with the marinated chunks and then tied into bundles. These are then put in the sun to dry, which takes four to five days.

in for the skinning and removal of the intestines. Since women are not allowed to slaughter, in my female-headed host family the butcher performed the actual slaughtering as well. The rest of the day the women were busy cutting up the meat. Everybody knew her task without being told.[1] I soon understood why Zahra laughed when I asked her why she did not go to the public bath before the feast: within an hour, we were all perspiring from the heavy work and our clothes were stained with blood. The ram had been slaughtered around eleven o'clock, but it was not until three in the afternoon that the family could sit down and consume the first meat: grilled liver. Most of the meat is consumed within a week, but some parts of the sacrificial ram are preserved, such as its tail, which is consumed on the occasion of the succeeding feast.

The Ashura

Exactly one month after the Great Feast, the *ᶜâšûrâ'* is celebrated on the tenth day of Muharram, the first month of the Islamic year. To Shiites, Ashura is important as the anniversary of the martyrdom of Husayn, the grandson of the Prophet. In the Sunnite interpretation of Islamic doctrine, the formal value of Ashura is restricted to its meaning as a voluntary fasting day which was probably initiated by the Prophet Muhammed to match the Jewish Day of Atonement (cf. chapter 1).

The celebration of Ashura concludes a transitional period of ten days between the old year and the new year. In Morocco, the first day of the new Islamic year is hardly celebrated. Children set off firecrackers and the newspapers report the king's attendance at the special prayer meetings in the mosque, but for my informants in the medina of Marrakech it is no occasion for congratulations or a topic of discussion. On the eighth day of Muharram the public baths in Marrakech are visited by people who thus conclude a seven-day mourning period. People who perform this mourning ritual abstain from washing themselves, combing their hair or using make-up. Mourning women try to keep the tasks of doing the dishes and laundry to a minimum, using only soft soap without scent. None of my informants perform the ritual mourning, but some remembered having mourned in their families when they were still young. Others had never heard of the mourning ritual.[2] The general atmosphere in the medina of Marrakech during the ten days leading up to Ashura is one of elation and merriment. On the square Jemaa al-Fna, rows of stalls are set up from which particular Ashura products are sold, such as different kinds of percussion

2. According to Westermarck (1926, II: 77), it was the Sherifs in particular, the descendants of the Prophet Muhammed, who performed the Ashura mourning rituals.

instruments, 'Ashura incense', 'Ashura soap', and large bags of raisins and nuts that go into the *krišlât*, the special sweets that women prepare. Other stalls sell toys. Like the 15th of Ramadan, Ashura is an occasion on which adults give toys and new clothes to the small children in the family. The town is immersed in the continuous noise of drumming produced by children who parade through the alleys playing their *te^{c}rîjas*, the vase-shaped drums bought for the Ashura. In the evening, teenage girls gather in the alleys to sing, dance and beat their drums to special Ashura songs. The singing may continue until two o'clock in the morning, but nobody complains about the noise.

On the Eve of Ashura, it is feared, those who work magic are particularly powerful. The magic that is performed on this night is believed to last a whole year. To protect their families, women burn the special Ashura incense at sunset and buy special soap to use as an antidote in case someone should fall ill. Most people will have consumed the special Ashura dish, a couscous prepared with the preserved tail of the sacrificial ram, in the afternoon preceding the Eve of Ashura. Those who have not, take this meal in the evening, after which women dress up and go to one of the numerous private parties that are organised by women on the night of Ashura. Jemma (1971: 102–3) describes Ashura meetings for men, who perform a percussion rite called *deqqa*, beating. I was told that few such meetings are held now and mainly involve groups of male adolescents. In former times groups from different quarters in Marrakech paraded through the medina while beating their drums. They came together on the big town square where a drum competition was held which lasted until the break of day. Women's parties also continue until daybreak. Many women allow themselves only a few hours of sleep, since the day following this festive night is believed to be one of the two best dates to visit the graveyard.[3] Women also believe that it brings prosperity to buy something on that day, preferably pottery. When the aunt of my hostess came back from her visit to the cemetery, she showed me the earthenware savings box that she had bought on the occasion, expressing the wish that she would save enough money to visit the festival of Mulay Ibrahim, which follows the celebration of the birth of the Prophet.

The Mulûd

The *mulûd* (*^{c}îd al-mawlid* or *mawlid an-nabî*), the feast of the birth of the Prophet, is celebrated on the twelfth day of Rabia One, the third month of the Islamic calendar. In many countries the most promi-

3. The other occasion is the day following the night of the 27th of Ramadan (cf. chs. 3 and 4).

nent element of the celebration is the recital of panegyrical poems about the birth of the Prophet in which his life and virtues are praised (cf. Combs-Schilling 1989; Tapper and Tapper 1987). Although celebrations of the birth of the Prophet are now largely accepted as an integral part of the Islamic ritual cycle, the *mulûd* has always met with opposition from purist movements which condemn it as a *bid^{c}a*, a religious innovation which contradicts the Tradition (Fuchs 1913–18: 419–22).

In the Maghreb, the *mulûd* was introduced by Abu al-Abbas al-Azafi (1162–1236) in his home town of Ceuta. By introducing the *mulûd*, he hoped to prevent the Muslims in this town from participating in the celebration of Christian festivals and to strengthen Muslim identity (Kaptein 1989: 105). The *mulûd* was proclaimed an official festival under the Merinide reign of Abu Yacub Yusuf (1286–1307), who thus tried to create religious legitimacy for his authority (ibid.: 115). By the second half of the fourteenth century the importance of the *mulûd* celebrations at the courts of sultans had diminished yet had become popular among the masses (ibid.: 146).

In present-day Marrakech, the celebration of the Prophet's birth is preceded by cleaning the house and visiting the public bath. On the eve of the feast some women prepare large platters of couscous which they take to the mosques for visitors – mostly men – who spend the night there to pray and recite the Koran. In my host family, nobody brought couscous to the mosque or spent the night praying, but at six o'clock in the morning I heard several women give three ululations. The Prophet is said to have been born at dawn, and women ululate to express their joy over his birth. As on the other official feasts, breakfast on the mulûd consists of a white porridge. The noon meal is copious and is preferably shared with relatives.

For many Marrakchis, the *mulûd* not only includes the birth celebration proper, but also the seven *mûsem*s, festivals at the shrines of saints, which take place a week after the celebration of the birth of the Prophet. In their view, these festivals do not just follow the *mulûd* by one week, but are part and parcel of the celebration of the *mulûd*. This can be illustrated by the fact that the trance sessions that are organised at the festivals are called *mulûdîya*s, to distinguish them from those which are organised during the month preceding Ramadan, called *še^{c}bâna*s.[4] The seven *mûsem*s differ in size and fame. The *mûsem* of Mulay Ibrahim, for instance, is of nation-

4. Cf. Jemma (1971: 104) who also describes the commemoration of the birth of the Prophet and the festivals that succeed it as belonging to the same celebration. He argues that the *mulûd* has absorbed pre-Islamic rites related to the winter solstice, which should explain the fact that the majority of the rites that mark the time of *mulûd* take place seven days after the celebration of the *mulûd* proper.

al importance while the *mûsem* of Tamsluht is regional and that of Lalla Mimouna is only of minor local importance. Small *mûsems*, such as that of Lalla Mimouna, last only one day, while the *mûsems* of Mulay Ibrahim and Tamsluht last a whole week.[5]

The main reason for visiting the *mûsems* is to attend *lîlas*, nights of trance-dancing (cf. chapter 2). Not all pilgrims who rent a room in Mulay Ibrahim or Tamsluht participate in these *lîlas*. Many come with a more general hope of benefiting from being so close to the saints. The more profane motive of 'a change of air' also plays a role.[6] The *mûsems*, therefore, not only attract devout pilgrims, most of whom are women, but also young men who seek distraction in watching the pilgrims, listening to big transistors, getting drunk and visiting prostitutes.

Seven days after the seven simultaneous *mûsems* in the Marrakech region, there is another *mûsem* in the medina of the city. This *mûsem* of Mul Ksur is concluded with a collective circumcision ceremony.[7] Marrakchis involved in local pilgrimages call the *mûsem* of Mul Ksur the *tâbi*^{c}, 'the seal' of the *mûsems*, which means that the visits to the other *mûsems* will only be valid after having visited Mul Ksur. It is the last important *mûsem* following the celebration of the birth of the Prophet and marks the beginning of the ritual low season, which lasts until Shaban, when the preparatory rites for Ramadan begin again.

The Celebration of Different Levels of Community

The Islamic Community at Large

Except for the Feast of Immolation, in none of the aforementioned feasts does the ideal of *tawḥîd* or unification of the Islamic community at large receive as much attention as it does during Ramadan. Performing the sacrifice relates Moroccans to the pilgrims in Mecca. Since Muslims over the entire world sacrifice, the Feast of Immolation symbolises the unity of the Islamic community. Except for the educated family in Gueliz, none of my informants referred directly to the sacrifice as a symbol of unification of the Islamic community. Yet, the sacrifice is seized upon as an occasion to reflect on differences between Muslims and non-Muslims. More than once, the

5. It is beyond the scope of this study to give a full description of these *mûsems*. Fernea (1976: 261–305) gives a vivid description of her visit to the *mûsems* of Mulay Ibrahim and Mul Ksur. For Mulay Ibrahim also see: Jemma (1971) and Legey (1926).

6. 'Going on holiday' is a Western phenomenon which only rich urban Moroccans can afford. For poorer Moroccans, the *mûsems* are occasions to escape the routine of everyday life. Cf. Reysoo (1988) for an account of the recreational aspects of *mûsems*.

7. Mul Ksur's real name was Abdallah Ben Udjal Al-Ghazuani. He was named Mul Ksur because he lived in a quarter of Marrakech called Al-Ksur, The Palace. Mul Ksur is one of the seven patron saints of Marrakech (cf. Castries 1924).

practice of sacrificing was compared with Christian and Jewish practices. For instance, several informants told me that Muslims have the feast of the ram and Jews have the feast of chicken. One male informant related how his mother had told him the following story:

> Each year on a particular day, all small Jewish boys in the *mellaḥ* (the Jewish quarter in Marrakech) were given a chicken to take care of. The next day, however, all chickens had disappeared and the boys were told that Muslims had stolen them. That afternoon, all Jewish families would eat chicken. This is how the Jews were taught to hate Muslims.

Women rarely refer to or discuss the Jews, who had lived in Marrakech before emigrating to Israel after Morocco's independence. The Great Feast, however, does invite such references. On the day of the feast, one of the women sharing our courtyard greeted my hostess with the words *ᶜîdkum jûᶜkum*, 'your feast is your hunger'. Both women laughed. Seeing that I did not get the joke, my hostess explained that the Jews used to ridicule Muslims during the feast with this formula. The idea behind it was that, although it was a holiday intended for people to enjoy a nice meal, they instead were busy the whole day processing the sacrificial ram into meat and had no time to eat.

Although mutton is generally associated with Muslims, adherents of other religions are also partially defined by their diet. While we were enjoying our grilled liver during the afternoon of the feast, the same woman who had made the joke gave me a thoughtful look and said: 'The problem with you Christians is that you eat pork. We eat mutton and the Jews eat chicken, but you eat pork.' Neither Ashura nor the *mulûd* were occasions on which informants compared their rites with contrasting rites and practices of non-Muslims.

The Moroccan Community

Emphasis on *al-waṭan*, the Moroccan community under the guidance of King Hassan II, is strongest on the occasion of the Feast of Immolation. The television broadcast of the sacrificial ceremony, during which the king is congratulated by Muslim ambassadors at the Feast of Immolation, and his public performance of the sacrifice, are similar to his promotion of nation-building during Ramadan. All stress his dual position of Commander of the Faithful and head of state. The Moroccan monarch is the only Muslim head of state who performs the sacrifice on behalf of his people (Combs-Schilling 1989: 222). The national level performance of the sacrifice was introduced during the early Alawi dynasty and has been carried out ever since the reign of Moulay Ismail (1672–1727). The innovation placed him in line with the Prophet Muhammed, who sacrificed on behalf of the Community of Believers. Combs-Schilling (1989: 222–3) convincingly argues that by making this link between himself and Muhammed, Moulay Ismail drew attention to his identity as blood descendant of the Prophet in order to support his legitimacy as rightful occupant of the Moroccan throne. In carrying out the act of communal sacrifice the present king draws on the same source of 'sacred performances' to claim legitimacy.

In 1982 and 1983 in particular, the king's emphasis on his dual authority was prominently displayed. The importance of the king as collective representation was dramatised when he sacrificed a ram on behalf of the whole Moroccan nation. He also 'released' others from this duty after passing a law forbidding individual sacrifices, as a measure to protect the weakened economy due to the prolonged drought. In 1988, the link between the religious atmosphere of the feast and the figure of Hassan II was again given extra emphasis when the king chose the week of the feast to launch his fundraising campaign for the Hassan II mosque in Casablanca, which is to be the largest mosque in the world after those of Mecca and Medina. Banners citing koranic texts, such as 'God will build a house in Paradise for him who builds a mosque', were suspended over streets, while the subject was discussed extensively in the newspapers and on television. Almost every day new figures on the amount of money donated by members of the royal family were provided.

As demonstrated by the importance that most of my informants attach to the king's sacrificial slaughtering, the policy of relating the feast to royalist and nationalist feelings is effective at least among the predominantly illiterate people, among whom I did my research. Some of my younger informants who had enjoyed a higher education were more critical of the king's claims to authority on this occasion. They accuse him of obscuring the real focus of the feast, which should be the commemoration of Ibrahim's faith. They explained that ignorant people confuse waiting for the signal of the local imam to slaughter with waiting for the king.

Significantly, the king does not claim any special attention on Ashura, nor does the occasion receive much attention in the media. According to my hostess, the king is against Ashura. When in 1988 Muharram was proclaimed, after only 29 days of the month Zu'lhijja, she was sure that this was one day too early and claimed that the king had deliberately moved the month of Muharram forward. In this way, Ashura would be celebrated one day in advance of its real date in order to reduce the power of magic.

The king's neglect of the celebration is consistent with the view of the majority of informants, according to whom Ashura is not an official religious feast. They emphasise that its celebration is a typically Moroccan phenomenon rather than one involving the entire Islamic community.

On the occasion of the *mulûd*, the king is back on television. He is shown attending the special prayer meeting in a mosque on the night preceding the morning the Prophet was born. The following day the newspapers publish the congratulatory telegrams which the king has received from other Islamic heads of state. In 1988 special attention was paid to the special prayer meeting for women, organised by one of the king's daughters.

Local Communities

Besides the emphasis on the king as Commander of the Faithful on the occasions of the Great Feast and the celebration of the birth of the Prophet, these celebrations deviate from Ramadan in that they do not emphasise the community of believers at large, but rather point to the stratification of this community.

Whereas during Ramadan solidarity between Moroccans is emphasised and differences in wealth are masked or denied, during the Feast of Immolation the importance of slaughtering as big a ram as possible creates an atmosphere of competition in which differences in wealth are accentuated. The size of a ram is an important indicator of status.[8] A divorced informant almost smuggled the small ram which she had bought for 400 dirham ($40) into her house, while another woman proudly paraded through her alley with an impressive ram which had cost her 650 dirham ($65). When we saw a big and fat ram on the market, the daughter of the divorced woman joked that the person who was going to buy it would probably take it out for a walk every day until the feast. In all families I visited, I was shown, and required to admire, their ram. Nearly everybody wanted me to compare their ram to the other ones I had seen, evidently expecting me to answer that theirs was the biggest or at least the fattest. I neither noticed nor heard of anyone who had distributed meat among the poor, as is done with special Ramadan food. All meat was consumed within the family.

The Great Feast is largely a family affair. The first and most important piece of meat to be shared by all family members is the liver. The liver is a highly valued organ in Morocco. Even more so than the heart, it is considered the seat of affection and compassion. For example, it is an expression of fondness to call someone

8. Cf. Combs-Schilling (1989: 224) who states that the size of the ram, especially that of its sexual organs, is a sign of the manliness of the purchaser. It also indicates how much he values his wife and children.

kebdatî, 'my liver'. Marrakchis are fond of pet- and nicknames, and *kbeyyedtî*, my small liver', is a popular pet name for aunts.[9]

Eating the liver of the sacrificial ram has important symbolic significance. It contains much *baraka*, divine power, and brings good luck for the next year, so one woman in our courtyard was very upset when in an unguarded moment a cat ran off with her skewer. Sharing the liver of the sacrificial ram is an expression of the close family bond. There is a skewer with liver for every member of the family. The skewers of those who cannot be present are kept for two or three days in case they should come and ask for 'their share (*ḥaqqhum*).

The celebration of Ashura accentuates the sexual differentiation of the Islamic community. My (female) informants stressed that the Ashura is particularly a festival for women and children. Indeed, girls and women enjoy certain prerogatives for the duration of the feast. For example, the conduct of the singing girls sharply contrasts with the modest behaviour normally expected of them, such as keeping their voices down, wearing *jellâba*s over their nightgowns when they go out, and remaining in the house after sunset. During the first ten days of Muharram the girls do not come out until eleven o'clock at night. They shout, sing and laugh loudly and tie scarves under their buttocks to accentuate their dancing movements. The songs they sing express the same defiance that can be seen in their faces:

> Hey, ho, congratulations to ourselves,
> this is yet the beginning.[10]

This chant is borrowed from soccer games, where it is sung by the (mostly male) spectators. Other songs are typical Ashura songs:

> the Eve of Ashura, we have no rulers,
> the feast of the [Prophet's] birthday,
> the men rule over us.

9. Cf. H. Geertz (1979: 341–6) who describes the broad choice of names available to Moroccans, out of which they single out a context in which to place a person and assess his or her social relationships. She argues that, contrary to men, women are not given nicknames and the limited range of naming contexts for women reflects the family-bound character of the women's world and suggests a culturally defined limitation on the assertion of individuality. My observation that women are often given pet-names confirms this view. Pet-names, such as 'my little eye', 'my little heart' etc., do not stress personal characteristics of the bearers. In almost every family women can be found who are called by these names. The contexts in which the pet-names are used are, therefore, of limited scope.

10. The text in Arabic is:
Hey, hû, mabrûk ᶜlînâ,
hâdi l-bidâya, mâ zâl mâ zâl

Oh, my Ashur,
my hair was loosened on you,
like the rope of a reel.[11]

The girls' freedom of movement and the contents of their songs are illustrative of the special rights and power that women claim on Ashura. Women were eager to tell me that, traditionally, this is the occasion on which men are supposed to buy new clothes for their wives. According to one informant, women were even able to sue their husbands if they refused to meet this obligation. She explained that this no longer holds true, since women have more freedom of movement and buy clothes more than once a year. Yet, most husbands still buy their wives a small present like a new scarf, a belt or a pair of slippers on the occasion of Ashura. In any case, women should be given, or buy, a *te^{c}rîja*, a vase-shaped drum, which is believed to prolong their lives by one year. Women also stress that husbands have no right to withhold permission for their wives to attend the parties held on the Eve of Ashura.

The magic performed on Ashura relates specifically to women who cast a spell on men to make them so 'crazy' with love that they surrender completely to their will. The third cited song, which the girls sing on their nightly gatherings during the first week of Muharram, alludes to this kind of power women can exert over men by seducing them with their beauty.

The extent to which men fear women's power of magic became clear to me when I was chaperoned on my way home from an Ashura party by the younger brother of my hostess and his friend. They were discussing the behaviour of a man who in their eyes had made himself look ridiculous by entering the house where the women's party was taking place several times to talk to his wife. One of the young men had heard somebody suggest that the woman had bewitched her husband. After a short silence his friend confirmed: 'The magic of Ashura is dangerous (*wâ^{c}er*)'.

Texts on the Ashura suggest that, in general, men share the female view. Oussaid (1988), for example, interprets the Ashura as a festival during which women and girls take revenge for the oppression they have been subjected to throughout their lives.

11. That is, as smooth and swift as a rope unwinding from its reel. According to one informant, this song is now not heard as often as it used to be in her youth (30 years earlier) when girls knew many more similar songs.

In Arabic, the words of these songs are:

lîlat l-^{c}âšúrâ', mâ ^{c}lînâ l-ḥukkâm
^{c}îd l-mulûd, yhekmû ^{c}lînâ- r-rjâl

'ahyâ ^{c}ešúrî
telqat ^{c}lîk š^{c}úrî
u š^{c}ûrî kîd ḥbâl l-jarâra

Recalling the celebration of Ashura in his home region of the Middle Atlas, he writes:

> Achoura était une fête religieuse pendant laquelle les filles de la tribu se faisaient belles et sortaient pour accoster les hommes et leur demander l'offrande. Plus que des biens, elles cherchaient le contact, l'évasion, le bonheur de prendre le temps de discuter avec un homme de leur choix. La fête de l'Achoura était celle de leur revanche sur l'oppression qu'elles subissaient le restant de leur vie. (Oussaid 1988: 140)

Although texts may not explicitly treat the character of the Ashura predominantly as a female affair, many allude to the theme of the power struggle between the sexes, which is also evident in my own material.[12] I would, therefore, argue that the feast of Ashura is a celebration of gender difference. More than during Ramadan, when, despite differences between men and women in relation to purity, on various levels of community emphasis is put on unity and differences between people are denied, during Ashura the categories of female and male in which the community at large can be divided are accentuated.

In fact, Ashura is a celebration of female power. Since in ordinary life women must obey their fathers and husbands and their power remains subordinate to that of men, Ashura is a rite of status reversal. Gender differences are accentuated by reversing the existing power relations between women and men. Rites of status reversal often occur in strict hierarchical societies. They provide a temporary release of tensions that arise if people live in conditions of extreme inequality. By turning the world upside down within the boundaries of extra-ordinary time and space, rites of status reversal make the dominant order visible, reaffirming its hierarchical principle at the same time (cf. Babcock 1978: 13–36; Turner 1969: 176).

The specific forms of female power which are celebrated during Ashura are disapproved of by both women and men: seductive power and sorcery are associated with evil and *jnûn*, spirits. The need to seek recourse in negatively valued magical practices illustrates women's lack of power in trying to get others to do what they want. As Jansen (1987: 119) puts it: 'Magic is a weak weapon in that it is individual, not very effective, and cannot address accepted

12. Cf. also Ben Talha (1965: 109); Fernea (1976: 218); Jemma (1971: 99) and Westermarck (1926 II:72). The texts cover different regions and different time-spans, which complicates comparison. Even accounts of the Ashura in Marrakech (Legey 1926; Jemma 1971; Fernea 1976) describe different practices. Only a few of these practices can be observed today. This raises the question how we are to deal with historical texts when analysing recent material. It also raises the issue of the flexibility of rites. Apparently individual elements of the rite can disappear or be introduced without causing a fundamental change in the ritual structure.

forms of dominance, just extreme abuses.' The theme of sexual differentiation recurs in the celebration of the birth of the Prophet. Although the *mulûd* is also a time for a family reunion around the lunch table, the *mulûd* is considered the special feast for men (cf. Jemma 1971: 108). The reason for this was quite obvious to my informants. One woman looked at me with surprise when I asked her why *mulûd* is the special feast for men. She replied: *ᶜlâš? n-nabî kân rajel!* 'Why? The Prophet was a man!'[13] Linking the commemoration of the key figure in Islam to men is yet another example of the view that men are better Muslims than women.

If the celebration of the Prophet's birthday proper is viewed as a special feast for men, the *mûsems*, following the celebration of the Prophet's birthday, are predominantly visited by women, although many men are also present.

Mûsems are generally denounced by young and educated people. Instead of accentuating an all-embracing community, these festivals, therefore, also exhibit the division between groups of people who adhere to the cults of the saints and those who do not.

The view that the *mulûd* is a special feast for men is not general to Muslim communities. In Turkey, women consider the commemoration of the birth of the Prophet a feast for women: their celebrations focus on the actual moment of the birth of the Prophet and identify with the mother of the Prophet, Amina (Tapper and Tapper 1987: 80). Nevertheless, there is an analogy in the way Turkish and Moroccan women participate in the celebration of the *mulûd*. In both cases, women are involved in ecstatic rituals which are disapproved of by the religious establishment. The services held by Turkish women are highly dramatic and emotional, and like Moroccan women during *mûsems*, the participants become excited and may sometimes fall into a trance-like state. Women's participation in trance cults can be seen as a critical commentary on gender hierarchy. By trance-dancing they express their problems which are thus publicly acknowledged (cf. Jansen 1987: 100).[14]

13. Invariably, my next question, whether the feast would have been a feast for women if the Prophet had been a woman, produced a roar of laughter among women. The idea that the Prophet might have been a woman was ridiculous to them. This question probably bordered on blasphemy, because some women were hesitant to answer it, although others went along with what to them was a joke and replied that, indeed, if the Prophet had been a woman, the birth celebration would have been the feast of women.

14. The preponderance of women in trance cults appears to be world-wide (Lewis 1971). Jansen (1987) suggests two explanations for this. First of all, in gender-stratified societies like those in North Africa and the Middle East, despite variations due to class, age and educational level of families, women are relatively subservient and have greater restrictions posed on them as a group than men (Jansen 1987: 99). Thus being more susceptible to social stresses and conflict, women may more often seek compensatory value in trance rituals than men. To explain the involuntary aspect of trance-dancing, Jansen adopts the argument of Kehoe and Giletti (1981), according to whom possession states may be symptoms of nutritional deficiency.

Purity

The theme of purification, which plays such a dominant role during Ramadan, is of less importance on the occasions of the other feasts. Although the person who performs the sacrifice must be pure for reasons of validity, and the house is cleaned to match that purity, the sacrificial rite itself has no purificatory value. In fact, performing the sacrifice has defiling aspects, due to the flow of blood by which it is accompanied and, I suspect, more generally due to its connotation with death. Here again, we see the same link between degrees of purity and the social hierarchy as discussed in chapter 5. The king slaughters a sacrificial animal from behind a white sheet that is held up to prevent splashes of blood from staining his garments. He does not wait to see the ram die, but walks away immediately after having cut its throat, so that the moment which all spectators have been waiting for passes quickly and the performance comes to an abrupt end. As I interpret this, the extreme composure that is associated with the purity and the high status of the king makes it necessary to avoid direct confrontation with the blood and the spasms of the agonised ram.

The same gender differences that were witnessed during Ramadan are operative here. While many men visit the public bath and dress in spotless white *jellâba*s, which express their purity, most of the women, who are busy processing the ram into chunks of meat for storage, wear old clothes and do not visit the bath until a few days after the feast.

There are two instances in which purification appears to play a role in the celebration of Ashura. First of all, those who have been mourning the first seven days of Muharram visit the public bath on the following day to perform the purification rite which concludes the mourning ritual. Secondly, as water collected at the break of day on Ashura is believed to have special powers, some people visit the public bath early in the morning. On the whole, however, purity plays a minor role on Ashura in comparison to the other feasts. Women do not give the house a special cleaning as they do before other feasts, and men do not wear white *jellâba*s on occasion of Ashura. Women who plan to attend a party on the Eve of Ashura may visit the public bath beforehand, but informants denied reference to possible religious motivations and offered the explanation of wanting to look and smell good. People who visit the cemetery must be in a pure state, which may also explain the fact that the public baths are more crowded than usual just before Ashura.

The significance of purity for the *mulûd* is comparable to its role for the Great Feast. In preparation for the feast the house must be cleaned, but the feast itself is of no purificatory value. Both men and women visit the public bath one or two days in advance, but as is the case for the Great and Little Feast, only men wear white *jellâbas* on the *mulûd*.

In order to visit the *mûsems*, a pilgrim should also be in a pure state, and many women carry white flags with the name of God written with henna – the colour white and henna being symbols of purity. Yet, according to my hostess, the areas where the *mûsems* are held are polluted by the disturbing presence of drunkards and prostitutes.

Religious Merit and Blessings

The close relationship between religious merit and blessings that was described for Ramadan also occurs on the other feasts. Where people work for *ajr, baraka* appears. During Ramadan, however, *ajr* is as actively sought as is *baraka*, while in the celebrations of the other feasts it is predominantly *baraka* which people seek to obtain.

Working for *ajr* is most recognisable during the Feast of Immolation. Indeed, performing the sacrifice is believed to render much *ajr*. In my host family, a few moments before it was slaughtered, the ram was made to eat henna and oats. Kohl was applied to its eyes in the hope of increasing the amount of *ajr* to be obtained by the sacrifice. As my hostess explained, the sacrificial ram goes straight to Paradise. Arriving there, beautified and having foods containing *baraka* in its stomach, God will know that the family by whom he was sacrificed took good care of him.[15]

People who cannot afford to buy a ram may sacrifice a ewe. The sacrifice of a ewe, however, is considered to render less *ajr* than that of a ram, albeit more than that of a goat, to which poorer people must resort. In the view of my hostess, offering anything other than a ram does not bring *ajr*, so that the only value in sacrificing a ewe or a goat comes from the meat to eat. Sacrificing a ram which

15. Another interpretation for the kohl that is applied to the eyes of the ram may be that it is thus made to resemble the ram sacrificed by the Prophet Muhammed, which had big black circles around the eyes (Combs-Schilling 1989). The embellishment of the sacrificial ram supports Combs-Schilling's contention that the ritual of the Great Sacrifice resembles the ritual of first marriage. Both the ram and the bride are embellished with kohl and henna, both are (dressed in) white and both are made to lie down and passively wait for a male to spill their blood. In the first case he accomplishes this by plunging the knife into the ram's throat, in the second case by plunging the phallus into the bride's vagina. Combs-Schilling (1989: 242) argues: 'The spilling of the bride's blood at the marriage ceremony verifies the male's dominance of biological birth, while the spilling of the ram's blood in the Great Sacrifice verifies the male's dominance of transcendent birth'. Bridegrooms are addressed in the same terms as the king, so that in both 'sacred performances' metaphorical merging occurs between individual men, the king, Muhammed and Ibrahim (ibid.: 251). She therefore concludes: 'Through the intermingling, the prince [of the Faithful, Hassan II] has his authority secured by being anchored in the persuasive immediacy of the household setting, while the heads of households have their authority elevated, made more general and more noble, by their association with the living prince' (ibid.: 252).

has lost an eye, has a broken leg, or is handicapped in any other way is invalid, and does not render *ajr*.

Westermarck (1926,II: 64) mentions the same discrimination between rams, ewes and goats and the importance of the ram's being in a good condition. However, he does not stress the lack of *ajr* but the lack of *baraka* of other sacrificial animals, compared to that of a ram. Here, again, we see the close tie between the *ajr*, which can be obtained by performing sacrifices or alms-giving, and the *baraka*, which is inherent in sacrificial food and alms (cf. chapter 6). On the basis of my data I conclude that both *ajr* and *baraka* play a significant role in the sacrifice. Compared to Ramadan, when, of the two concepts, *ajr* is of greater importance, during the sacrifice more attention is focused on *baraka*, as argued by Westermarck.

As we have already seen, the liver is believed to contain much *baraka* and must be shared by all family members. In fact, the whole sacrificial ram is a vessel of divine grace. Hence the importance that, in accordance with the prescriptions, the sacrificial animal be *ṣḥîḥ*, healthy and free of any bodily defects.[16]

The blessedness of the sacrificial ram gives rise to a wide array of local beliefs related to the distinctive powers of particular parts of its body. Like many *baraka*-related issues, most beliefs of my Marrakchi informants concerning the powers of the sacrificial ram are related to the themes of marriage, fertility and health. For example, while the ram was still bleeding to death, my hostess dipped her finger in the blood flowing from the cut and applied marks on the foreheads of the children and all the unmarried females to assure them a good partner.[17]

Obtaining *ajr* and *baraka* are also a part of the celebration of Ashura, albeit to a far lesser extent than during Ramadan and the Feast of Immolation. It is the occasion on which well-to-do people, in particular merchants, pay the *zakât*, the alms tax stipulated by Islamic law, and thus gain *ajr*. Pious people who practise the voluntary fasting recommended for Ashura also collect *ajr*. Like the 27th of Ramadan, Ashura is a date upon which *ajr* can be obtained by visiting the cemetery. The water collected at sunrise is believed to originate from the sacred source Zemzem at Mecca and contains much *baraka*. Besides bathing in it, some people store a bottle of the blessed water as a cure for illnesses. Ashura incense and Ashura

16. As in ch. 5 the link between *ṣḥîḥ* and *baraka* confirms Douglas's argument about the relation between sacredness and the condition of being complete or intact (Douglas 1966: 70–3).

17. Combs-Schilling (1989: 230) offers an alternative interpretation of this act. Just as Ismail's life was saved by the blood of the sacrificial ram, the dots of blood are applied to children in the hope that like Ismail they may grow into adulthood.

soap are also believed to contain *baraka* and are kept for the same purpose.

The celebration of the *mulûd* may also render *ajr* and *baraka*. As is the case on the 27th of Ramadan, attending the prayer meeting in the mosque during the night of the Prophet's birth yields *ajr*, as does the distribution of couscous among those praying there and the poor. Giving money to the men who parade the camels through the town is considered a form of *ṣadaqa*, alms-giving, which is also believed to yield *ajr*.

Most activities related to the festivals of saints, however, focus on obtaining *baraka*. Significantly, my hostess stated that in former days one could earn *ajr* by visiting the *mûsems* of Mulay Ibrahim and Tamsluht, but, due to the large numbers of drunken men and prostitutes now present at the festivals, this is no longer the case and only *baraka* can now be obtained. This came as a shock to her aunt, who visits the festival of Tamsluht every year and has always thought she was earning religious merit.

For many pilgrims it is of utmost importance to spend the night in the vicinity of the saint's shrine and benefit from the sojourn in his *baraka*-permeated surroundings. For the same reason the nights of trance-dancing are organised in the immediate area of the shrine, so that the saint's *baraka* can be implored to protect those who are possessed by spirits.

Recognition of the Feasts within Dominant Islam

There are two points in which the religious feasts I describe in this chapter differ significantly from the fast during Ramadan. Firstly, in general, people have less thorough knowledge of the 'correct' way to perform the rites, and secondly, there is a greater diversity in the interpretations of the celebrations.

The beliefs and practices related to the *baraka* inherent to the sacrificial ram, for example, were all recorded in the medina of Marrakech and in the squatter area outside the city wall on the right bank of the river Issil. When I discussed them with the members of the wealthy family in the *ville nouvelle*, they were both amused and irritated.[18] They knew about these practices and the mother of the family confessed that she had adhered to them in the past as well. However, her husband, a koran scholar, had forbidden her to engage in them and ordered her to restrict herself to the 'true Islam'. She now rejects such practices and associates them with 'those poor people who live within the city walls'. Her son added that these peo-

18. Their amusement derived from the fact that such old traditions still exist, while their irritation was related to their fear that I should learn wrong things about Islam and would present a distorted picture of Morocco in my book.

ple do not have any education and therefore do not know true Islam, 'they exaggerate'. He saw the willingness of poor people to put themselves into debt in order to buy a ram as another example of their ignorance and argued that God disapproves of people who go to such extremes. Mother and son explained that the true Islamic meaning of the sacrifice was to follow Ibrahim's example and express one's faith. People in the medina also described the basic meaning of the sacrifice as an expression of faith. In their view, however, their practices do not conflict with this meaning.

This is but one example of the way in which the celebration of the Great Feast demonstrates a greater variety of interpretations and practices than I encountered during Ramadan. Another example relates to the stringency of the regulations. Slaughtering an animal on the day of the Great Feast is *sunna mu'akkada ^{c}alâ al-kifâya,* obligatory for free Muslims who can afford to buy one (Mittwoch: 1913–38: 444–5). The addition *^{c}alâ al-kifâya* characterises the sacrifice as a collective duty. In Morocco, nearly every family sacrifices. Even poor people take great pains to come up with enough money to buy a sacrificial animal. Some informants were not aware of the basically voluntary character of the sacrifice but considered it a religious duty for everyone. When I confronted my Marrakvchi hostess with the rule that the sacrifice is only obligatory for people who can afford it, she responded that there is a difference between practices which are 'just' *sunna,* and practices which are *sunna mu'akkada,* imperative or definite, almost as obligatory as *mafrûḍ* (cf. chapter 1 note 6). As she interprets it, the fact that the sacrifice is *sunna mu'akkada* means that it is compulsory.[19] Another example concerns the prescriptions according to which a single person must sacrifice a sheep. For ten persons or more a camel or a cow may be sacrificed (Mittwoch 1913–38: 444–5). Moroccan informants stated that the sacrificial animal should ideally be a ram, and the religious value of other animals is downplayed. Furthermore, the prescriptions state that only the person who has bought the sacrificial animal obtains *ajr*. In the view of my informants, the *ajr* is equally shared by husband and wife.

The belief of many people that one should not sacrifice ahead of the king is yet another example of different interpretations of the rules. According to one informant, a premature sacrifice is *ḥarâm,* but others hesitated and stated that it is only 'not good' to slaugh-

19. It is significant that in Morocco more people perform the sacrifice than the five daily prayers; the latter are more compulsory according to doctrinal prescriptions. This over-evaluation of the sacrifice may be general for North African Islam: in an article where he situates the Algerian observance of the fast among the other pillars of Islam, Benkheira (1986: 46) unjustly mentions the sacrifice and omits the prayers among the religious duties.

ter one's ram before the king does. Most women were convinced that to slaughter ahead of the king renders the sacrifice invalid, such that it does not yield any *ajr*. Two women insisted that the meat of a ram which is slaughtered before that of the king will rot immediately. Some educated informants claimed that the signal of the local imam is the only correct point of reference for the exact timing of the sacrifice. In a sense, even the sacrificial practice, as I witnessed it in Morocco, runs counter to the prescriptions. In the week following the sacrifice, people who have sacrificed a ram engage in conspicuous consumption, eating lavish meals with a lot of meat for lunch and dinner and sometimes even for breakfast. Very few people distribute meat among the poor as alms, although in the prescriptions it is stipulated that the sacrificer may enjoy a third of the animal and should give away the rest (Mittwoch 1913–38: 444–5). According to my informants, only rich families sometimes sacrifice two rams, bringing one to the mosque to be distributed among the poor.

I would argue that the existence of interpretations and practices which are at variance both with each other and with doctrinal prescriptions can be explained by the fact that the official regulations are not as stringent as those relating to the fast. The latter is compulsory for all adults and anyone who breaks it without valid reason is not only sinning but also transgressing Moroccan (Islamic) law (cf. chapter 4). The prescriptions concerning the sacrifice are not regulated by law. They are less binding and therefore open to more ambiguity and personal interpretation.

Compared to Ramadan and the Feast of Immolation, Ashura is of little significance according to the Islamic doctrine. It is only mentioned as a recommended day for voluntary fasting. This may explain the incomplete knowledge informants had about the religious status and origin of the beliefs and practices associated with the feast. A case in point is the mourning ritual that precedes the celebration of Ashura. Most women agreed that mourning is 'against Islam or *ḥarâm*. Few people had ideas about the meaning of mourning. Even informants who in the past had practised mourning were not sure whose death was being mourned. Some suggested the mourning was for Ibrahim, who had been captured and burned by Jews. This is also how they explained the origin of the *ščâla*s, the bonfires that are lit in the medina and in some houses on the Eve of Ashura.[20] When I told a group of women about Shiite mourning rites in memory of Husayn, they were indignant that I compared Moroccan mourning with Shiite practices and insisted that Shiites

20. In the past, almost every alley lit a bonfire on Ashura and there were competitions between groups of boys playing the vase-shaped drums (cf. Legey 1926).

were not true Muslims but *kâfirîn*, infidels. However, two girls remembered having learned in school about the commemoration of Husayn on Ashura. They suggested that those who practise ritual mourning probably mourn over the Prophet's grandson without realising the background of their practice. This version is consistent with the view of a woman from the squatter area who stated that the ritual mourning was to commemorate the death of the sons of Lalla Fatima, the Prophet's daughter. The woman did not know their names or personal histories. In the 1920's Westermarck (1926, II: 78–9) encountered various explanations for the practice of ritual mourning across Morocco. In Fes people mourn over Hassan and Husayn, the sons of Ali, the Prophet's son-in-law. The Ait Wäryager claimed they mourn the Prophet's death, while the Ulad Bu Aziz stated that the mourning was for Baba Ashur. In Westermarck's view, Baba Ashur personifies the Old Year. He argues that the mourning rites are pre-Islamic New Year's rites which were later adjusted to fit Islam. Jemma (1971: 99) offers the same explanation.

The fact that, in many respects, the ritual structure of Ashura does not resemble that of the other religious feasts seems to confirm this hypothesis. For instance, it is not considered necessary to take purifying measures, such as cleaning the house or visiting the public bath, in preparation for the feast; neither the mosques nor the shrines play a role in the Ashura celebration; and people do not visit relatives and close friends to congratulate them on the occasion of the feast. When women were asked about these differences, some declared 'Ashura does not belong to religion'. When people are asked to mention the feasts of the Islamic year, Ashura is, none the less, mentioned among the others, and as we have seen in the section on *ajr* and *baraka*, the celebration clearly has religious connotations. This may explain why some informants, when asked about the religious status of the feast, took the vague position that *câšûrâ' men d-dîn u mâšî men d-dîn*, 'Ashura is part and not part of religion'.

It is interesting that the significance of the vase-shaped drums on Ashura is not cast in Islamic terms. One adds another year to one's life by every drum bought or received on Ashura, and breaking a drum on Ashura is a bad omen. This is one example of the specific powers which are believed to be effective on Ashura, but are not explained in Islamic terms: a girl born on Ashura has no hymen and people should not get married on Ashura, because they will have the same number of quarrels as the number of drums that are beaten on that date. This is consistent with the ambiguity expressed by women about the religious status of Ashura.

Considering the ambiguity and vagueness that surrounds the celebration of Ashura in Morocco, it would be very interesting if more historical research were conducted into the background of the practices and beliefs described here. Without further research, it would be problematic to speculate about the pre-Islamic nature of the festival. To do so would risk adopting the often unjust bias, embraced by both dominant Islam and various anthropological studies, which links practices that conform to prescriptions of orthodox Islam with men and those which contain more heterodox elements with women.

Without suggesting any causal connection between the two, it is noteworthy that it is precisely Ashura – the celebration of female power – which is marginal in the cycle of religious celebrations. As the king's neglect of the festival demonstrates, participation in the Ashura celebration is not highly regarded. Neither purity, the prestigious virtue which is more associated with men than with women, nor the mosque, the sacred space where primarily men gather, play a significant role. Apparently, the rite of status reversal cannot be carried to such an extent that it includes religious inversion. Consistent with the emphasis during Ashura on the negatively valued female power of magic and seduction, the feast is marginal in the cycle of religious celebrations. The celebration of Ashura therefore not only affirms women's subordinate position in society, but also reinforces the view that women's religious worth is inferior to that of men.

In contrast, the day on which the Prophet's birth proper is commemorated, which is viewed as predominantly a feast for men, is highly valued as an Islamic holiday. Yet, it is not accompanied by much ritual. The prayer sessions in the mosques are of a voluntary character. For many people, the celebration consists of only a good meal and a family reunion.[21] The rites related to the seven *mûsem*s that conclude the week of the *mulûd* are much more elaborate. Yet, the ritual knowledge of my informants was only vague and fragmented. Unlike the prescriptions concerning the fast, which people are always eager to learn more about, nobody seemed to be bothered by the fact that they had no overall view of the events making up these festivals. For example, time and again I was told that on the seventh day of the *mulûd* there would be seven *mûsem*s in the Marrakech region. Nobody could name all of the seven *mûsems*, however. Seven is a number of symbolic significance, which plays a role in many Moroccan Islamic practices.[22] Apparently, the number of *mûsem*s held simultaneously is more meaningful than exact knowl-

21. I attended the *mulûd* in Sidi Slimane in 1984 and in Marrakech in 1988. On neither occasion was the the ritual celebration organised by the monarch, as Combs-Schilling (1989: 157–74) describes it, referred to by informants and I suspect that it is of minor or no importance in their own celebration of the *mulûd*.

22. For example, on the seventh day after birth a name-giving party is held for babies. In Marrakech, as in other Moroccan places, there is a ritual of visiting seven saints and all feasts are considered to last seven days (cf. Westermarck 1926 for more examples).

edge of their names.[23] Another example concerns the futile journey the aunt of my hostess made to the place where she thought the religious orders would gather that day to leave for Mulay Ibrahim and Tamsluht. She found the square empty. Latifa did not seem disturbed by the fact and tried again the next day, this time with more luck.

As was the case with some of the rites connected to the Feast of Immolation, the religious status of the rites that make up the *mûsem*s is ambiguous. For a considerable number of people, especially for those who attend the festivals themselves, the *mûsem*s belong as much to Islam as the other feasts. For example, some of my informants made references to the *ḥajj* when we discussed the *mûsem*s. According to the aunt of my hostess, a minimum of seven visits to the festival of Mulay Ibrahim or Tamsluht equals the performance of the pilgrimage to Mecca. She therefore called these *mûsem*s 'the *ḥajj* of the poor'. My rich informant who lives in the *ville nouvelle* of Marrakech also associated *mûsem*s with poor people, but contrary to Latifa, she contends that *mûsem*s are against Islam and that many of the activities which take place there are *ḥarâm* or forbidden. She mentioned the slaughtering of the camel as a case in point. Before her marriage, she used to attend the *mûsem* of Mulay Ibrahim and had noted how the camel had been slaughtered by a man sitting on a horse who had beheaded her with a single stroke of his sword. This, she argued, defies the Islamic prescriptions for slaughtering. Moreover, the camel's skin was cut into very small pieces which were sold. This is even more *ḥarâm:* the *kiswa*, the black embroidered cloth covering the Kaaba in Mecca, is the only item that may be thus sold.[24]

Ramadan as a Condensation Symbol

In one way or another, one or several of the key concepts that shape the practice of fasting during Ramadan also feature in the celebration of the other religious feasts. Yet, in none of the feasts is the combination of community feelings, purity, *ajr* and *baraka* articulated as clearly as during the fast.

23. My hostess and her friend knew six names:
i. Sidi Ferz (countryside)
ii. Mulay Ibrahim (countryside)
iii. Mulay Abdallah Ben Husayn and Mulay Bu Brahim (Tamsluht)
iv. Sidi Hmed Ben Nasr and Lalla Mimouna (cemetery Bab Debagh)
v. Sidi AbdelAziz (biggest market-place)
vi. Sidi Hmed Zawia (Bab Khamis)

24. Although this lady vehemently rejected *mûsems*, she wanted me to tell her all about my visit to the *mûsem* of Mulay Ibrahim. The eagerness with which she posed her questions gave me the impression that, although she has learned to disapprove of *mûsem*s due to the influence of her late husband, she is still emotionally involved with the practices of what she called *n-nâs š-šeᶜbîyîn*, 'the folk people' or popular mass.

The emphasis which during Ramadan is put on different levels of community can be recognised during the other feasts, but more often differences between various categories of Moroccans are accentuated rather than those between the communities of Muslims and non-Muslims. The latter only receives attention during the Feast of Immolation. During Ramadan, the ideal of the Islamic community at large is represented, while in the other celebrations the stratification of the community is brought to the fore. The Great Feast demonstrates that the *umma* accommodates rich and poor people, while Ashura stresses that Muslims are either men or women. Sexual differentiation is repeated in the celebration of the *mulûd*. This is also the occasion during which differences between people who adhere to the cults of the saints and those who reject such practices are stressed most.

Aside from the celebration of the Ashura – when it is of almost no significance – purification is a recurring element in the other feasts. It is, however, only so as a pre-requisite for making the practices related to the feasts valid, and not, as is the case in Ramadan, the goal or result of such practices.

During all feasts, instances in which *ajr* is collected can be identified. Yet, at no stage is gaining religious merit so actively sought by people as during Ramadan. For the other feasts the main focus is on *baraka*. This suggests that *ajr* is closely related to the concept of purity, while *baraka* is less dependent upon it. Although transmitters of *baraka* should be protected against pollution, people can benefit from their divine power even when they are not in a ritually pure condition. My hostess's view that visiting the *mûsems* no longer renders *ajr* because of the presence of impure drunkards and prostitutes confirms this claim.

The data also suggest that *ajr* can mainly be obtained through practices which are closely linked to formal religious duties, while the range of rites that render *baraka* is much broader. This, however, does not imply that ajr is exclusively linked to formal Islamic practices and *baraka* to local ones. As the examples in chapter 6 demonstrate, activities undertaken for the purpose of obtaining *ajr* during Ramadan, such as bringing couscous to the mosque, and visiting the graveyard, are part of Moroccan tradition.

The crucial feature which distinguishes the performance of the fast from the other feasts is the stringency of its regulations. Of all the festivals that make up the ritual cycle, Ramadan is the only feast that is linked directly to a religious duty incumbent upon every mature Muslim, and the only practice which is regulated by Moroccan law. This may explain the specific preoccupation with *ajr* during Ramadan. Keeping the fast is viewed as one of the conditions for entering Paradise, and working for *ajr* is also aimed towards securing one's place in Paradise. The celebration of the Feast of Immolation and the birth of the Prophet are classified as *sunna,* recommended, while the religious status of the Ashura is ambiguous. While participation in these celebrations may enhance one's chances of going to Paradise, neglect does not necessarily forfeit them. Because of the voluntary character of these rituals it is less important for people to have thorough knowledge of the 'correct' way to perform them. This is related to a greater diversity in the native interpretations of the celebrations. There are more local beliefs and practices linked to the Feast of Immolation, the Ashura and the birth of the Prophet which are denounced by educated Moroccans who adhere to dominant Islam than is the case with activities developed during Ramadan. This may also partly be explained by the fact that the spirits, who play a prominent role in many of the (magical) practices rejected by adherents of formal Islam, are believed to be absent during most of Ramadan.

Significantly, it is predominantly women who are engaged in practices that are ignored or denounced by those who claim to represent formal Islam. Where they are excluded from prestigious participation in formally approved rites, women turn to other activities which grant them religious gratification. More particularly, they seek compensation for the *ajr* that they cannot earn through participation in the prestigious and formally approved rites by engaging in activities which are believed to render *baraka.* Islamic prescriptions, for example, prohibit the performance of the sacrifice by women, but since they are the processors of the meat, women are in a position to exploit fully the *baraka* inherent to the sacrificial animal. Due to the lack of formal religious education and, more indirectly, the association of the mosque with men, it is difficult for uneducated women to earn *ajr* through participation in the prayer meetings on the night when the birth of the Prophet is commemorated. Women's high participation in the *mûsem*s that follow may likewise be interpreted as a compensational search for *baraka*.

We can now better understand the preoccupation of women with performing deeds for *ajr* during Ramadan, when circumstances for collecting religious merit are more favourable for women. Comparison with the other feasts also sheds more light on the special significance of fasting for women as a highly prestigious activity in which they can participate on a more equal basis with men than in the formally recognised activities of the other feasts.

eight

The Liminal Month: Ramadan as a Ritual Complex

Human beings have the need to create order and classify their experiences. All societies have rituals which draw attention to the boundaries between basic categories. Liminality is a time and space of withdrawal from ordinary classification. It refers to a kind of 'no man's land' or 'betwixt-and-between' situation (Turner 1977: 37). Since normal modes of social action are suspended temporarily during liminality, it can be regarded as 'potentially a period of scrutinization of the central values and axioms of the culture in which it occurs' (Turner 1969: 156). Thus, room is created for the members of a society to reorganise their basic assumptions into new meaningful wholes (Myerhoff 1982: 129).

In this chapter I will analyse the relations between the notions of *umma*, *ṭahâra* and *ajr* by viewing them as specific articulations of liminality. The first section focuses on aspects of the fast that may be interpreted as attributes of liminality, while the following sections deal with the boundaries marked by fasting. It will be argued that the first fast of children can be interpreted as a rite of passage which initiates them into Muslim adulthood. The meaning of fasting Ramadan as an individual rite of passage is subordinate to its meaning as a collective calendrical rite, which marks the beginning of the cycle of religious celebrations.

Themes of Liminality

Umma as Communitas

The ideal of the Islamic community, which people strive to live up to during Ramadan, resembles the liminal situation which Turner has labelled 'normative communitas'. Turner argues that since ordinary categories of classification are abandoned during liminality, the roles and statuses by which people are normally differentiated also cease to exist, allowing them to form a relatively undifferentiated *comitatus,* communion of free and equal individuals. When this pure form of existential *communitas* is organised in an enduring social system this results in normative communitas (Turner 1974: 169).

To describe the social relations between people during Ramadan in terms of *communitas* would be to present an idealised image of the situation. The mere existence of rules which prescribe proper fasting behaviour implies a distinction between people who abide by them, and those who do not. Even though I estimate the number of non-fasters to be low among the people of my fieldwork, it is common knowledge that among certain categories of people, such as university students and the modernised elite, there are more people who do not practise fasting. They either withdraw from social life by leaving their homes less often or by fleeing the country. The number of Moroccans visiting the Spanish enclave of Melilla, for instance, increases considerably during Ramadan.[1]

More importantly, the fasting community remains more than 'rudimentarily structured and differentiated' (Turner 1969: 96). The frequency with which Hassan II is pictured in the mass media during Ramadan not only reaffirms his religious leadership but enhances nationalist feelings (cf. chapter 4). As a result, fasting becomes closely associated with Moroccan identity under the leadership of the Moroccan monarch. In this way the Moroccans who fast distinguish themselves from other Muslims, which runs counter to the supposition that *communitas* unites all members of a community.

Boundaries between fasting Moroccans also persist. Although my informants emphasise the shared hunger of both the rich and the poor, this is less trying for people of substance who can afford to let others work for them during the fasting month and who may spend a considerable part of the day sleeping. People who are not so well off have no means of taking it more easy during Ramadan. Also, despite the fact that women and men communicate more freely during Ramadan, gender differences concerning purity, patience and reason are prominent during the fasting month.

Furthermore, the relations between fasting people are not always as harmonious as Turner would have us believe in his description of *communitas* during liminality. After sunset most people have regained their spirits and may be cheerful and warm-hearted, but during the day many fasting Moroccans are more irritable than usual and avoid others in order to prevent quarrels or fights. While the newspapers generally emphasise the positive effects of fasting on social relations, critical articles about the moodiness of people

1. H. Driessen, personal communication.

who fast also appear under headings such as: 'Entre l'humeur et l'humour' (*Le Matin du Sahara*, 5.5.87: 6), 'Les secrets de la bonne humeur' (*Le Matin du Sahara*, 28.4.87). Several articles openly describe tense situations that arise during Ramadan, for example:

> Dans la rue ou dans les lieux de travail, des visages fermés et des corps abattus marchent au ralenti. Les regards vides se croisent sans même se reconnaître. Seul et unique souci généralisé: L'attente de l'heure de la rupture du jeûne en pensant à sa dose de nicotine, en rêvant de sa tasse de café ou en songeant, tout simplement, à une boisson gazeuse bien forte pour digérer ce que l'on a engouffré la veille! . . . ('L'esprit du jeûne', *Le Matin du Sahara*, 20.4.88: 8)

These examples of how social relations that exist outside Ramadan affect the way in which people relate to each other during the fasting month, confirm Sallnow's criticism of Turner's use of the concept of *communitas* for the liminality of pilgrimages. He contends that the simple dichotomy suggested in Turner's model between structure and *communitas* 'cannot comprehend the complex interplay between the social relations of pilgrimage and those associated with secular activities'. Despite the general ethos of egalitarianism, intra-group collectivism was matched by inter-group differentiation established through competition and reciprocity (Sallnow 1981: 176–9). Likewise, although it is certainly appropriate to stress the importance of an *umma*-ethos during Ramadan, this does not result in the eradication of differences between those who propagate or pursue it. Therefore, in so far as *communitas* features in the fasting ritual, through the emphasis on the Islamic community, it does so only as the vocabulary of liminality.

Umma, Ajr and Ṭahâra as Liminal Sacredness

In nearly all first discussions about Ramadan, people summed up the central value of Ramadan in the statement that it is *š-šhir l-mbârak*, 'the blessed or sacred month', or, in the words of the more educated, *š-šhir l-karîm*, 'the noble of distinguished month'. The second formulation alludes to the fact that during Ramadan people transcend their ordinary existence. In terms of liminality, sacredness can generally be translated as: that which is 'set apart', 'protected from the outside' or 'on one side' (cf. Douglas 1966: 8; Turner 1974: 241).

The emphasis on *umma* during Ramadan is one manifestation of the extra-ordinary character of the fasting month. By striving to live up to the ideal of the Muslim community, social life is 'set apart' from its regular course on earth. For one month, people act as if they could create 'Paradise on earth'. Even if people feel that these aspirations may be too high, in their perceptions, at least, the road to Paradise is shorter during Ramadan than during the other months of the year; those who die go straight to Paradise and for those who remain on earth a place in Paradise becomes more attainable by performing religious deeds for *ajr*. The boundaries between Paradise and earth even fade temporarily during the *laylat al-qadr*, The Night of Measure, when the heavenly gates open and may be seen by those who pray on the rooftops of their houses. This night is the most sacred night of Ramadan and, in fact, of the whole Islamic year.

The central value of purity can also be viewed as a theme of liminality; the many purification rites that are performed in relation to the fasting month protect its sacredness from the profane. As was described in chapter 2, during the last few days of Shaban, women perform elaborate purificatory activities to rid the house of the defilements of everyday life and prepare it for the sacredness of Ramadan. However, the passage from Shaban to Ramadan is not one from a state of absolute impurity to a state of complete purity. During the other months, Muslims are pure while non-Muslims are impure, and men are more pure than women. Fasting Ramadan is not simply conceived of as a state of sacredness and purity, but rather as a process of purification which reaches its climax during The Night of Measure.

After the apex of sacredness during The Night of Measure, steps are taken to leave the sacred situation and return to normal life. In Marrakech I did not notice women giving the house a thorough cleaning again as in Berkane, but in both towns the public baths were once again crowded during the last few days of Ramadan. The same applies to the markets, where people could be seen buying new clothes to wear during the feast that would conclude the fasting month. Caution is taken to keep the sacredness of Ramadan apart from ordinary existence. The prohibition to fast on the first day after Ramadan is one such measure. Another is the recommendable purification on the day of the concluding feast.

The sacredness of Ramadan can also be recognised in the fear of pollution. Nearly all 'polluting' circumstances which threaten the validity of the fast focus on bodily orifices, with prime concern for the mouth as boundary marker of the body. Any food or drink entering the mouth renders the fast invalid. Vaginal penetration and discharge of sexual fluids are equally defiling, as are menstrual blood and the fluids that leave the body at delivery. In Marrakech less tangible transgressions of the orifices leave some room for doubt, but in Berkane strong fragrances penetrating the nostrils, objectionable words escaping the mouth or entering the ears, and sensual stimuli entering the eyes are considered no less *ḥarâm* or taboo.

The reason why these orifices become taboo during the fast can be understood by turning to Douglas's (1966; 1970) analysis of body symbolism. She argues that the functions of the different parts of the body, and the way these are related to each other, offer a source of symbols for other complex structures. As the vulnerable points where the boundary of the body is transgressed in the discharge and penetration of substances, the orifices are particularly apt to represent precarious boundaries of other structures. The taboos surrounding the fast therefore serve to impose clear boundaries where they would otherwise be less distinct. A closer examination of the term *ḥarâm,* by which all the abovementioned situations are condemned whilst fasting, confirms this argument. In Moroccan Arabic the meaning of *ḥarâm* varies from 'forbidden' in religious discourse, to 'shameful' or 'damnable' in daily speech. In Standard Arabic, the root meaning of *Ḥ.R.M.* connotes the liminal qualities of 'being set apart', sacredness, protection and taboo. Under the entry of *ḥarâm,* Wehr (1976: 171) includes the following meanings: forbidden, unlawful; offence, sin: inviolable, taboo; sacred; cursed. Especially illustrative is the combination *al-arḍ al-ḥarâm,* which denotes 'no man's land', 'neutral territory'. *Ḥarâm* is a somewhat ambiguous term, for it can be interpreted as 'forbidden' in the sense of unclean, as well as 'forbidden' in the sense of ultraclean (Denny 1985: 70).

Although there are many instances in the course of everyday life during Ramadan when fasting people may hesitate or differ in opinion over whether their actions are *ḥarâm* or not (such as wetting an envelope with one's tongue to seal it, treating grazes with iodine, applying deodorant at night which keeps odours away through the fasting day), one thing is clear to everybody: food, drink and sexual contact are strictly forbidden. In terms of liminality, the taboo on such acts that are part of ordinary existence is a symbolic device to create dichotomies which separate the sacred sphere from the mundane (cf. Durkheim 1961: 468).

Dichotomies, Ambiguities and Inversions

To eat is normal, not to eat is extraordinary. This kind of play upon dichotomies can be recognised at many points during the fast. Some of the dichotomies are repeated daily:

fasting	—	eating and drinking
sexual abstinences	—	sexual activity
scarcity	—	abundance
self-control	—	indulgence
prohibition	—	obligation

Other dichotomies separate Ramadan from the other months:

trust	—	hostility
impotence of spirits	—	power of spirits
purity	—	impurity
sacredness	—	profanity

The opposition between these social categories operating in normal life may be accentuated in several ways; they may be exaggerated, rendered ambiguous or inverted. There are also dichotomies which highlight different categories of people:

men	—	women
adults	—	children
Moroccans	—	foreigners
Muslims	—	non-Muslims

The difference between these dichotomies and the opposites which were mentioned earlier is that they are more absolute: although children become adults, foreigners may become Moroccans and non-Muslims may convert, other exchanges are impossible: as a rule, men do not become women, Moroccans do not become foreigners and Muslims can formally not become non-Muslims without risking the death sentence.

The patterning of activities during the daily alternation between fasting and feasting contains aspects of inversion: normally, most eating takes place during daytime, as does going out and visiting friends. During Ramadan, eating and most social calls are postponed until night. Usually, during the nights the streets are empty and after eleven most people have gone to sleep. During Ramadan, the streets are crowded at night and people are awake during most of the night, while during daytime they sleep more and longer than normally.

Despite these changes, some activities are carried out as usual, so that people must cope with the paradox of continuing their daily routines and engaging in activities specific to the ritual of fasting; although working hours are adjusted, children still go to school and people continue to do their work, bothered as they may be by hunger and a lack of sleep due to their nightly activities. The general effect of the daily shift between fasting and feasting is therefore an inversion and a blurring of the boundaries between the patterns of activities considered fit for the day and the night.

Although the classification of activities into certain parts of the day becomes somewhat ambiguous during Ramadan, the temporal concepts 'day' and 'night' are more distinct than ever. To understand this, we have to look at the way urban Moroccans reckon clock time. People have to combine the 'Western' system of reckoning time by the hour, and the Muslim system by which the day is divided into five intervals corresponding to the five prayers.

Men almost invariably wear a watch. I suspect their frequent dealings with government institutions which employ Western clock time has made it necessary for them to adopt this system of keeping track of time. Far fewer women have watches, some of whom wear one only as a piece of jewellery when they go to a party. Although not every woman can tell time with a watch, most are able to give a rough estimate of the hour of the day. To arrange activities and meetings with friends, however, women do not employ Western clock time. One of the two basic distinctions they make is between *n-nhâr*, 'the day' and *l-lîl*, 'the night'. The day is further divided into *ṣ-ṣbâḥ*, 'the morning', and *l-*^{c}*ešîya*, 'the afternoon'. To divide the lapse of time between *ḍ-ḍhûr*, 'midday or midday prayer' and 'the night', the intervals between the prayer times are used as terms of reference. Women may arrange with friends to go to the public bath *be*^{c}*d ḍ-ḍhûr*, 'after the midday prayer' or visit each other for tea *m*^{c}*a l-*^{c}*eṣr*, 'around the afternoon prayer'. Girls should come home *m*^{c}*a l-mġurb*, 'around the sunset prayer', and children are sent to bed *mûr (be*^{c}*d) l-*^{c}*šâ'*, 'after the evening prayer'. These designations are only approximations, and the time intervals gradually merge into one another. When a woman has arranged to visit her friend 'around the afternoon prayer' she may arrive half an hour before or after the muezzin has announced the prayer time from the mosque. In fact, all her friend will know for certain is that she will arrive closer to the afternoon prayer than to the midday prayer or the sunset prayer. Since the prayers are related to sunrise and sunset, the times of the prayers vary across the seasons. The exact prayer times are published in the newspapers.

During Ramadan, all indicators of time are subordinated to the distinction *qbel l-mġurb–mûr (be*^{c}*d) l-mġurb*, 'before sunset' – 'after sunset'. Contrary to normal times, when the call of the muezzin is only used as a vague designator of time intervals, during Ramadan all attention is focused on the exact moment of sunset. *L-mġurb beḍ-ḍebt*, 'sunset exactly' marks the conclusion of a day of fasting and the beginning of a night of feasting, and it is considered objectionable to postpone breaking the fast after the announcement of sunset. No gradual passage of day into night is allowed.

Besides these changes in the categories of time, there are also instances of ambiguity and inversion with regard to the boundaries between people of different status. A case in point is the sexual distribution of space. In normal circumstances women and men spend much of their time in segregated spheres. Women spend most of their time within the private space of the house, while public female spaces include the public bath and the cemetery. Men occupy most other public spaces but in return spend little time at home. When they do, they usually remain apart from their female kinfolk.[2] The conjugal bed is the only space that is shared by husband and wife. During Ramadan this pattern is turned upside down. Partners sleep in separate beds but otherwise the spatial boundaries between women and men are blurred. Women move in the streets more freely. They do so even at night, when in normal times no decent woman should leave the house. Men spend much more time in the house during Ramadan and may even invite men who do not belong to the family into their homes.

An even more striking instance of reversal occurs during the first night of Ramadan, when children parade through the alleys of Marrakech, beating drums and singing chants in which they mock the adults who have to give up vices such as drinking and smoking during Ramadan (cf. chapter 3). This licence contrasts strongly with the deference children are expected to show at normal times. It is an example of a rite of status reversal, in which groups or categories of persons who habitually occupy low status positions in the social structure exercise ritual authority over their superiors, who in return, must accept with good will their ritual degradation (Turner 1969: 167). By reversing roles, the social categories and forms of grouping that are usually taken for granted and considered unchanging are made visible (ibid.: 176).

The distribution of the *zakât al-fiṭr,* the obligatory donation of food, exemplifies a tendency in liminality to make those who are socially marginal ritually central (cf. Turner 1974: 233).[3] What makes marginal individuals suitable for this is that, like liminal personae, they are 'betwixt and between'. Unlike liminars, however, the ambiguity of marginals is structural; they do not have the cultural assurance that their ambiguity will be resolved (Turner 1974: 233). All persons who are entitled to receive wheat on the concluding feast of Ramadan show attributes of such 'structural liminality' or have 'infamous occupations', performing tasks that place them at the outskirts of the community or handling (human) waste (cf. Blok 1981). The *ġeyyât,* oboist, and *neffâr,* trumpeter, for instance, are outside when most people are inside, and find themselves detached

2. I have given a more elaborate account of the distribution of space between urban Moroccan women and men in Buitelaar (1986). For further reading on the subject of women and space, see S. Ardener (1981).

3. For reasons of simplification I depart from Turner (1974: 233), who distinguishes between outsiders, marginals, and the structurally inferior. Here 'marginals' is used in the broad sense of those who fall between the structural arrangements of the social system or who occupy positions on the fringes of society.

from the commmunity when they occupy their position on top of the minaret, half way between heaven and earth. Due to their association with the mosque and the performance of religious duties, the *ġeyyât* and the *neffâr* are respectable persons compared to two other alms-receiving individuals whose occupations take them out into the streets when other people are asleep: the *beyyât,* the night watchman, and the *mûl z-zbel,* the garbage collector. Handling 'matter out of place', left-overs and waste, the status of the garbage collector is even lower than that of the watchman. His association with uncleanliness resembles that of another category of alms-receiving individuals: the women who work in the public bath. Not only do these women handle human waste and operate in the liminal space of the public bath, but they deviate from the Moroccan value that women should not operate in the public sphere or work for money.[4] The midwives who come to the door to collect their share of the wheat are associated with the liminality inherent to giving birth.

The social status of the marginal people who receive wheat towards the end of Ramadan is ambiguous. On the one hand they are despised for their association with dirt and being outsiders. On the other hand, the indispensability of their activities to the protection of order is recognised and to a certain extent respected. It is this ambiguity that makes these people so suitable as subjects of ritual attention by which the liminality of Ramadan is expressed.

If liminality 'represents the midpoint of transition in a status-sequence between two positions' (Turner 1974: 237), the next question to be answered is what kind of patterns of social space and time Moroccans distinguish through the fast.

The First Fast

Most of the people whom I talked with had recollections of the first time they had fasted Ramadan. One or two years before they began full participation in the fast, they had fasted one to three days around the 27th of Ramadan. Although boys may receive some special treatment on this occasion, the ceremony organised for girls at the end of their first fasting period is usually much more elaborate; they are dressed and sometimes carried around on a table like a bride. To break the fast, their mother gives them a date and a glass of milk, which are the same symbolic foods offered to brides.

In his seminal book on rites of passage, Van Gennep (1960: 175) pointed out that the importance of 'first time' activities is universal and states that everywhere they are accompanied by special rites.

4. Cf. Buitelaar (1985b) and Jansen (1987) for an account of the liminality of the public bath and the women who work in it.

The ceremony marking the first fast may be interpreted as such a 'first time' rite of passage by which the participants are separated from childhood. Although the 'neophytes' are separated from younger children, they do not yet belong to the adults who fully participate in the fast. Being 'betwixt and between', they are situated in an ambiguous and indeterminate situation which characterises the transitional phase of a rite of passage. This partly explains why the girls are dressed and treated as brides; their situation resembles the liminal position of a bride, who no longer belongs to the category of girls, but, until the consummation of the wedding, does not yet belong to the category of women either.

Being lifted off the ground, in this case being carried on a table, is a recurring feature in rites of passage.[5] It is a spatial expression of liminality, emphasising the extraordinary position occupied by the novice. Literally lifted out of her previous position, her floating in the air symbolises that she is neither here nor there, belonging to neither one category nor the other, until she is integrated into the social structure again, where she will occupy a new position with new duties and a new status.

Although this holds true for a bride, who becomes a woman very soon after she is put down on the ground, the lifting of girls who have completed their first fasting day only alludes to their liminality. Like boys who have performed the first fast, they remain in a liminal position over an extended period of time before they join the community of people who fast regularly. This may vary from one or two years in the case of girls, to several more in the case of boys, depending on when they are considered to have matured. For girls this is related to the onset of menstruation, roughly at the age of fifteen (cf. Davis and Davis 1989: 45). For boys, indicators of maturity are less clearly defined. Male informants of Davis and Davis named beard growth and adult physique as signs of maturation. In practice, by the age of seventeen most males observe the fast.

Since all mature Moroccans are expected to fast, Ramadan is a symbolic marker of beginning adulthood.[6] When a person begins to observe the fast, it confirms that she or he has grown up to meet the responsibilities of being a full-fledged member of the Muslim community. In this sense, Ramadan can be interpreted as a rite of initiation or status elevation. However, after the ceremony following the first accomplished fasting day, neither the liminal position

5. Cf. Westermarck (1926, I: 240) who mentions that pilgrims returning from Mecca ride rather than walk and are carried over the threshold of their house. In Western culture the tradition of the bridegroom lifting his bride over the threshold of their new house can be interpreted in the same vein.

6. Maturation and observing the fast are so closely linked that Davis and Davis (1989) used information on the number of Ramadans fasted as a measure for physical development in their research on adolescence.

of the initiates nor their first complete observance of the fast receives any ritual attention. Since most rites of passage are invested with rich mid-liminal symbolism, one can ask why so little symbolism accompanies the transition from the status of a child who has accomplished the ordeal of fasting one or two days, to that of a fully grown fasting member of the Muslim community.

The answer lies in the fact that participation in the fast is only an intermediate step in the development towards Muslim adulthood. Although 'fasting makes the Muslim' (cf. chapter 4), in the views of Moroccans the requirements of Islam are only completely met at marriage: *z-zawâj ykemmel d-dîn*, 'marriage completes the religion' and *z-zawâj nuṣṣ d-dîn*, 'marriage is half of the religion' are popular sayings. Furthermore, only at marriage is a person held fully responsible for her or his actions as an adult. Unlike the flaws of married people, a mishap of someone old enough to observe the fast but not yet married may be laughed off as a whim of youthful behaviour.

For males, the transitional phase between having been accepted as a grown-up fasting member of the community and marriage to confirm adulthood extends over a longer period of time than for females. Both in Marrakech and in Berkane, 18 is considered the ideal age of marriage for females and 25 for males. For the latter, the age of marriage in practice is higher. Given the high rate of unemployment, it is difficult for many males to accumulate the capital needed for the marriage payments at an early age. In the past, the age difference for marriage was even larger, because females married younger. As a result, the first observance of the fast by girls corresponded more closely with marriage and her status as an adult and full member of the Muslim community. This explains why the ceremony that concludes the first fasting day is more elaborate for girls than for boys. For a girl, the significance of the occasion as a sign that adulthood and marriage are close at hand is more evident.

Also, for girls the ceremony is the first occasion which marks the development of their Muslim identity. For boys, the first step in acquiring religious identity is circumcision, which may take place any time between the ages of two and six. Like the bride-like treatment of girls on the occasion of their first fasting day, the ceremony that boys undergo at circumcision contains aspects that resemble rites for bridegrooms. The symbolic lifting from the ground, as observed at the ceremony of the first fast for girls, also occurs in this rite.[7]

7. Although circumcision rites vary regionally, certain features appear to recur: the boy to be circumcised is dressed like a bridegroom and a stick with mint and a white cloth such as normally carried in bridal processions is put at his side. Rich families let their son circumambulate the mosque on horseback. In rich and poor families alike, the boy is not allowed to walk. Before circumcision he should be carried by his mother; after circumcision preferably by his paternal grandmother (cf. Reysoo 1985: 48; Westermarck 1926, I: 240).

In both cases the allusion to a wedding establishes a link between this first step in the development towards adulthood and Islamic identity, and marriage as the concluding step in this process. Although complete observance of the fast during Ramadan symbolically marks the beginning of adulthood, it represents only an intermediate phase in the process of reaching Islamic adulthood. Its significance as a rite of initiation is therefore subordinate. The first fasting day is accompanied by ritual precisely because it is 'the first time [that] counts' (Van Gennep 1960: 175). The transition to complete observance of the fast needs only little ritual attention, as the definite passage into Islamic adulthood occurs at marriage, which is accompanied by much more symbolism characteristic of life-crisis ritual.

Fasting as a Calendrical Rite

The significance of the fasting month as an individual rite of initiation into Islamic adulthood is subordinate to its significance as a collective calendrical rite. Fasting is not a practice that individuals perform only once in a lifetime to symbolise their incorporation into society; it is an annually recurring ritual in which most adult Moroccans participate. The annual round of life and the familiar flow of time is disrupted by it. For an entire month, time is ordered in an extraordinary fashion which has a stong impact on all spheres of social life.

To assess the significance of fasting Ramadan as a time-ordering ritual we must locate its position within the various Moroccan patterns of accounting for time (cf. Leach 1961: 135).[8] Like most Moroccans living in urban areas, Marrakchis have to find their way through two different kinds of calendar time, the Gregorian solar calendar and the Muslim lunar calendar (cf. Eickelman 1977).[9]

The Gregorian calendar is used in government institutions and business offices. Most people are familiar with the French names and the sequence of the months of this calendar, and most of my informants were aware of the year and month of the Gregorian calendar they were living in. Despite this knowledge, the Gregorian calendar is rarely used as a frame of reference by which events in the past are remembered; least of all by illiterate people, many of

8. Our experience of time has many aspects: repetitive time, for example the coming and going of seasons; irreversible time, such as the experience that we are ageing; the pace at which time passes; the relation between past, present and future, which may be circular, linear or pendular time; calendar and clock time, etc. (cf. Leach 1961; Eickelman 1977). Here, we are primarily concerned with the way events in the immediate past and present are classified within the categories of calendar time.

9. The lunar calendar is 354 or 355 days long. Therefore, over a period of 36 years, there is a complete cycle of intersection between the Muslim lunar calendar and the Gregorian solar calendar.

whom, especially older people, do not know their own age or the year in which their children were born.

The exact details of the Muslim lunar calendar are less known to Moroccans than those of the Gregorian calendar, the divisions of which are forced upon them in all contacts with government and commercial institutions (cf. Eickelman 1977: 45). Paradoxically, the Muslim calendar is of greater significance as an instrument for organising time and categorising events within personal histories. The Classical Arabic names of the Islamic months are hardly known by the illiterate. The names of most months have been substituted by Moroccan Arabic ones:

	Classical Arabic	Moroccan Arabic	Moroccan terms in English
1.	*muḥarram*	*^{c}ašûr*	the Tenth (day of the new year, Ashura)
2.	*ṣafar*	*šaye^{c} ^{c}ašûr*	following the Tenth
3.	*rabî^{c} al-awwal*	*l-mulûd*	the Birth (of the Prophet)
4.	*rabî^{c} aṯ-ṯânî*	*šaye^{c} l-mulûd*	following the Birth
5.	*jumâdâ al-ûlâ*	*jamâd*	Jamad
6.	*jumâdâ al âḵira*	*jamâd t-tânî*	Jamad II
7.	*rajab*	*šihr l-ġufrân*	the month of Forgiveness
8.	*ša^{c}bân*	*še^{c}bân*	Shaban
9.	*ramaḍân*	*ṛemḍân*	Ramadan
10.	*šawwâl*	*l-^{c}îd ṣ-ṣgîr*	the Little Feast
11.	*ḏû al-qa^{c}da*	*bîn l-^{c}iyâd*	between the Feasts
12.	*ḏû al-ḥijja*	*l-^{c}îd l-kbîr*	the Great Feast

The names that in daily talk have been substituted for the official doctrinal names demonstrate the social significance of the Muslim calendar for Moroccans. Most Moroccan names are derived from the position of the specific month *vis-à-vis* the religious feasts. Indeed, the annual religious cycle provides the main frame of reference by means of which my informants order events in the immediate past and future, for example: 'She got married just before Ramadan'; 'My sister will be coming for the Great Feast'; 'School begins again just before the Ashura'. Since school semesters are based on the Gregorian calendar employed by the state, this last quotation is a telling example of the way in which this system for keeping track of time, so distant from the experience of Moroccans, is made sense of by relating it to temporal categories represented by the cycle of religious feasts, which more closely reflect cultural experience.

Only four months have retained their formal names in Moroccan Arabic. *Jamâd* and *jamâd t-tânî* may be considered dialectical adaptations of *jumâdâ al-ûlâ* and *jumâdâ al- âkira* which have not undergone semantic change. This can be explained by their position within the religious cycle; the distance between these two months and the nearest religious feasts is too great for them to be associated with these feasts. They constitute the 'low season' of the religious cycle.

Shaban and Ramadan have retained their original names for the opposite reason; they mark the beginning of the religious 'high season', which extends from Shaban to Mulud and reaches its apex in the period between Ramadan and the Great Feast. While the other religious feasts are restricted to fixed dates within the months named after them, the activities associated with the fast extend over the whole of Shaban and Ramadan. Furthermore, Shaban and Ramadan are distinguished from the other months as the two 'most blessed months' of the year. Together these factors may explain why the names of these two months have not been transformed in Moroccan Arabic in order to link them to the religious activities occurring then; stating their names is equal to summing up the sacredness and the activities associated with them.

Since Shaban is blessed primarily because it is the preparatory month to the fasting month, Ramadan stands out most in relation to all other months of the Muslim calendar. This is expressed in the statement *remḍân š-šihr l-mbârak*, 'Ramadan is the blessed month'. The special character of Ramadan is the basis for its key significance in the Moroccan classification of time (cf. Eickelman 1977). When I asked my informants to list the religious feasts, they invariably mentioned Ramadan first, naming the other feasts in chronological order from this starting point. In their view, the religious cycle begins with Ramadan and ends with the Mulud. This is confirmed by the way in which the celebration of each feast contains an aspect which links it to the next. The starting point of this chain of links is the end of Ramadan; people who have received *fiṭra*s, the wheat handed out as alms towards the end of Ramadan, store this wheat until the Great Feast. It is then prepared in the bread that is eaten with the meat of the sacrificial sheep. In Marrakech it is a tradition to preserve the tail of the sacrificial sheep, which on the occasion of Ashura is served with couscous. On the night of the Ashura, women and girls sing a song in which they state that they will not be ruled by men until the advent of Mulud. Only the trance nights held shortly after Mulud do not anticipate the next feast as clearly as the events that link the other feasts, in reference to which the next feast is always mentioned. The celebration of Mulud marks the beginning of the religious 'low season', lacking the impulses of *baraka*, blessedness or sacredness, which are supplied at short intervals by the feasts preceding it. I, therefore, prefer to view the trance nights concluding Mulud as a preventive measure which placates the spirits, who have more freedom of action during the period of decreased blessedness. Subsequently, the 'farewell parties' for the spirits performed in Shaban mark the end of the period of their free reign and the new beginning of a period of increased blessedness.

Even though it is the ninth month of the Islamic year, Ramadan is associated with the beginning of a new year; breakfast on the day concluding the fasting month was offered to me with the words 'eat the first breakfast of the New Year' (cf. Buskens 1987: 121).[10] The Islamic New Year proper is celebrated on Ashura. The celebrations of Ramadan and Ashura share several characteristics which the other feasts lack. Both are marked by a fasting period (albeit compulsory in the first case and voluntary in the second); both are accompanied by children playing vase-shaped drums;[11] on both occasions women can safely leave their homes at night; visiting the cemetery is part of both rituals; both are occasions for alms-giving; both are occasions of great anxiety regarding magical practices. These parallels suggest that both celebrations beginning the new year are linked. Yet, Ashura only plays a minor role in the classification of time. Recent years are counted back based on the number of Ramadans rather than the number of Ashuras that have passed. The passing of years according to the Gregorian calendar is likewise neglected. The significance of Ramadan as the principal means by which Marrakchis give temporal shape to their experiences, and its quality as marker of the beginning of a new religious cycle, make it the most important calendrical rite for Marrakchis and for most urban Moroccans.

One tentative suggestion to explain the fact that Ramadan plays such an important role in Moroccan time reckoning may be that it is a reaction to the introduction of European time reckoning in Morocco by the French. This kind of time reckoning is still employed by Moroccan government institutions. Although adjustments have been made to accommodate the Friday prayer meeting in the mosque, Morocco is one of the few Islamic countries in the Middle East where the government has not restored Friday as the day on which its institutions are closed, but has maintained Saturday and Sunday as the official weekend. This raises the question whether the fast has always been important in the Moroccan cycle

10. Ramadan has been interpreted as a kind of New Year celebration by many Western scholars studying Islamic texts, which has led to an elaborate debate concerning the origin of the fast of Ramadan (cf. Wagtendonk 1969).

11. Cf. Needham (1967: 611) who describes the general use of percussive instruments to mark transitions.

of religious celebrations, or whether it has become so as contacts with non-Muslim peoples intensified and Moroccans increasingly felt the need to reassert their Muslim identity. Since there is hardly any historical evidence on the practice of fasting, let me, by way of conclusion, offer some suggestions for further research.

The fact that in Morocco a strong taboo is placed on breaking the fast while this is much less the case in other countries in the Middle East, such as Egypt and the former Yemen Arab Republic, suggests that the interpretations of the fast are closely interwoven with local patterns of experience. Morocco's geo-political position on the border of the Islamic world may be a factor in explaining the importance attached to fasting as a marker of Muslim identity.

Combs-Schilling (1989) demonstrates how Morocco responded to the European assaults when, during the fourteenth and fifteenth centuries, an economic and military crisis ravaged the country by returning to the foundations of Islamic faith. The reconstituted monarchy emphasised the bloodline which tied them to the Prophet Muhammed. The Saadian sultan al-Mansur, who ruled Morocco from 1578 to 1603, introduced the monarch's performance of the sacrifice on behalf of his people during the Feast of Immolation and the celebration of the birth of the Prophet. Deverdun mentions that the same sultan also introduced the practice of organising religious lectures during Ramadan. After reading the Koran he would distribute alms among the poor (Deverdun 1959: 426). This suggests that the preoccupation with boundaries which characterises the practice of fasting reflects the recurrent struggles of the Moroccan dynasties to maintain and protect the precarious boundaries of their Islamic states and keep Western Europe at bay.

Fasting has always been a general phenomenon in the region. The Jews and Christians against whom the Muslim identity had to be reasserted also practised fasting. Much as the celebration of the *mulûd* was introduced in Morocco as an Islamic counterpart of the Christian celebration of Christmas (cf. Kaptein 1989), the Islamic practice of fasting Ramadan may have been emphasised to counter the Jewish and Christian forms of fasting.[12]

If more historical evidence would support this hypothesis, the same line of thinking might be extended to explain why many of the activities which Berkanis denounce as *ḥarâm* or forbidden during the fast are merely *makrûh* or objectionable from a Marrakchi perspective. It might be that these variations can partly be explained by the different roles the towns have played in Moroccan history.

12. A parallel may be drawn with the initial institution of the fast, which developed in reaction to Jewish and Christian fasting practices (cf. ch. 1).

Fes and Marrakech have been the two centres of Morocco for nearly nine centuries. The dynasties which founded Marrakech and chose it for their capital were all religiously inspired: Almoravid and Almohad are derived from the Arabic *al-murâbitûn*, 'Those who are tied to God', and *al-muwaḥiddûn*, 'Those who believe in the Oneness of God', while the Saadians and Alawites claim descent from the Prophet Muhammed. Also, as early as the eleventh century, Marrakech became a major centre for religious learning (cf. Eickelman 1985). In this context, Marrakchis have developed a strong historical awareness of their own political-cultural and Muslim identity.

On the other hand, Berkane lies on the periphery of the Moroccan state and owes its existence to the French Protectorate. The French interpreted the northern people's rejection of the political legitimacy of the sultan as a sign that the Berbers had only been Islamicised superficially. Berbers spoke their own language instead of Arabic, the tongue of Islam, which endorsed the idea that, at heart, Berbers were not Muslims. This justified the promulgation of the *Dahir Berbère* or Berber Policy in 1930, as a result of which Berbers no longer fell under Islamic law, but under 'tribal law'. Tribal leaders were appointed, who were supervised by the French (cf. Bidwell 1973; Burke 1972). The Berber policy became the target of Moroccan nationalism.

The tendency of Berkanis to interpret the prescriptions of the fast more strictly than Marrakchis may reflect a need to reassert membership in the community of Moroccan Muslims. Fasting, with its quality of *tawḥîd*, unification of all Muslims, may have gained special significance for reaffirming Moroccan Muslim identity.

On the other hand, the strict observance of the fast and other doctrinal prescriptions by Berkanis may also be a more recent phenomenon. According to De Mas (personal communication), it is only since the early 1970s that many mosques have been built in this part of Morocco. He attributes the intensified religiosity to the influence of fundamentalist organisations that have been active in the region. In the 1970s and 1980s, the town of Nador, with which Berkane has close contacts, was the seat of two fundamentalist organisations (Tozy 1984: 306). This may at least explain the extreme strictness displayed by the members of my host family in Berkane. When he was in his late teens, the youngest son (now in his mid-twenties) had been a member of the 'Muslim brothers', as his mother called it. She was very negative about his experiences. 'They' had put powerful and bizarre things into her son's head until he was unable to think properly. He quit school and spent the entire day praying in the mosque. He even refused to attend his sister's wedding, since singing and dancing was *ḥarâm* in his view. My hostess was very glad that after three years her son 'had recovered from his illness'. Despite this negative attitude, it is possible that the members of my host family have been influenced by their son and brother and have been taught by him to be more strict in their interpretations of the prescriptions.

Conclusion

In this study, I have described Ramadan in Morocco by addressing two issues: first, what it is that makes fasting a meaningful act for Moroccans, and second, in what ways the practice of the fast is embedded in the Moroccan world-view. To this end, I have analysed three notions through which Moroccans construct the practice of fasting. Performance of the fast distinguishes Muslims from non-Muslims. Simultaneously going through the extraordinary, repetitive routine of fasting at daytime and feasting at nighttime connects Muslims over the entire world, marking off the *umma* or community of believers who express their loyalty to God by following his Prophet Muhammed. This unification of the Islamic community is emphasised not only at the level of the Greater Umma encompassing all Muslims. Notions of *al-waṭan*, the (Moroccan) nation, and *qarâba*, 'closeness', are likewise stressed, the former through restoration of Moroccan traditions and the prominent role King Hassan II has created for himself to play during Ramadan, the latter through the intensified sociability of kin, friends and neighbours.

More than any other act of worship, fasting during Ramadan permeates all spheres of life, public and private. Women's participation is more manifest in the fast than in other collective rites, in which men appear to be the leading actors. Expressing membership of the *umma* through fasting is, therefore, of special significance to women. Consistent with the distribution of responsibilities between the genders, women are most active in exchanging Ramadan delicacies and visits among the *qurâb* or 'close ones'.

Another key notion in performance of the fast is *ṭahâra*, purity. Not only must fasters be in a pure condition for their fast to be valid, but performance of the fast itself is seen as a physical and moral purification process with beneficial effects on health. The notion of *ṭahâra* is linked to the notion of *ṣaḥḥa,* health. Fasting is believed to 'clean' the stomach and to allow vital organs to come to a rest. Fasting involves both the body and the mind: people who fast ideally focus on God and avoid arguments. As a reward, past sins are forgiven by God at the end of Ramadan. This moral purification not only affects fasting individuals, but also brings about a regeneration of society at large.

In the case of women, the purification process is hampered by menstruation. Their compulsory breaking of the fast during the days that they are in this impure state is interpreted as a sign of weakness and their compensatory fasting later in the year is not valued as highly as fasting during Ramadan. Women have developed several strategies to make up for these restrictions, one of which is working harder for *ajr*, religious merit, than men.

Ajr is the third notion which shapes people's fasting activities and their interpretation thereof. The *ajr* that is earned by performing religious deeds will be credited on the Day of Judgement, thus facilitating one's entrance into Paradise. Ramadan is the pre-eminent month to undertake acts for *ajr*, since it is believed to be an effect of the sacredness of the fasting month that good deeds are rewarded twice as much as during the other months of the year.

Praying the special Ramadan prayers and spending the night of the 27th of Ramadan in the mosque reciting the Koran are ways to earn *ajr* that are specific to men, while women tend to perform good deeds for *ajr* by distributing *ṣadaqa* or alms, usually in kind. They also emphasise that *ajr* is earned by demonstrating *ṣabr* or patience, which they conceive of as a specific female quality.

On an analytical level, the three notions of Islamic community, purity and religious merit are part of a complex configuration. Not only does each of the terms refer to a set of related notions, but they are also interrelated: purity is only attainable by members of the Islamic community, while religious merit can only be collected by those who are in a pure state. On a more abstract level, they have in common the characteristic of realising, in one way or another, unification. The native term for unification, *tawḥîd*, was mentioned by informants in relation to the quality of the fast of approaching the ideal of *umma*. As a doctrinal concept, *tawḥîd* refers to the oneness of God and the unification that believers seek with Him by total submission and service. I would argue that the entire practice of fasting can be interpreted as an exercise in unification. Linking Muslims everywhere in the world in a joint action of alternately fasting and feasting, the fast unifies the Islamic Community. The conscious effort to abstain not only from eating, drinking and sexual contacts but also from quarrelling and sinful thoughts is an example of the unification of the body and the mind. Since it brings one's possible place in Paradise closer within reach, *ajr* can be interpreted as a kind of unification of life on earth and the afterlife in Paradise.

While one or several of the themes of various levels of community feelings, purity and religious merit can be recognised in Moroccan celebrations of other Islamic feasts (the Feast of Immolation, the Ashura or New Year's celebration, and the celebration of the birth of the Prophet), the way these notions combine in the celebration of the fasting month is unique.

Despite the fact that Moroccans express the meanings of the fast in terms of universal Islamic values, the combination and especially the articulation of these values must be understood against the background of the Moroccan world-view. The soup called *ḥrîra* has come to symbolise the 'Moroccan way' of fasting, and every night during Ramadan, many bowls of *ḥrîra* are taken across the streets to be handed out to poor fellow Moroccans, so that they can share in the joy of the moment during which the whole Moroccan nation breaks the fast by consuming this traditional soup.

King Hassan II's pointed presentation of himself during the fast as Commander of the Faithful and blood descendant of the Prophet is another powerful example. Telescoping representations of Muhammed, the state and the family, Hassan II becomes an archetypal man: he is the popular representation of collective self, the symbol of Moroccan identity. As in other important rituals, the monarch has become the centre of the fast. He acts like the father of a large family, the Moroccan people, on behalf of which he attends the annual Ramadan conference with other representatives of the *umma.*

The strong accent on purity during Ramadan is probably a regional phenomenon. Fasting is a practice which invites associations with purification, but the extent to which purity is emphasised in Morocco is exemplary of the general preoccupation with purity in the Maghreb (Mauretania, Morocco, Algeria, Tunisia, Libya). Public baths, for example, were introduced under the influence of the Ottoman Empire, but nowhere in the Middle East have they become as popular as in Morocco and Algeria. Large numbers of the urban population in these countries visit the public bath once a week. For reasons of impurity, Muslims in the Maghreb are more strongly opposed to Christians who touch the Koran than are Muslims in the Levant. For the same reason, in Morocco non-Muslims are denied access to mosques. The first Resident-General of Morocco, Lyautey, first imposed this interdiction in order to avoid tensions. It is worth noting that the prohibition has remained valid in contemporary Morocco, while similar restrictions do not exist for most mosques in the Levant. One reason for this is that the Malikite school of Islamic law, which is followed in the Maghreb, puts more emphasis on the concept of *ṭahâra* than the other law schools do. Subsequently this preoccupation with purity may have been reinforced by the European domination. By protecting themselves against the impurity of unbelieving invaders Maghrebian Muslims could reassert Muslim identity and claim religious superiority while being subordinated economically and politically.

Claiming purity may, indeed, be an expression of dominance. The fact that men wear white overcoats on the concluding feast of Ramadan while women generally do not is an example of men's general dominance in gender relations that finds symbolic expression in an interpretation of *ṭahâra,* which is more highly valued in men than in women.

The preoccupation of women with performing deeds for *ajr* is a counterbalance to the different appreciation of the religious worthiness of men and women. The specific forms of the deeds which women perform for *ajr* must also be understood within the context of Moroccan values of food-sharing and hospitality.

The view that *baraka* and *ajr* are two sides of the same coin illustrates how Moroccan patterns of communication with the divine reflect the way they arrange transactions with each other. Furthermore, because the notion of *ajr* is paired to the notion of *baraka,* it has become 'Moroccanised'. In the Moroccan interpretation of *baraka,* the presence of saints who mediate between God and individual believers plays an important role. *Baraka* may be actively sought and passed on to others. Likewise, people actively seek *ajr* by performing religious activities. In some cases, it is also believed possible to pass it on to others. The activities that women perform to gain *ajr* are less often strictly private acts of piety than activities concerned with the well-being of others. This confirms the general tendency that women's religious activities are immediate and personal, and focus on the well-being of family members and other 'close ones'. In the way that Moroccan women perform deeds for religious merit, *ajr* has thus become a more concrete notion than in doctrinal explanations, in which the concept of *ajr* is highly abstract, referring to a direct and individual relation between God and the person who seeks *ajr.*

The local practices and interpretations of the fast which are described in this study often digress from, but do not necessarily contradict the prescriptions for fasting. That most Moroccan women give the house a thorough cleaning before the fast begins and sleep separated from their husbands during Ramadan are examples of a strong preoccupation with purity which goes beyond purification rules but does not conflict with them. The same applies to the special significance of patience and alms-giving in the religious experience of women and their preoccupation with working for *ajr.*

The way these concepts shape women's fasting activities demonstrates that, as active participants in what is usually labelled 'official Islam', women may articulate meanings which are not central to dominant Islam but are not contradictory to it either. It is therefore a misrepresentation to draw a rigorous distinction between 'official Islam' and 'informal Islam' and conflate it with the sexual dichotomy.

As Tapper and Tapper (1987: 72) argue, different aspects of the religious system may be the province of one sex or the other. The husband of the woman who stated that fumigation of the house on the evening of the 27th of Ramadan is a precaution against spirits who are released during that night, thought it necessary to reject his wife's explanation in the presence of a Western researcher whom he assumed to know the tenets of 'true Islam'. Nevertheless, he did not forbid his wife to carry out the fumigation rite as I presume he would have done had he really been convinced that the practice was against the doctrinal prescriptions. Also, distribution of the *zakât al-fiṭr* is considered a responsibility of the male head of the household towards his family, while it is women's responsibility to attend to the well-being of deceased relatives by cleansing their graves on the day of the 27th Ramadan and distributing alms on their behalf. On the basis of the data, we may conclude that when women are excluded from religious activities which are highly valued within dominant Islam, they may develop alternative activities. On the night of the 27th of Ramadan, for example, men gather in the mosque and earn *ajr* by reciting the Koran throughout the night, while women visit saints and implore *baraka* through their mediation.

The analysis of *umma, ṭahâra* and *ajr* as themes of liminality yields an insight into the way these central notions of the Moroccan world-view are reproduced and regenerated. Normal patterns of classification fade or are turned upside down during Ramadan. This has the effect of drawing attention to the basic assumptions that underlie Moroccan conceptions of the world. Individuals who for the first time participate in the fast learn what it means to be a full member of the Islamic community. The liminality of Ramadan also brings to the fore how far daily life has strayed away from the ideals of the Islamic community. As the most important collective calendrical rite, fasting offers the opportunity to purify and restore the disturbed social order.

Liminality not only functions to reproduce world-views, but may also provide room for adjusting them to changes in the experiences of people. The indeterminate nature of liminality offers room for scrutinising basic assumptions about the world and reorganising them into new meaningful wholes. This raises the question whether the basic values of the Islamic community, purity and religious merit have always been as important in the performance of the fast, or whether they have become so as contacts with non-Muslim peoples intensified and Moroccans increasingly felt the need to reassert their Muslim identity. The fact that al-Mansur was the first sultan to organise religious meetings during Ramadan at a time when Morocco's sovereignty was threatened by European powers, seems to suggest this may have been the case. Answering this question would require an investigation into the history of the performance of the fast in Morocco and comparisons with fasting practices elsewhere in the Islamic world.

Appendix: The Folly Fast

The purport of this book has been that performance of the fast is serious business; in the view of Moroccans, fasting is a sacred duty to which all one's activities during the blessed month should be devoted.

Notwithstanding the grave importance of the fast, Moroccans are gifted with the virtue of mocking their own fasting practices time and again, be it in jokes, in television programmes or, as will be demonstrated in the following cartoons, in newspapers.

The cartoons which I append here are taken from the daily newspaper *L'Opinion*. The strength of each of these cartoons is that they present images which most Moroccans will identify with their own fasting experiences.

Some cartoons point to the social control which people exert on one another to make sure that everyone keeps the fast:

The following three cartoons illustrate that fasting is paradoxically accompanied by a preoccupation with food, more particularly with the special Ramadan soup *ḥrîra,* the comsumption of which marks the Moroccan way of breaking the fast:

In the next cartoons, the preoccupation with food is paired with another 'hot issue' during Ramadan: the problem of sleeping during daytime:

A popular joke which people like to make during the last half hour before sunset marks the breaking of the fast is that during Ramadan, time is divided into two different speeds: during daytime the clock goes tick ... tock, ... tick ... tock, while at nighttime it goes ticktock-ticktockticktock. The experience of time is also the subject of the next cartoons, which illustrate how difficult the last few moments before the breaking of the fast may be and how anxiously people are waiting for the call from the muezzin that the fast may be broken:

People who do not live close to a mosque have to rely on more modern devices, such as an alarm clock or radio, to determine the exact moment to break the fast:

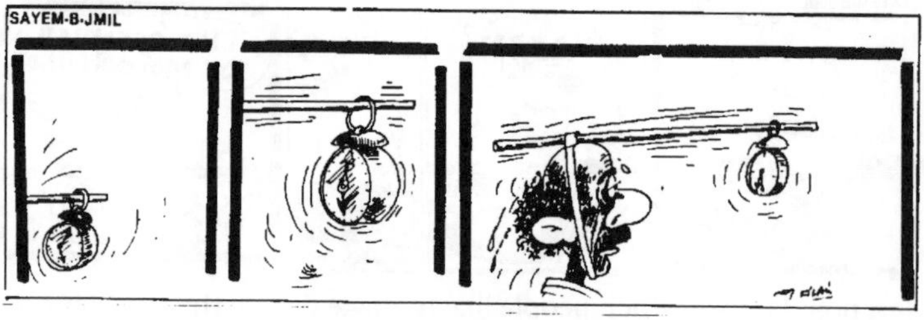

Towards the end of Ramadan, all attention is focused on the appearance of the new moon, which marks the conclusion of the fasting month. Note that in the final cartoon, a man is thinking of the beer he will be able to drink if he and his friends succeed in 'catching' the new moon:

ÇA Y'EST. JE L'AI TROUVÉ

SAYEM.B.JMIL
JE L'AI EU
JE DESCENDS
LE VOILA! ON PEUT FAIRE LA FETE

Bibliography

Abu-lughod, L. (1986), *Veiled Sentiments. Honor and Poetry in a Bedouin Society*. Berkeley and Los Angeles: University of California Press

Akhmisse, M. (1985), *Médecine, Magie et Sorcellerie au Maroc*. Casablanca: Benimed

Alami, A. (1988), Le Caractére éducatif du jeûne est prouvé. *Le Matin du Sahara*. 24.4.88: 3

Annuaire Statistique (1989), *Annuaire Statistique du Maroc*. Rabat: Direction de la Statistique

Antoun, R. (1968), The Social Significance of Ramadan in an Arab Village. *Muslim World*, LVIII: 36–42 and 95–104

____ (1976), Anthropology. In: L. Binder (ed.) *The Study of the Middle East*. New York: Wiley & Sons

Arberry, A. (1955), *The Koran Interpreted*. London: George Allen & Unwin Ltd. (2 vols)

Ardener, E. (1972), Belief and the Problem of Women. In: J. S. la Fontaine (ed.) *The Interpretation of Ritual*. London: Tavistock

____ (1975), The Problem Revisited. In: S. Ardener (ed.) *Perceiving Women*. London: Dent/Mallaby Press; New York: Halsted Press

Ardener, S. (1975), Introduction. In: S. Ardener (ed.) *Perceiving Women*. London: Dent/Mallaby Press; New York: Halsted Press

____ (1981), *Women and Space. Ground Rules and Social Maps*. London: Croom Helm

Aslam, M. and Assad, M. (1986), Drug Regimens and Fasting during Ramadan: A Survey in Kuwait. *Public Health*, 100: 49–53

Babcock, B. (1978), Introduction. In: B. Babcock (ed.) *The Reversible World. Symbolic Inversion in Art and Society*. London: Cornell University Press

Ben Talha, A. (1965), *Moulay-Idriss du Zerhoun. Quelques aspects de la vie sociale et familiale*. Editions Techniques Nord-Africaines

Ben Yusif, D. (1990), *Al-ṣawm*. (in Arabic). Casablanca: Najah al-jadida

Benkheira, M. H. (1986), Jouir du rite: remarques sur l'islam populaire urbain dans l'Algerie independante. *Peuples méditerranéens*, no. 34: 37–47

Berrada, A. (1988), Délit de Ramadan. 222, Boulevard Cachecroûte.

Kalima, no. 25: 54–5
Bidwell, R. (1973), *Morocco under Colonial Rule. French Administration of Tribal Areas 1912–1956.* London: Frank Cass & Co.
Blanc, F. (1977), *Recueil de textes juridiques. I. CODE PENAL.* Casablanca: Librairie-papaterie des écoles
Blok, A. (1981), Infame beroepen. *Symposion,* III(1, 2): 104–28
Boughali, M. (1988), *Sociologie des maladies mentales au Maroc.* Casablanca: Afrique Orient
Bousquet, G. (1935), *Précis elémentaire de droit Musulman (mâlékite et algérien) conforme au programme de Certificat de Législation Algérienne.* Paris: Librairie Orientaliste Paul Geuthner
____ (1960), *Le droit Musulman par les textes. Précis de droit Musulman. Tome II.* Alger: Maison des Livres
Bowen, J. (1990), Salat in Indonesia: The Social Meanings of an Islamic Ritual. *Man* (N.S.), 24: 600–19
Bruijn, J. de (1984), De instellingen van de islam. In: J. Waardenburg (ed.) *Islam. Norm, ideaal en werkelijkheid.* Weesp: Het Wereldvenster
Buitelaar, M. (1985a), Over baden en bidden. De religieuze betekenis van de hammâm voor Marokkaanse vrouwen. In: W. Jansen (ed.) *Lokale Islam. Geloof en ritueel in Noord-Afrika en Iran.* Muiderberg: Coutinho
____ (1985b), Door baden herboren. Het *hammâm*-bezoek als rite de passage. *Publicatie-reeks Vakgroep Culturele Antropologie,* no. 18. Nijmegen: Katholieke Universiteit Nijmegen
____ (1986), Ruimteverdeling en grensoverschrijdingen. De bewegingsruimte en sociale kontakten van vrouwen in Marokko. *Tijdschrift voor Vrouwenstudies,* 7(2): 206–19
Bukari, al- (1862), *Al-Sahîh,* ed. L. Krehl. Leiden: Brill (translation used here: *Traditions Islamiques.* Paris: Imprimerie Nationale, 1903, 4 vols)
Burke, E. IIII (1972), The Image of the Moroccan State in French Literature: A New Look at the Origin of Lyautey's Berber Policy. In: E. Gellner and C. Micaud (eds) *Arabs and Berbers. From Tribe to Nation in North Africa.* London: Duckworth
Burton, R. (1964), *Personal Narrative of a Pilgrimage to al-Madinah and Meccah.* Memorial Editions. New York: Dover Publications
Buskens, L. (1986), *Beknopte bibliografische notitie omtrent de Ramadan.* Nijmegen: Unpublished paper
____ (1987), *Ramadan in Marokko. Betekenis en structuur van een ritueel.* Nijmegen: Katholieke Universiteit Nijmegen
Bynum, C. (1986), Introduction: The Complexity of Symbols. In: C. Bynum, S. Harrell and P. Richman (eds) *Gender and Religion: On the Complexity of Symbols.* Boston: Beacon Press
Castries, H. de (1924), Les Sept Patrons de Merrakech. *Hesperis,* 4(3):

245–305

Chelhod, J. (1973), A Contribution to the Problem of the Pre-eminence of the Right, Based Upon Arabic Evidence. In: R. Needham (ed.) *Right and Left: Essays on Dual Symbolic Classification*. Chicago: Chicago University Press

Chemoul, M. (1936), Les Institutions Musulmanes: le jeûne. *Bulletin de l'Enseignement Public du Maroc,* no. 149: 403–25

Chottin, A. (1923), Airs populaires receuillis à Fes. *Hesperis,* 3(2): 275–85

____ (1927), Note sur le 'Nfir'. *Hesperis,* 7(3): 376–81

Christian, W. (1989), *Person and God in a Spanish Valley.* New revised edn. Princeton, NJ: Princeton Univerity Press

Claisse, A. (1987), Makhzen Traditions and Administrative Channels. In: I. W. Zartman (ed.) *The Political Economy of Morocco.* New York: Praeger, pp. 34–58

Cohen, A. (1985), *The Symbolic Construction of Community.* London: Tavistock

____ (ed.) (1986), *Symbolising Boundaries. Identity and Diversity in British Cultures.* Manchester: Manchester University Press

Combs-Schilling, M. (1989), *Sacred Performances. Islam, Sexuality and Sacrifice.* New York: Columbia University Press

Conférences Religieuses (1988), *Conférences Religieuses du mois de Ramadan.* Rabat: Ministère de Habous et des Affaires Islamiques

Crapanzano, V. (1973), *The Hamadsha. A Study in Moroccan Ethnopsychiatry.* Berkeley: University of California Press

Daoud, Z. (1988), Marrakech. A la croisée des chemins. *Lamalif,* no. 198: 42–4

Davis, S. (1983), *Patience and Power. Women's Lives in a Moroccan Village.* Cambridge, MA: Schenkman

Davis, S. and Davis, D. (1989), *Adolescence in a Moroccan Town. Making Social Sense.* New Brunswick and London: Rutgers University Press

Denny, F. (1985), Islamic Ritual. Perspectives and Theories. In: R. C. Martin (ed.) *Approaches to Islam in Religious Studies.* Tucson: University of Arizona Press

Deverdun, G. (1959), *Marrakech des origines à 1912.* Rabat: Editions Techniques Nord-Africaines (2 vols)

Douglas, M. (1966), *Purity and Danger.* London: Routledge & Kegan Paul

____ (1970), *Natural Symbols.* Harmondsworth: Penguin

____ (1975), *Implicit Meanings. Essays in Anthropology.* London: Routledge & Kegan Paul

Durkheim, E. (1961), *The Elementary Forms of the Religious Life.* Glencoe, IL: Free Press (French edn 1912)

Dwyer, D. (1978a), *Images and Self-Images. Male and Female in Moroc-*

co. New York: Columbia University Press
____ (1978b), Women, Sufism and Decision-Making in Moroccan Islam. In: L. Beck and N. Keddie (eds) *Women in the Muslim World*. Cambridge, MA: Harvard University Press
Dwyer, K. (1982), *Moroccan Dialogues. Anthropology in Question*. Prospect Heights, IL: Waveland Press
Eickelman, D. (1976), *Moroccan Islam. Tradition and Society in a Pilgrimage Center*. Austin: University of Texas Press
____ (1977), Time in a Complex Society: A Moroccan Example. *Ethnology*, 16: 39–55
____ (1981), *The Middle East. An Anthropological Approach*. Englewood Cliffs, NJ: Prentice-Hall
____ (1985), *Knowledge and Power in Morocco. The Education of a Twentieth-Century Notable*. Princeton, NJ: Princeton University Press
____ (1987), Religion in Polity and Society. In: I. W. Zartman (ed.) *The Political Economy of Morocco*. New York: Praeger
Faithorn, E. (1975), The Concept of Pollution Among the Káfe of the Papua New Guinea Highlands. In: R. Reiter (ed.) *Toward an Anthropology of Women*. New York: Monthly Review Press
Fallers, I. (1974), Notes On An Advent Ramadan. *Journal of the American Academy of Religion*, 42(1): 35–52
Fernea, E. (1969), *Guests of the Sheik. An Ethnography of an Iraqi Village*. Garden City, NY: Anchor Books
____ (1976), *A Street in Marrakech. A Personal Encounter with the Lives of Moroccan Women*. New York: Anchor Books
Fuchs, H. (1987), Mawlid. Mawlid al-nabî. *First Encyclopedia of Islam*, vol. V: 419–22
Geertz, C. (1968), *Islam Observed. Religious Development in Morocco and Indonesia*. Chicago and London: University of Chicago Press
____ (1973), *The Interpretation of Cultures. Selected Essays*. New York: Basic Books
____ (1976), 'From the Native's Point of View'. On the Nature of Anthropological Understanding. In: K. Basso and H. Selby (eds) *Meaning in Anthropology*. Albuquerque: University of New Mexico Press
____ (1983), *Local Knowledge. Further Essays in Interpretive Anthropology*. New York: Basic Books
Geertz, C., Geertz, H. and Rosen, L. (1979), *Meaning and Order in Moroccan Society. Three Essays in Cultural Analysis*. Cambridge: Cambridge University Press
Gellner, E. (1969), *Saints of the Atlas*. Chicago: Chicago University Press
Gennep, A. Van (1960), *The Rites of Passage*. Chicago: Chicago University Press (French edn 1909)

Ghazali, al- (1955), *Ihya ᶜouloum ed-Din ou Vivifacation des sciences de la Foi* (analyse et index: G. H. Bousquet). Paris: Librairie Max Besson

Gluckman, M. (1960), *Essays on the Ritual of Social Relations*. Manchester: Manchester University Press

Goitein, S. D. (1966), Ramadan, The Muslim Month of Fasting. In: S. Goitein (ed.) *Studies in Islamic History and Institutions*. Leiden: Brill

Grunebaum, G. von, (1958), *Muhammedan Festivals*. London and New York: Abelard-Schuman

Hofmann, N. (1978), *Der islamische Festkalender in Java und Sumatra unter besonderer Berücksichtigung des Fastenmonats und des Fastenbruchfestes in Jakarta und Medan*. Bad Honnef: Bock und Herchen

Instruction Islamique *(1984), Instruction Islamique, 1ére-4éme Année secondaire*. Royaume du Maroc, Ministére de l'Education Nationale. Rabat: Librairie el Maârif (4 vols)

Ishaq Kalil, Bin (1956), *Abrégé de la loi Musulmane selon le rite de l'Imam Mâlek* (trans. G. H. Bousquet). Alger: Editions Algériennes EN-NAHDHA

Jansen, W. (1987), *Women without Men. Gender and Marginality in an Algerian Town*. Leiden: Brill

Jeffery, A. (1962), The Section on Fasting, from the Sahih of Al-Bukhari. In: A. Jeffery (ed.) *A Reader on Islam. Passages from Standard Arabic Writings Illustrative of the Beliefs and Practices of Muslims*. The Hague: Mouton

Jemma, D. (1971), *Les Tanneurs de Marrakech*. Memoires du C.R.A.P.E. XIX. Alger: Centre National de la Recherche scientifique

Jomier J. and Corbon, J. (1956), le ramadan, au Caire, en 1956. In: *Mélanges. Institut dominicain d'études orientales du Caire*, 3 (1956): 1–74

Kaptein, N. (1989), *Het geboortefeest van de profeet Mohammed. Oorsprong en verspreiding in het Nabije Oosten tot het begin van de 7e/13e eeuw; invoering en geschiedenis in de Maghrib en al-Andalus tot aan de dood van al-Wansarisi (914/1500)* (unpublished dissertation). Leiden: Rijksuniversiteit Leiden

Keesing, R. M. (1989), Exotic Readings of Cultural Texts. *Current Anthropology*, 30(4): 459–79

Kehoe, A. and Giletti, D. (1981), Women's Preponderance in Possession Cults: The Calcium-Deficiency Hypotheses Extended. *American Anthropologist*, 33: 549–61

Lane, E. (1842), *An Account of the Manners and Customs of the Modern Egyptians written in Egypt during the Years 1833–1835*. London: Ward, Lock

O.N.C.F

RABAT VILLE

12-06-95

1643 99 60231K70575

VILLE

PORT

T . N . R 1CL

PLEIN TARIF

ller retour PRIX : 92,00 DH

retour est valable 2mois

ntrole Aller	controle Retour

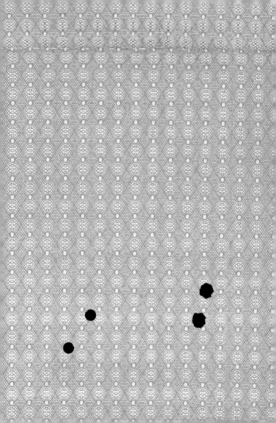

Leach, E. (1961), Two Essays Concerning the Symbolic Representation of Time. In: E. Leach, *Rethinking Anthropology*. London: Athlone Press

____ (1968), Ritual. In: D. Sills (ed.) *Encyclopedia of the Social Sciences*, vol. 13: 520–6. New York: The Macmillan Company and The Free Press

____ (1976), *Culture and Communication*. Cambridge: Cambridge University Press

Lech, C. (1979), *Geschichte des islamischen Kultus. Rechtshistorische un hadit-kritische Untersuchungen zur Entwicklung und Systematik der ᶜibadat. Band I: Das Ramadan Fasten. Erster Teil*. Wiesbaden: Harrassowitz

Leemhuis, F. (1984), Soenna. In: J. Waardenburg (ed.) *Islam. Norm, ideaal en werkelijkheid*. Weesp: Het Wereldvenster

Legey, D. (1926), *Essai de Folklore Marocain*. Paris: Librairie Orientaliste Paul Geuthner

Lentjes, W. (1981), *Marokko als ontwikkelingsland*. Goirlese werkgroep. Den Bosch: Malmberg

Lewis, J. (1971), *Ecstatic Religion. An Anthropological Study of Spirit Possession and Shamanism*. Harmondsworth: Penguin

Loeffler, R. (1988), *Islam in Practice. Religious Beliefs in a Persian Village*. Albany: State University of New York Press

MacCormack, C. (1980), Nature, Culture and Gender: A Critique. In: C. MacCormack and M. Strathern, *Nature, Culture and Gender*. Cambridge: Cambridge University Press

Maher, V. (1974), *Women and Property in Morocco. Their Changing Relation to the Process of Social Stratification in the Middle Atlas*. Cambridge: Cambridge University Press

Mandleur, A. (1972), Croissance et urbanisation de Marrakech. *Revue de Géographie du Maroc*, 22: 31–60

Mauss, M. (1970), *The Gift. Forms and Functions of Exchange in Archaic Societies* (trans. Ian Cunnison). London: Cohen & West

Mernissi, F. (1975), *Beyond the Veil. Male-Female Dynamics in a Modern Muslim Society*. New York and London: Schenkman

____ (1977), Women, Saints and Sanctuaries. *Signs*, 3(1): 101–12

Mittwoch, E. (1987), cîd al-adhâ. *First Encyclopedia of Islam*, vol. III: 444–5

Moore, H. (1988), *Feminism and Anthropology*. Oxford: Polity Press

Morsy, M. (1983), *La Relation de Thomas Pellow. Une lecture du Maroc au 18e siècle*. Synthese no. 12. Paris: Editions Recherche sur les civilisations

Munson, H. Jr (1984), *The House of Si Abd Allah. The Oral History of a Moroccan Family*. London: Yale University Press

____ (1986), The Social Base of Islamic Militancy in Morocco. *The Middle East Journal*, 40(2): 267–84

Muslim, (1955–56), *Al-Sahîh*. Cairo (5 vols)

Meyerhoff, B. (1982), Rites of Passage: Process and Paradox. In: V. Turner (ed.) *Celebration. Studies in Festivity and Ritual*. Washington, D.C.: Smithsonian Institution Press

Nabhan, L. (1991), *Das Fest des Fastenbreches (cîd al-fitr) in Ägypten. Untersuchungen zu theologischen Grundlagen un praktischen Gestaltung Islamkundliche Untersuchungen* Band 147. Berlin: Klaus Schwarz Verlag

Needham, R. (1967), Percussion and Transition. *Man* (N.S.), 2: 606–14

Noin, D. (1970), *La Population Rurale du Maroc*. Paris: Presses Universitaires de France

Ortner, S. (1974), Is Female to Male as Nature Is to Culture? In: M. Rosaldo and L. Lamphere (eds) *Women, Culture and Society*. Stanford, CA: Stanford University Press

____ (1984), Theory in Anthropology since the Sixties. *Comparative Study in Society and History*, 26: 126–66

Oussaid, B. (1988), *Les Coquelicots de l'Oriental. Chronique d'une famille berbère marocaine*. Casablanca: Les Editions Toubkal

Peets, L. (1988), *Women of Marrakech*. London: Hurst

Peters, J. (1984), Tafsier en ilm al-hadieth (Koran exegese en Traditiewetenschap). In: J. Waardenburg (ed.) *Islam. Norm, ideaal en werkelijkheid*. Weesp: Het Wereldvenster

Peters, R. (1984), Fikh (Rechtswetenschap). In: J. Waardenburg (ed.) *Islam. Norm, ideaal en werkelijkheid*. Weesp: Het Wereldvenster

Qayrawani, Ibn Abi Zayd, al- (1975), *La Risâla ou Epître sur les éléments du dogme et de la loi de l'Islam selon le rite mâlékite* (texte arabe et traduction francaise avec un avant-propos, des notes et trois index par L. Bercher). Alger: Editions populaires de l'Armee

Rabinow, P. (1975), *Symbolic Domination. Cultural Form and Historical Change in Morocco*. Chicago: University of Chicago Press

Reysoo, F. (1985), Een collectieve besnijdenis in Noord-West Marokko. In: W. Jansen (ed.) *Lokale Islam. Geloof en ritueel in Noord-Afrika en Iran*. Muiderberg: Coutinho

____ (1988), *Des Moussems du Maroc. Une Approche anthropologique de fêtes patronales*. Nijmegen: Katholieke Universiteit Nijmegen

Roog, S. (1988), *Alleen vogelmelk ontbreekt . . . Een onderzoek naar purifikatierituelen tijdens de ramadan in een Turks dorp*. Nijmegen: Katholieke Universiteit Nijmegen

Rosen, L. (1984), *Bargaining for Reality: The Construction of Social Relations in a Muslim Community*. Chicago: Chicago University Press

Ruska, J. (1987), Sabr. *First Encyclopedia of Islam*, vol. VII: 25–7

Sallnow, M. J. (1981), Communitas Reconsidered: The Sociology of

Andean Pilgrimage. *Man* (N.S.), 16: 163–82
Schacht, J. (1964), *An Introduction to Islamic Law.* Oxford: Clarendon Press
____ (1969), Adjr. In: H. Gibb *et al.* (eds) *The Encyclopedia of Islam. New Edition,* vol. I. Leiden: Brill/London: Luzac & Co., p. 209
Schimmel, A. (1983), The Sufis and the *Shahada.* In: R. Hovannisian and J. Vryonis Jr (eds) *Islam's Understanding of Itself.* Malibu, CA: Undena Publications
Schwerdtfeger, F. (1982), *Traditional Housing in African Cities. (Zania, Ibadan, Marrakech).* Chichester: John Wiley & Sons
Sebti, M. (1985), L'habitat des douars de Marrakech: un héritage compromis. *Annales de Géographie,* no. 521: 63–85
Seddon, D. (1981), *Moroccan Peasants. A Century of Change in the Eastern Rif 1870–1970.* Folkstone, Kent: Dawson
Snouck Hurgronje, C. (1888–89), *Mekka.* Leiden: Brill
Soudan, F. (1987), Rencontre Hassan II/Chadli. Un sommet pour deux monologues. *Jeune Afrique,* no. 1376, 20 May 1987: 8–19
Tabari, al- (1901), *Tarik al-rusul wal-muluk,* ed. J. Goeje. Leiden: Brill
Tapper, N. and Tapper, R. (1987), The Birth of the Prophet: Ritual and Gender in Turkish Islam. *Man* (N.S.), 22(1): 69–92
Tozy, M. (1984), *Champ et contre champ politico-religieux au Maroc* (Thèse Pour le Doctorat d'Etat en Science Politique). D'Aix-Marseille: Université de Droit, d'Economie et des Sciences D'Aix-Marseille
Tritton, A. (1987), Tahara. *First Encyclopedia of Islam,* vol. VII: 609. Leiden: Brill
Troin, J. (1975), *Les Souks Marocains.* Aix-en-Provence: Edisud
Turner, V. (1968), *The Drums of Affliction. A Study of Religious Processes among the Ndembu of Zambia.* Oxford: Clarendon Press
____ (1969), *The Ritual Process. Structure and Anti-Structure.* New York: Ithaca
____ (1973), Symbols in African Ritual. *Science,* 179: 1100–5
____ (1974), Passage, Margins, and Poverty: Religious Symbols of Communitas. In: V. Turner, *Dramas, Fields and Metaphors. Symbolic Action in Human Society.* Ithaca and London: Cornell University Press
____ (1977), Variations on a Theme of Liminality. In: S. Moore and B. Meyerhoff (eds) Secular Ritual. Assen and Amsterdam: Van Gorcum
Waardenburg, J. (1979), Popular versus Official Islam. In: P. Vrý-hoff and J. Waardenburg (eds) *Official and Popular Religion.* The Hague: Mouton
____ (1984), Inleiding. In: J. Waardenburg (ed.) Islam. *Norm, ideaal en werkelijkheid.* Weesp: Het Wereldvenster

Wagtendonk, K. (1968), *Fasting in the Koran*. Leiden: Brill
____ (1984), Grondslagen van de islam. In: J. Waardenburg (ed.) *Islam. Norm, ideaal en werkelijkheid*. Weesp: Het Wereldvenster
Watt, W. (1970), *Bell's Introduction to the Qur'an. Completely Revised and Enlarged by W. Montgomery Watt*. Edinburgh: Edinburgh University Press
Wehr, H. (1976), *A Dictionary of Modern Written Arabic* (ed. J. Milton Cowan). Wiesbaden: Harrassowitz
Westermarck, E. (1926), *Ritual and Belief in Morocco*. London: Macmillan & Co. (2 vols)
____ (1930), *Wit and Wisdom in Morocco*. London: Routledge & Sons
Zaki Yamani, M. A. (1987), Fasting and Feasting: Some Social Aspects of the Observance of Ramadan in Saudi Arabia. In: A. Al-Shahi (ed.) *The Diversity of the Muslim Community. Anthropological Essays in Memory of P. Lienhardt*. London: Ithaca
Zartman, I. W. (1987), King Hassan's New Morocco. In: I. W. Zartman (ed.) *The Political Economy of Morocco*. New York: Praeger
Zein, el- (1977), Beyond Ideology and Theology: The Search for the Anthropology of Islam. *Annual Review of Anthropology*, 6(1977): 227–54

Glossary

ajr = religious merit
al-ᶜîd al-kabîr = feast concluding Ramadan
amîr al-mu'minîn = Commander of the Faithful
baraka = divine power
bint = girl
ᶜaql = reason
ᶜâšûrâ' = tenth day of the Islamic new year
ᶜšâ' = light meal eaten in the evening
ᶜulamâ' = religious scholars
ḏbîḥa = ritual slaughtering
derdeba = night of trance dancing
fatwâ = formal religious opinion, religious decree
fḍîla = preferred day of Ramadan
fiqh = jurisprudence
fiṭra = measure of wheat distributed at the end of Ramadan
fqi = Koran scholar
fṭûr = breakfast
gassa ṣ-ṣâbirîn = dish of the enduring people
ġeyyât = oboist
ġusl = major ritual ablution
hilâl = first crescent of the new moon
ḥajj = pilgrimage to Mecca
ḥarâm = forbidden, taboo
ḥammâm = public bath
henna = henna, plant used to colour the hair or skin red
ḥrîra = Moroccan tomato soup
jinn (jnûn) = spirit(s)
jellâba = Moroccan overcoat worn outside the home
kuḥl = kohl, antimonium, used as make-up around the eyes
laṭâfa = kindness
laylat al-qadr =27th Ramadan, in which the Koran was sent to earth
lîla = night of trance dancing
mafrûḍ = obligatory
makrûh = reprehensible
mġurb = sunset
mqeddma = female leader of Gnawa team

muṣallâ = square used for open-air prayers
mûsem = annual festival at a saint's shrine
neffâr = trumpetplayer
neṣrânî(ya) = Christian
nîya = intention
nqî = clean
qarâba = closeness
qurâb = the close ones (relatives and friends)
ṛemḍân = Ramadan
rukn al-muftî = Moroccan television programme treating religious issues
s-seb^{c}*a u* ^{c}*ešrîn* = 27th of Ramadan
siḥr = magic
sḥûr = nightly meal eaten during Ramadan
sunna = customs or traditions of the Prophet; recommendable conduct
še^{c}*bâna* = Shaban party
šahâda = Muslim Creed
šarî^{c}*a* = Islamic law
šebbakîya = Ramadan cookies
šerrât = scarification treatment
šîḵa = professional female dancer and singer
ṣabr = patience, endurance
ṣadaqa = alms
ṣalât = five daily prayers
ṣaleḥ = a holy or pious man
ṣawm = fast
ṣeḥḥa = health
ṣḥîḥ = healthy
tarâwîḥ = Ramadan prayers
tawḥîd = unification
te^{c}rîja = vase-shaped drum
ṭahâra = purity, purification
umma = Islamic community
usbû^{c} *al-*^{c}*îd* = the week following the feast
weṣt ṛemdân = the day in the middle of Ramadan
yawm aš-šakk = the day of doubt
zakât = alms
zakât al-fiṭr = obligatory donation of food at the end of Ramadan

INDEX